CHRISTIAN GNOSIS

CHRISTIAN GNOSIS

CHARLES W. LEADBEATER

EDITED WITH A FOREWORD BY
STEN VON KRUSENSTIERNA

INTRODUCTION AND NOTES BY
RICHARD SMOLEY

QUEST
BOOKS

Theosophical Publishing House
Wheaton, Illinois • Chennai, India

Quest Books
Theosophical Publishing House
P. O. Box 270
Wheaton, IL 60187-0270

www.questbooks.net

Cover design by Beth Hansen-Winter

Library of Congress Cataloging-in-Publication Data

Leadbeater, C. W. (Charles Webster), 1854–1934.
Christian gnosis / Charles W. Leadbeater; edited with a foreword by Sten von
Krusenstierna; introduction and notes by Richard Smoley.—1st. Quest ed. 2011.
    p.   cm.
Includes bibliographical references and index.
ISBN 978-0-8356-0895-4
1. Liberal Catholic Church—Doctrines. I. Von Krusenstierna, Sten. II. Smoley,
Richard. III. Title.
BX4795.L45L43 2011
230'.48—dc22   2011003640

5   4   3   2   *   13   14   15

Printed in the United States of America

CONTENTS

DIAGRAMS

Introduction to the Second Edition

by Richard Smoley

Today the word *gnosis* provokes a cavalcade of associations. It can mean a kind of spiritual experience akin to enlightenment. It can refer to the ancient Christian mystical schools of the early centuries AD or even to a spate of new religious movements that lay claim to the ancient Gnostic heritage.

For Charles W. Leadbeater, whose essays constitute this volume, the meaning of *gnosis* is different. In ancient Christianity, he tells us, *gnosis* was a "technical term. It did not mean ordinary wisdom, but the special religious teaching to those who are at the stage of the perfect" (p. 88). He quotes the apostle Paul: "We speak the wisdom of God in a mystery, even the hidden wisdom, which God ordained before the world unto our glory" (1 Cor. 2:7).[1] And he goes on to argue—echoing the great Church Father Origen—that this "hidden wisdom" could not have been the teachings of exoteric Christianity, since these were widely known even to the ancient public.

It is this "hidden wisdom" that is the topic of this book. It would be foolish of me to spell out these ideas in an introduction, since Leadbeater himself does so clearly and at length, but as a preliminary it would be helpful to say something about these teachings and their context, as well as about the man who presents them.

Charles Webster Leadbeater was born in Stockport, England, in 1854 (some sources have given this date incorrectly as 1847). He started his career as a bank clerk, but, thanks to a vocation to the priesthood and help from an influential relative, he was able to pursue theological studies and was ordained as a priest in the Church of England in 1879. In

1883 he joined the Theosophical Society, which had been formed in 1875 with the partial object of exploring "the hidden mysteries of nature and the latent powers in man."

One aspect of the Theosophical Society that especially appealed to Leadbeater was its claim that it had been founded under the inspiration of hidden Masters of Wisdom, individuals on earth who were possessed of certain extraordinary powers (such as clairvoyance and telekinesis) and who were in communication with the founders of the Society, notably H. P. Blavatsky and Henry Steel Olcott. Leadbeater wanted to be the disciple of such a Master and even wrote a letter to that effect, transmitted through a "spirit guide" in March 1884. In October of that year, he received a reply—a letter written in blue pencil and signed "KH"—the initials used by Koot Hoomi, one of the Masters. In it Koot Hoomi told him what was involved in the discipleship he sought. The letter also suggested that Leadbeater visit India "for a few months."

At the time Leadbeater had no personal ties in England, so he resolved to go to India and stay there indefinitely. He arrived at the end of 1884. The following year he embarked upon a course of study (which he mentions occasionally in this collection) that enabled him to develop certain psychic faculties, notably clairvoyance. This faculty would inform much of his writing for the rest of his life.

Leadbeater became a close associate of Annie Besant, who had joined the Theosophical Society in 1889 and would become its leader in the following decade. Together with Besant, Leadbeater conducted inquiries into the psychic realms that led to such works as the 1895 collection *Occult Chemistry*, in which the authors described their visions of subatomic particles (objects that were still unknown to science, which still regarded the atom as an irreducible entity). Other works inspired by his research include *The Astral Plane, Invisible Helpers, The Other Side of Death, Man Visible and Invisible,* and *The Chakras.* These last two proved to be particularly influential, and to this day there are very few New Age books on the subtle bodies of man or the chakras that are not more or less directly influenced by Leadbeater.

In 1906, Leadbeater fell afoul of accusations of sexual impropriety with young boys. Evidently he had—very much against the mores of the time—advised them to masturbate. Whether he did anything more is rather hard to determine, but, in any event he left the Theosophical Society in 1906 and pursued his own occult researches for the next three years, until Annie Besant, at this point the president of the society, invited him to return. He did so and settled at the society's world headquarters at Adyar, near Madras (today's Chennai), India. In 1909 he took an interest in a young Brahmin boy, Jiddu Krishnamurti, foreseeing that he would display remarkable qualities. Besant agreed, predicting that Krishnamurti would serve as a vehicle for the new "World Teacher" who was destined to come and inaugurate a new cycle for humanity. Krishnamurti was taken up by Besant and Leadbeater and given the finest English education available at the time. The Theosophists even formed a society, the Order of the Star, to promote Krishnamurti's work as World Teacher.

The predictions for Krishnamurti did have some validity. He became one of the most influential spiritual teachers of the twentieth century but in the opposite way to what Besant and Leadbeater had expected. In 1929, in a famous speech, "Truth Is a Pathless Land," he dissolved the Order of the Star. "You can form other organizations and expect someone else," he told his followers. "With that I am not concerned, nor with creating new cages, new decorations for those cages. My only concern is to set men absolutely, unconditionally free."[2]

Undaunted by this reversal, Leadbeater continued his work and promoted the concept of a new, previously unknown member of the hierarchy of adepts: the World Mother, whom he also mentions in *Christian Gnosis*. He died in Perth, Western Australia, on March 1, 1934.

Such are the bare facts of Leadbeater's life. To understand their relationship to this present work, we need to begin with his clairvoyant experience while observing the Christian sacraments. He noticed that even when an uninspired priest was performing a mass in front of an ignorant congregation, certain "thought-forms" of an unusual nature were created. He would discuss this experience in a number of works, notably *The Science of the Sacraments*, which gives a thorough description of these astral thought-forms and even related them to certain well-known types of church structure.

Leadbeater began to turn these ideas into practice in 1915. At this point, the English Theosophist James Wedgwood (1883–1951) came to Sydney. Wedgwood had been ordained as a priest by Arnold Harris Mathew (1852–1919), Old Catholic Archbishop of Great Britain, who, by his secession from the Old Catholic Church of Utrecht, was considered to be a "wandering bishop" in an independent sacramental line.

The concept of wandering bishops and independent sacramental lines may sound peculiar, but it is extremely important for placing *Christian Gnosis* in the context of Christianity as a whole. The idea comes from a peculiarity in Roman Catholic doctrine: an ordinary priest can be unfrocked—that is, he can be stripped of his role and his office—but a bishop cannot be unconsecrated. (The correct terminology is that a priest is ordained, whereas a bishop is consecrated.) A bishop remains a bishop even if he "wanders"—that is, separates himself from the Church. Stephan A. Hoeller, bishop of the Ecclesia Gnostica in Hollywood and himself the holder of an independent sacramental lineage, explains the concept thus: "Due to an early tradition, articulated but not invented by St. Augustine, the orthodoxy and validity of apostolic succession were not considered identical. Bishops could be heretics, yet could exercise their office as stewards of the sacraments in a valid manner. This doctrine (known as the Augustinian doctrine of orders) has been held to this day by the Roman Catholic Church. Provided the 'wandering ones' held the same intentions when ordaining their successors as those traditionally held by sacramental Christendom over the ages, they could pass on their sacred powers and administer the sacraments in a manner that the popes would recognize as valid."[3]

Holders of these traditions included bishops of the South Indian Church, which traces its origins to the apostle Thomas, and the Old Catholic Church of Holland, the first bishop of which was consecrated in 1724 and which is still (somewhat grudgingly) granted status as a legitimate apostolic church by Rome. It was in the Dutch Old Catholic line that Mathew held his episcopate. Mathew had also consecrated Frederick Samuel Willoughby as a bishop (although he suspended him from the English branch of the Dutch Old Catholic Church because of a scandal involving homosexuality), and Willoughby in turn consecrated Wedgwood in 1916. Wedgwood and Leadbeater formed the Liberal Catholic Church, also in 1916, with Wedgwood as first Presiding Bishop.

While the strands of the wandering bishops' lines can become extremely hard to sort out, the basic picture is clear. The Liberal Catholic Church was intended to serve as a combination of the Catholic sacramental heritage with a theology that was close to that of Theosophy. While there is no formal connection between the Liberal Catholic Church and the Theosophical Society, in practice there is much overlap, and many Liberal Catholic clergy are Theosophists.

This background helps explain what we have in this volume, which hews quite closely to many aspects of Catholic practice and even doctrine but interprets them in Theosophical terms. Indeed much of this book consists of a line-by-line exegesis of the great Catholic creeds—particularly the Nicene and Apostles' creeds—in light of this thought.

Certainly Leadbeater's theology diverges from traditional Catholic teaching in any number of respects. One of the most notable ones is the nature and person of Christ. Unlike Catholicism and Eastern Orthodoxy, which, over the course of innumerable church councils, pieced together a view of the dual nature of Christ as truly God and truly man, Leadbeater's Christology entails a version of adoptionism. That is, Christ and the man Jesus are not identical in the sense that orthodox theologians would understand: to Leadbeater, the Christ is a discarnate being known as the World Teacher, who has taken incarnation on many occasions and who, in the first century AD, took over the physical person of the disciple Jesus when the latter was baptized by John. (Besant and Leadbeater apparently believed that the same World Teacher would use the human form of Krishnamurti in the same way.)

Still other teachings that Leadbeater advances in these essays depart from conventional Christian thought: reincarnation, karma, and evolution. Reincarnation has always had a shadowy place in Christian teaching: it is difficult to find any specific condemnation of it by any of the great Church councils—which were generous in their anathemas against most other doctrines—but, on the other hand, none of the Church Fathers taught it, and most of them denounced it, even Origen, whom Leadbeater—incorrectly, in my view—presents as an advocate of the teaching. Origen did believe in the preexistence of the soul, and while some passages in his writings seem to incline toward reincarnation, it is also the case that he repudiates it specifically and vigorously on a number of occasions. (See my endnote on the subject.)

The idea of evolution is also absent from Christianity and indeed from Western esoteric thought until the nineteenth century. I do not mean the Darwinian view of the evolution of species, but the evolution of the individual spirit in its descent from the unseen realms to the world of matter and its slow but inevitable return to its source. As Theosophy—and Leadbeater—depict this process, this evolution entails numberless incarnations, each of which contributes slowly and perhaps infinitesimally to the development of the Ego—(the Theosophical term for the permanent, immortal "I" as opposed to the perishable body and personality). Esoteric study and development accelerates this process but does not fundamentally alter it. Nor, apparently, can this evolution be reversed: a human soul, no matter how corrupt or evil, cannot return to the state of a plant or an animal.

Personally, I find it difficult to find anything but the faintest traces of the doctrine of evolution in esoteric thought, Eastern or Western, before the advent of Theosophy in the late nineteenth century. While the Eastern religions do teach reincarnation, they do not as a rule present it in an evolutionary context. According to them, the living spirit—what some Eastern schools call the *jiva* or "life principle"—can and does pass through endless incarnations, as a man, as a god, as an animal. But it does not evolve or develop; it is trapped in this endless cycle and returns to these states over and over again. This is, in fact, the Wheel of Kama—of life and death—that is presented in so many Buddhist works of art. Only enlightenment can take one off this whirligig. Thus evolution, in this sense, is most likely an innovation introduced by Theosophy in the wake of scientific discoveries of the nineteenth century. If it existed as a part of the "hidden wisdom" before this point, it was very hidden indeed.

I mention these ideas only as examples; Leadbeater himself spells out many of his other doctrinal positions, all the while emphasizing that, unlike the Catholic Church, the Liberal Catholic Church does not insist upon adherence or belief on the part of its communicants; it administers the sacraments as a service to all those who seek them out.

It would be inappropriate to lengthen this book further by any more discussion of Leadbeater's theological ideas or of the circumstances by which this book was created; these are outlined in the foreword by Sten von Krusenstierna, late Presiding Bishop of the Liberal Catholic Church, who assembled these writings into this volume.

I need only say something about the present edition. This volume contains the full text of Leadbeater's writings in *The Christian Gnosis* as published by St. Alban Press in 1983. (The definite article in the title has been left out as a concession to the current taste for brevity.) I have omitted a short biography of Leadbeater by Krusenstierna, although I have relied on it for the biographical sketch in this introduction. I have not cut or changed Leadbeater's text in any way, except to alter the punctuation, particularly the internal punctuation of sentences. For example, Leadbeater's use of commas to separate parts of compound sentences and relative clauses is different from early twenty-first century usage, so I have modified these to some degree. In every case, however, I have taken pains to avoid changing the meaning or even the nuance of the original text. I have made the capitalization of words more consistent and changed spellings to accord with American orthography. I have also added references for some citations, including biblical quotations that Leadbeater did not

identify. Leadbeater's biblical citations are indicated by parentheses ();
mine are inserted in square brackets [].

The endnotes come from three sources. Some are Leadbeater's own;
some were added by Sten von Krusenstierna; the rest are my additions.
These are indicated with the initials CWL, SVK, and RS, respectively.
In the case of my notes, I have not attempted to give exhaustive an-
notations of every concept or figure mentioned by Leadbeater; I have
focused on identifying things that may seem unclear to the contemporary reader.

Finally, two acknowledgments are in order. First, I would like to
thank Jeffrey Forth, former national secretary of the Theosophical Society in America, who first brought this book to my attention. I would
also like to thank Graham Wale, Presiding Bishop of the Liberal Catholic Church, for his gracious help and permission in allowing Quest
Books to reprint the work.

This is an age of acute interest in the "hidden wisdom" of Christianity and in the truths that lie behind the official doctrines. Written nearly
a century ago, Leadbeater's essays in this volume still present a readable,
clear, and inspiring introduction to this Christian gnosis.

Richard Smoley
Wheaton, Illinois
November 2010

Richard Smoley's books include *Inner Christianity: A Guide to the Esoteric Tradition; Conscious Love: Insights from Mystical Christianity; Forbidden Faith: The Secret History of Gnosticism; The Dice Game of Shiva:
How Consciousness Creates the Universe; The Essential Nostradamus;* and
Hidden Wisdom: A Guide to the Western Inner Traditions (with Jay Kin-
ney). Formerly the editor of *Gnosis: A Journal of the Western Inner Traditions,* he is currently editor of *Quest: Journal of the Theosophical Society
in America* and of Quest Books.

FOREWORD

BY STEN VON KRUSENSTIERNA

C. W. Leadbeater's consecration to the episcopate in 1916 at the age of sixty-two was followed in the next ten years by an amazingly creative literary output from his hand. The Liberal Catholic Church was not the only object of this activity; in addition to such remarkable works as *The Science of the Sacraments* and *The Hidden Side of Christian Festivals* there were books on such different subjects as *The Hidden Life in Freemasonry*, *The Masters and the Path*, and *The Chakras* published during this period.

In the foreword to *The Science of the Sacraments* (first edition, 1920) Bishop Leadbeater wrote: "I have not of set purpose introduced any statement of the theological belief induced by the wider knowledge gained by this development of faculty, though indications of them inevitably peep through here and there. If time is given to me, I hope later to prepare a second volume dealing with that side of the question."

In other contexts he mentions his intention of producing a volume containing an interpretation of Christian doctrine and giving the theological outlook of the Liberal Catholic Church.

In 1924, the Rev. F. W. Pigott (later to become the third presiding bishop of the Liberal Catholic Church) visited Sydney, where he was consecrated as regionary bishop for Great Britain and Ireland. Like Bishop Leadbeater himself, Bishop Pigott had previously been a priest in Anglican orders; he was also well versed in the theology of the period. Bishop Leadbeater gave him the as yet unfinished manuscript of his "theological" book to obtain his opinion.

After reading a few chapters, Bishop Pigott returned it to him with the remark that it was "not theology." Bishop Leadbeater, who had great confidence in Pigott, put the manuscript away with the remark, "then we had better forget all about it." That is the story as Bishop Lawrence Burt, at that time a priest and master of ceremonies at the pro-Cathedral of St. Alban in Sydney, told me many years later. Bishop Pigott also mentions the incident in *The Liberal Catholic* of April 1954:

> A book of Christian theology was written by him at about, or soon after, the time of the writing of *The Science of the Sacraments*, *The Hidden Side of Christian Festivals* and a masonic book. In the year 1924 the theological book in typescript was handed to me when I was at Sydney to read and, presumably, to comment upon. I read only a few chapters, then gave it up. It was mostly a very Leadbeaterish harangue against a variety of Christianity which by then was obsolete or at least obsolescent amongst Christians of education. It was rather a sort of Christianity which perhaps does or did survive amongst Salvation Army teachers but not amongst the more refined and thoughtful congregations. So I advised that it be not published, and apparently it never was published.

However, it is obvious that Bishop Pigott himself felt that a book on theology was needed, for, on the ship on his way back to England, he wrote *The Parting of the Ways*, a book which for many years was the main source of theological study for Liberal Catholic clergy.

With the great changes which took place in Christian theology after the Second World War, several bishops, including myself, felt that Bishop Leadbeater's unpublished book, if it could be found, might still contain much useful material. A search for the manuscript was begun. It was finally located by Bishop Charles Shores at the headquarters of the Theosophical Society at Adyar, Madras, where Leadbeater had spent the last four years of his life. With the permission of the president of the Society, copies were made, one of which was sent to the presiding bishop at the time, Dr. A. G. Vreede, who had eight chapters from the manuscript—after some editing—published in *The Liberal Catholic* in various issues from 1961 to 1963.

A copy of this manuscript forms the basis of this book. In addition, I was given at a later date, among other material, a number of chapters from the book. Some of these chapters contain additional material. As far as can be established, the original manuscript contained twenty-two chapters. The whole manuscript appears to be unfinished and contains perhaps a half or two-thirds of the contents originally planned by the author. No name had yet been given to the work.

When going through Bishop Leadbeater's papers, including copies of talks and articles, I formed the opinion that most of his writings could be placed into four different categories:

1. Handwritten material: This is written by Bishop Leadbeater himself in ink or pencil in small, clear handwriting on scraps of paper, sometimes on the backs of envelopes, giving the impression that it must have been written at odd moments.

2. Dictated material: This was dictated by him to assistants or secretaries and usually taken down in shorthand. Many of his clairvoyant investigations were taken down in this way by Ernest Wood and others and later edited for publication.

3. Lectures, talks, or sermons: During his period in Australia (1914–1930), there were nearly always secretaries present who took down his talks in shorthand. He usually spoke from notes. The typewritten lecture or sermon was later corrected by himself or by one of his literary assistants, such as Professor Wood or the Rev. Herbrand Williams. Some of these were published as articles in various journals such as *The Liberal Catholic* or *The Theosophist*.

4. Question-and-answer sessions: These were a common feature during his days in Sydney. At one time they were weekly occurrences which usually took place at the pro-Cathedral of St. Alban or at Leadbeater's residence, The Manor, Mosman. This material was also taken down in shorthand and later typed. Some of it was edited by his literary assistants and either condensed into articles or published as "Questions and Answers" in *The Liberal Catholic*.

Most of his later works contain material drawn from all the four sources mentioned. The present work is no exception. The talks and sermons usually have a more vivid style than the written or dictated sources. An example of this is the delightful chapter "About God," which is a shortened version of a talk given to a group on the shore of the Pacific Ocean.

In 1978, the present editor, after several requests, decided to make an attempt to complete the manuscript and prepare it for publication. This proved much more difficult and took much longer than anticipated, especially since my only qualification for this task was a deep appreciation of C. W. Leadbeater's writings. I have also been somewhat hampered by lack of time and by my lack of proficiency in the English language. As editor, I had to attempt to conceive what would have been the intention of the author if he had completed the book himself. Some guidance was found in articles published in *The Liberal Catholic* between 1924 and 1930. There were indications that some of these would have been included in the proposed work.

The main sources from which the book as now presented has been compiled are:

1. The eighteen chapters of the unfinished manuscript;
2. Articles in *The Liberal Catholic* covering subjects not dealt with in the original manuscript;
3. Some unpublished talks and sermons to which the editor had access.

The purpose of adding material of the last two categories was to try to complete the work by giving a fuller coverage of Liberal Catholic teaching as propounded by Bishop Leadbeater. This has, however, not been fully achieved because of lack of suitable material on some subjects. The resulting work is definitely not a book on theology in the usual sense (Bishop Pigott was quite right in this), but it is "theological" insofar as it deals with such subjects as God, Christ, man, and the universe and contains definite interpretations of the ancient doctrines of the Church.

Two chapters in the original manuscript, in which the author refutes the "hell and damnation" doctrines held by many Churches in the nineteenth century, have been omitted. Also a chapter entitled "Why is Christianity Not More Successful?" and another, entitled "God's Attitude Towards Man," which was published in the September 1929 issue of *The Liberal Catholic*, have been omitted as being no longer relevant. Some of the chapters and articles have been severely edited, mainly to avoid duplication of subject matter. Some of the material contained in various chapters of the original manuscript can also be found in *The Christian Creed* and has been omitted. Even so, some duplication here and there has been unavoidable. As far as possible. the original script has been followed. A title for the book had to be chosen, as the manuscript had no title.

We are much indebted to the Rev. John Clarke for his valuable advice and assistance in the final editing of this work.

> + *Sten von Krusenstierna*
> *Presiding Bishop*
> *Liberal Catholic Church*
> *Easter 1983*

AUTHOR'S PREFACE

Long ago I was taught many things by certain great oriental teachers; I verified a number of these facts for myself by investigation and by experiment, and so I pass them on to you with confidence that I am not misleading you. Yet it is not because I say so that you should believe these things; if you accept them, it should be because they seem to you inherently reasonable.

This is no new doctrine. Two thousand five hundred years ago, people questioned the Lord Buddha as to which of the many forms of religious teaching was correct. "What are we to believe? There are many systems of philosophy; which of these do you recommend?"

The answer of the Enlightened One was admirable, for was he not, after all, the wisest man on earth? "Do not believe in a thing," he said, "merely because it is said, or because it has been handed down from antiquity. Nor in rumors as such." (How many people accept rumors without the slightest attempt to verify them!) "Do not believe in the writings of sages, merely because sages wrote them; do not believe in fancies which you may suspect to have been inspired by a deva [that is, do not believe in supposed spiritual or angelic inspiration] nor in inferences drawn from some haphazard assumption you may have made." (People often jump to a conclusion from which they build up a whole system of inferences, while the basis, founded on the merest imagination, may be wrong from the beginning.) "Do not believe because of what seems an analogical necessity," because an analogy which holds good in one case does not necessarily hold good in another.

"Do not believe on the mere authority of your own teachers. But believe when the writing, doctrine, or saying is corroborated by your own consciousness. For thus I have taught you, not to believe merely because you have heard; but when you believe of your own consciousness [that is, when it agrees with your own reason and common sense], then act accordingly and abundantly."

That is a very fine statement for any religious teacher to make. When you know for yourself, that is best of all; failing this, you can only take the best possible hypothesis—you can only accept that system which you see and feel to be reasonable and coherent, that which best accounts for all the various phenomena which you see before you.

What we put before you here seems to us to follow that system. You may accept it if it seems so to you also; but if you find some other system which seems to account for things better, you must assent to that. Short of actual knowledge, there is a definite intuition of the truth that comes sometimes to a person. Generally it is quite safe to be guided by that, for it usually comes from an eager leaping out of the soul towards a truth which it had known in other lives.

I base my confidence on what I know and what I have seen. May you all attain equal knowledge and equal certainty! That is the true basis, I believe, of religious faith—knowledge (when you reach it), and, in the meantime, your own reason and common sense. For God has given us our intellect, and He must mean us to use it with regard to the highest science of all—the science of our religion, the study of our relation to Himself.

The Author

PART ONE

The Divine Plan: Evolution

1

ABOUT GOD

Because we are still comparatively unevolved, any god that we could fully understand would not be much of a god. We are better acquainted with things below—with animals, trees, and rocks. Now and again we meet a man whom, in an expansive moment, we might acknowledge to be greater than ourselves; but, as a general rule, we are rather inclined to think that we are as good as anyone else if not a great deal better.

There is a certain danger of being conceited when we compare ourselves with things "beneath" us. We are proud, for example, of our intellect. But those who have come to know something of the Masters realize, first of all, that their own boasted intellect is merely the first rudiments of one; in comparison with the Masters' it is as the slight lessening of the darkness which comes before the dawn. Further insight reveals that, in fact, we have nothing that we can truly call our own. Our intellect, together with our other good qualities, is but a dim reflection of the powers of the Logos shining through.

The Masters tell us that they themselves, with their wonderful powers which seem to us so godlike, are but as dust under the feet of still higher beings. We cannot fully appreciate these Great Ones; still less can we comprehend the Logos. As for *Parabrahma*, the Absolute, He is not personal in any way; He is not what we would call an existence.

Of the Absolute nothing whatever can be rightly said save He is not this, He is not that; He cannot be defined on any plane that we have ever imagined or thought. As the Buddha put it, "Look not for Brahm or the beginning there." However earnest the seeker, He can never be grasped. "Veil after veil may lift but there must be veil after veil behind." It is useless to speculate; *Brahma* can be understood only on His own level.

The Logos

When we speak of God we mean, for all practical purposes, the Logos of our solar system. The Logos is more comprehensible than the Absolute because He has risen by slow degrees from our own humanity. The physical matter in the sun and in the planets of our system forms His physical body; the astral matter within the limits of the system is His astral body; the mental matter is His mental body. Thus we are all part of Him. We are part, too, of the "seven Mighty Spirits before [His] throne" [Rev. 4:5] through whom He pours Himself out into His universe. That is to say, the astral matter which makes up our astral bodies is also astral matter of one or other of the Seven Spirits. The force which flows out from the Logos reaches us principally through one of those seven channels, and so it is said that we belong to the Ray of which that particular Spirit is the head.

All that we have been taught about God—all that is good and beautiful—is true of the Solar Logos. But we have also heard a great deal about God that is far from good. Men have said that He is capable of anger and jealousy, that He slaughtered thousands of people at different times because they did something of which He did not approve or failed to do something that He ordered. But the truth is that we all come from Him, we all belong to Him, and we are all on our way back to Him.

God is, and can only be, good. His laws are made for our evolution and our helping; He does not change His laws or outrage them, so if we break them certain effects are bound to follow. The suffering that results to ourselves is not inflicted by Him; it is the natural consequence of our own actions. On the other hand, the Great Ones, who have been men like ourselves and have risen from our humanity, assure us that by working according to the law (which is the law of evolution) we shall one day stand where they do now.

Our Solar Logos has a life of His own among His peers. Each of His worlds sends up to Him a stream of devotion, and He in turn pours back upon it a great flood of spiritual influence. That stream, flowing through space, caused initially by the devotion of His people, forms, as it were, the seven-stringed lyre of Apollo, which He plays upon as one plays upon a harp. This music of the spheres ascends to the Great Logos as the praise and glory which is due to Him.

Our sun is a sun of the fourth order; therefore our Logos is a Logos of the Fourth Order. Just as our planets depends upon their sun and derive from it the life which sustains them, so does our Solar Logos (and perhaps millions of others like Him) depend upon a Solar Logos of the Third Order. And the thousands of Logoi of the Third Order depend upon a Logos of the Second Order; He, in His turn, "circles around" one of the First Order, and those of the First Order depend upon *Parabrahm*. We have been told these things, but in reality they can have very little meaning for us since they are so far beyond the world of our present experience.

It is good to remind ourselves that, in fact, even the things we think we understand are a very long way from our comprehension. Take the most ordinary things around us; we do not know how a tree grows, for instance. We know that it absorbs certain elements from the earth, but how it turns these into bark and leaves nobody really understands. We think we know things, and if we can name them and stick a label on them we are then quite sure that we have mastered them. But, as a matter of fact, there are very few things which we understand completely.

The Solar System

The solar system may be likened to a lotus flower. By raising one's consciousness to a higher level one may see that the planets—those spheres of fire—circling round the sun are like the tips of the lotus petals, or like the tips of the fingers of a hand. Most of the petals grow under the water—only the tips emerge, and where they break the surface they appear to be separate. The sun, floating in space, might represent the pistil among the stamens. Or it might be seen as the center floating overhead, a reflection of that which is the heart of the flower down below. The planets are linked together, not only fundamentally but subordinately. They are all, as it were, part of one great calyx.

When the Logos begins to form a system, His first step is to delimit the sphere of His activities, which extends far outside the orbit of the outermost planet of the system-to-be. Having made His limit, it is said that He then thinks the whole of His system into existence on what, to Him, corresponds to our mental plane. He determines the number of planets and satellites that He will bring into being, and the stage of development that shall be reached on each set of worlds. He makes, in fact, a gigantic and detailed thought-form of the complete system.

In Greek philosophy, the thought-form is built up in the intelligible world. This thought-plan is not exactly a mold into which matter is poured; it is rather an existence on that high plane which is brought down, bit by bit, to the lower planes as the great Beings who are working under the Logos require it as a pattern.

It is in reference to the intelligible world that we say everything exists in the beginning. The physical world does not exist at that stage, but its plan in the mind of the Logos has existed from the time when He resolved to form this system. Each part, as has been said, is brought down into manifestation as it is needed.

The Logos builds His system out of matter. The one thing which penetrates everywhere, as far as we know, is what the scientists call the ether of space. Theosophists call it *koilon*.[4] What we call matter is built out of bubbles blown in this substance. In *The Secret Doctrine* there is the statement that "Fohat digs holes in space." When I first read that many years ago, I thought of each "hole in space" as a solar system. When I came to know a little more, I concluded that the "holes" which Fohat "dug" are these tiny bubbles of infinitesimal smallness.

There are some 14,000 millions[5] of these bubbles in an ultimate physical atom. Eighteen of those atoms make up a chemical atom of hydrogen, the lightest of our elements.

To us, the bubbles may seem to be absolutely empty, but the breath of God is within them, and no power that we know can alter them in any way. An ancient Indian writing tells us that the Logos (not the Logos of our solar system) breathed into these bubbles and that thus it is His breath out of which everything is built. If He were to choose to draw in His breath, at that instant everything would fall into nothingness because the bubbles would have disappeared. St. Augustine declares that "If God were to cease from speaking the Word even for a moment, heaven and earth would vanish."

2

THE DESCENT INTO

The Trinity

W e must now try to understand something about the nature of the Deity and His manifestation in matter, which, as far as we are concerned, means the making of our solar system. All religions put forth some kind of theory to explain the origin of man and of the worlds, and most agree in describing the manifestation of the Deity as threefold. The Absolute (of whom we can know nothing except that He is) is the supreme God who rules over millions of universes. It is said that the process of cosmic evolution is similar to that of our solar system and that even in the absolute Logos or Deity there is the same threefold manifestation. We cannot actually know that, because the Absolute is so far above anything that we can see or touch; we can only infer that it must be so from what we see at lower levels.

In the case of our own solar system it is certain that we have this threefold manifestation because it is possible to look back and to see what has happened in the past. It is possible to see how the forces are flowing now, and from that we can deduce that there must be three centers of activity—three such aspects through which the force flows; three Persons, as it is stated, in one God.

It would be well, first, to define the word "person." It is derived from two Latin words, *per*, "through," and *sona*, "a sound."[6] It therefore signifies "that through which the sound comes." The name was first given in Rome to the mask which was worn by a minor actor or supernumerary who played several parts. He would, for instance, play the part of

9

dier in one act, a man in the crowd in another, a policeman in a third. Only the principal actors dressed their part fully. The supernumerary wore an ordinary peasant's dress and changed only his headdress and his mask, which indicated the particular part he was playing at the time. If, for example, he were acting the part of a soldier, he would wear an appropriate mask and a soldier's helmet.

The mask was the *persona* because the sound of the actor's voice came out through it. The three Persons of the Blessed Trinity are in reality three manifestations or aspects of the One God. Even that is not quite correct because they are more than mere aspects—a theory long ago condemned by the Church as heresy.

However, it is as near as we can come to representing this mystery to ourselves to say that in these three parts which the Deity plays He is represented by three Persons. We may employ analogies, but we must do so with care; they may help a little but it is well not to push them too far. To take a very simple analogy, we can imagine one man as the mayor of a city, the manager of a bank and, at the same time, the colonel of the local militia. In these three parts he would wear three different sets of clothing and, though he would act whatever part he was representing at a given moment, still he would always be one and the same man. Now the three Persons of the Blessed Trinity are very much more than that, but They may be thought of as God acting in different directions or in different capacities. This is indeed only a small part of the truth; the whole truth cannot be grasped at our present stage.

Our Solar System

It is difficult for us to imagine anything antecedent to our solar system.

One theory concerning the origins of our system is that two suns came into collision, striking one another, not head on, but glancingly, and thus set the planets in motion round the sun in their present orbits. That may or may not be true, but the reality goes a great deal further than that. Each solar system, as we learn from occult study, is the physical body, the expression of a Deity or Logos, and it may be that, in some cases, He indeed gathered the material for His physical body by means of such a collision. At any rate, in the case of our own solar system, occult investigation has shown that the Logos first decided upon a point where He could make His system, and then set up a great vortex into which He drew matter out of surrounding space and proceeded gradually to ensoul it. We do not know much about the original condition of that matter, but it appears that at a certain stage in the proceedings there is only atomic matter; that is to say, the atoms lie far apart and equidistant and are not in any way aggregated to make forms of any sort whatever. We do not know it as a definite fact, but they may be thought of as floating in empty space as motes float in a sunbeam. They are, however, indescribably smaller than any motes we can see with our physical eye. Ancient philosophy sometimes called this primordial matter "virgin matter," meaning that it was not yet interpenetrated or affected by the stream of life from the Logos.

The Planes of Matter

Occult investigation has further shown that in our solar system there are seven great planes or levels of matter and that man possesses bodies corresponding to, and by which he is able to contact, each one of them. There is the physical world, which we know, to a certain extent, as far as its lower subdivisions are concerned; the astral plane, which is the world in which feelings are expressed; the mental plane, which is built of the matter set in motion by our thought; the intuitional plane; the spiritual plane, where the triple spirit of man manifests itself; the monadic plane, where the Monad, the divine spark in man, resides; and finally the divine plane, on which is the triple manifestation of the Logos.

Each of these planes is divided into seven subplanes. They must not be imagined as lying one above the other like the shelves of a bookcase; rather must we think of them as filling the same space and interpenetrating one another just as air and water in a bottle of aerated water take up the same space, because the air "crowds in" between the molecules of the water. If we pour sugar into the aerated water, we have solid particles floating among the liquid and the gaseous matter; air, water and solids now interpenetrate each other and occupy the same space. In like manner, the different types of the matter of the solar system interpenetrate one another. When spirit ensouls matter, it comes into the finer matter first and gradually energizes matter of increasing density. We call this a "descent" because it is coming nearer to the physical-plane matter.

When the Deity of the solar system manifests Himself in these planes, He appears as threefold upon that highest division which we call the divine plane. It is obviously impossible to picture this divine manifestation in any way, for it is entirely beyond our power either of representation or comprehension. In our limited consciousness we imagine the Three Persons as separate, yet They are really one. The first manifestation, which in Christian terminology is called God the Father, remains always at that highest level; the second—God the Son—descends one level and manifests Himself on the sixth or monadic plane. The Third—God the Holy Ghost—descends yet further to the higher part of the spiritual plane. The Holy Trinity is often spoken of as manifesting as Power, Wisdom, and Intelligence. The Father is said to be the Creator, and yet He creates through the Son; that is to say, Power is exercised through Wisdom, and both Father and Son, as Power-Wisdom, work through Intelligence. Another definition of the three Persons is Will, Wisdom, and Activity, and in that case we may think of the Holy Ghost as the "Arm of the Lord" outstretched to do His work.

Now we find the same arrangement in the soul of man on the lower part of the spiritual plane. On the plane below—the intuitional—two principles manifest, giving rise to the intuitive nature. On the higher mental, there appears only one, manifesting as the intelligence. These three principles in man (which we call spirit, intuition, and intelligence) not only represent or reflect the three Persons of the Blessed Trinity, but in some way that as yet we cannot fully comprehend they *are* that Blessed Trinity. God is in every man, and every man is a manifestation of Him, even to the extent of mirroring in his soul that mysterious arrangement of three who yet are one. Here, then, we have the true meaning of the saying that God created man in His own image—not the physical body of man, but the constitution of his soul reproducing with marvelous exactitude the method of divine manifestation.

The Three Outpourings

It is from the Third Person—the Holy Ghost—that the first movement towards the formation of the system comes. In the Jewish account of the Creation we are told that at this stage the Spirit "brooded upon the face of the water" of space or the seas of matter (Latin *maria*, plural of *mare*, "sea"). As soon as the Holy Spirit descends, this matter, which before was inert, unproductive or "virgin," at once begins to show signs of life. Through His glorious vitality, the atoms, which were all alike and equidistant, are awakened to new powers of attraction and repulsion and form aggregations and combinations of all kinds, bringing into existence the lower subdivisions of each level until we have, in full activity, the marvelous complexity of the forty-nine subplanes of our system.

When the field has thus been prepared for its activity, the second great outpouring of the Divine Life begins—the outflow of what is sometimes called monadic essence. This comes from the Second Person of the Trinity—God the Son. Slowly and steadily, but with resistless force, this mighty influence pours itself in great waves downwards through the various planes, giving to matter further powers of combination and making for itself forms or bodies out of that matter, each successive wave spending a whole aeon in each of the seven kingdoms of nature. It thus ensouls in succession what are called the three elemental kingdoms in which the spirit, moving downwards, immerses itself at last in physical matter and passes into the mineral kingdom. Having thus reached the lowest point of its destined course, it turns to begin its grand upward sweep towards divinity, pressing onward through the vegetable and animal kingdoms until it reaches the human kingdom, where it meets the outpouring from the First Person of the Blessed Trinity.

The life of the Second Person ensouls all these lower kingdoms until it reaches the human kingdom, where that which has been the ensouler becomes, in its turn, the ensouled, for from that vivified matter which has acted as a soul for the animal is formed the causal body of man. It is into the causal body, then, that the Third Outpouring from the First Person, God the Father, descends, and so the individuality, the Ego, of the man is formed.

It used to be thought that man was the only reasoning animal. Assuredly, man has a far better brain than an animal, but anyone who has kept a pet dog or cat and made a friend of it knows that along certain lines the higher domesticated animals do reason and deduce one thing from another. The animal, while alive, is a separate soul just as much as any man, but when its body dies its soul is no longer a permanently separate entity. It remains as a separate thing in the astral life for some considerable time, but after that it goes back into what is called the group soul, whereas the man's soul, when the body dies, passes through various intermediate stages and then returns to take another body. Man is a separate entity, a living soul, forever. That is the difference between the lowest man and the highest animal. And so we are told in the Bible that the spirit of the beast goeth "downward"—that is, back again into his group-soul but "the spirit of man goeth upward" [Eccl. 3:21] and eventually attains union with the Monad or Spirit.

Nothing in this great system is lost. If it is true that the Second Outpouring is, as it were, absorbed into the first, without that second the first could not have been. All that has been gained by the Second Outpouring is transferred into and welded into the first. This is put clearly in the *Quicunque vult*:[7] "yet he is not two, but one Christ; one, not by conversion of the Godhead into flesh; but by taking the Manhood into God."

14

Divine Energy

The Deity sends forth from itself various forces or forms of energy. There may be many of which we know nothing, but there are some which have been observed. It is not easy to find the origin or source of some of these forces, for they descend from planes higher than those which are accessible to us. But all power is divine power and comes forth from one or another of the three aspects of the Logos.

We find, too, that a great many of these forces—light, heat, electricity, and certain rays described in scientific experiments—appear to be variants of the same force and under certain conditions they can be changed one into the other.

Apart from the group of forces just mentioned, we find another force which we call the life force and which long ago subdivided itself to a great degree. It comes forth at the Second Outpouring from the second aspect of the Logos, through millions of channels, showing itself on every plane of our system, yet fundamentally it is one and the same force. On the intuitional or *buddhic* plane, it displays itself as the Christ-principle which gradually unfolds itself within the soul of man.

This force must not be confused with the force of vitality or *prāna,* which pours forth from the sun and is an expression of the first or Father aspect of the Logos. The vitality itself is not life but is necessary for the maintenance of life in a form.

Another distinct force, coming forth from the third aspect of the Logos is called the Serpent Fire, known in India under the name of *kundalini.* This force is the same as that which emanates from the Holy Ghost at the First Outpouring, but now it is on its path of return. On its outgoing path, it forms out of the bubbles in *koilon* the atoms which are used as building stones by the Second Outpouring in the creation of living forms. On its return path—in the form of the Serpent Fire—it plays a part in the evolution of the bodies of all living creatures.

We know all these forces as distinct and separate on the physical plane, but this does not mean that they may not be connected at a higher level. There is much that one knows on higher planes that simply cannot be put into language down here.

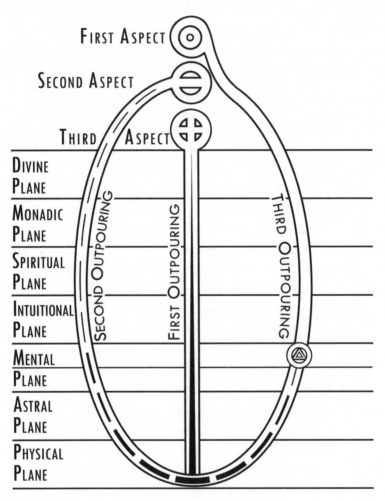

Diagram 1. The Three Outpourings

This diagram shows the seven planes of our system. The symbols used to designate the three Persons of the Trinity are of great antiquity. The First Person—the Father— is symbolized by a point within a circle; the Second Person—the Son—by a horizontal bar within a circle; and the Third Person—the Holy Spirit—by a cross within a circle. They are placed outside time and space, only the streams of life and force flowing from Them are shown descending into our system of planes. The First Outpouring, coming from the Third Person—God the Holy Ghost—is shown as a straight line descending to the lowest and densest plane, vivifying matter on its way. The Second Outpouring, emanating from the Second Person—God the Son—is that stream of life sent out into matter already vitalized by the First Outpouring and is shown descending to the lowest point in matter, after which it rises until it reaches the mental plane. In both of these outpourings the divine life becomes more veiled as it descends into matter (shown darker in the diagram). The Third Outpouring, coming from the First Person—God the Father—descends only as far as the intuitional plane, and its link with the Second Outpouring is symbolized by a triangle within a circle, representing the individual triune soul of man, the reincarnating Ego. The force of the Third Person also rises again after touching its lowest point in matter, but now in the form of what is called the Serpent Fire or *kundalini*, so we must imagine that the vertical line in the center returns upon its path.

3

MADE IN THE IMAGE OF GOD

We are told that God made man in His own image. Some have held this to mean that it is the physical body of man which is made in the likeness of the physical body of God. But that cannot be so, for God has no physical vehicle, unless we accept the manifestations of the solar system on the physical plane as the physical manifestation of God. That, indeed, they are, since there is nothing which is not God. He not only permeates everything, but He literally *is* everything. All the spirit, all the power, all the energy in the world is the Divine Spirit and Power and Energy, and the very matter through which it acts is only another manifestation of Him. It is literally true that there is nothing but God at all levels from the highest to the lowest, for it is the Divine Life itself which surrounds us everywhere. But when it is said that God made man in His own image, it is the man himself—the soul—to which we refer, and not the physical body.

How can the soul of man be made in the image of God? There are Three Persons in that ever-Blessed Trinity, and yet those Three are One. The same phenomenon appears in man. But man is threefold in another sense, as we are told in the New Testament. He is made up of body, soul, and Spirit; but it is not in this way that he is three in one. It is rather the soul itself which is triple, which has three aspects or manifestations.

The Spirit in man is the divine power of the Godhead in him, the divine energy leaping forth directly from Him at a tremendously higher level than anything we can understand.

There are seven different planes of nature, which are sometimes called "worlds" or "heavens." Thus we find references in the Bible to other and higher worlds, as when St. Paul speaks of having been caught up into the third heaven [2 Cor. 12:2], showing that he recognized at least three higher states than this earth.

Most people think of heaven as a place of happiness and delight, and so it is, for all higher levels are in every way better, more joyous, and less restricted than the physical plane. But, strictly speaking, "heaven" means that which is "heaved up" or raised above us; therefore any state higher than our own might be spoken of as heaven, and it is in that sense that we speak of the "seven heavens" or the seven conditions higher than this physical life.

The Spirit

The Spirit of man—the divine spark which is part of the divine fire—rests on a plane so high that at our present stage of evolution we cannot respond to it.

Further on in our evolution, when we have more fully developed our powers, we shall come clearly and definitely into touch with that Spirit, and we shall know that we are God and that God is in us. But for the present we are nearly at the bottom of the ladder that will take us to that stupendous height. The evolution before us is so vast that what we have already achieved will seem to us as nothing when we look back upon it from the immense heights of that distant future.

There are those who approach this most profound of all subjects with the firm conviction that they are capable of understanding it fully. God alone understands it fully and because, in a sense, we also are God, we shall begin to comprehend it fully when we have developed to the full "measure of the stature of the fullness of Christ" (Eph. 4:13). At present we are but children in these studies. We can understand enough to guide us in our daily living; we can always understand enough to show us the next step which we have to take, and that is enough for us at the moment.

The Spirit itself, which we sometimes call the Monad, exists on a plane which is far beyond the reach of our consciousness. The first contact which we can make with it is on a plane below its own, where it shows itself as threefold. Then, in its further downward movement, it puts out a very small part of itself into a much lower level, and that is what is called the soul, or Ego, in man. This soul or Ego passes on from life to life at its own level—a level very much lower than that of the Spirit, but still much higher than our life on this physical plane.

The Soul

The soul contains within itself the triple manifestation of the Spirit. It is said that God the Father remains on His own level and that God the Son descends into incarnation and takes upon Himself the robe of flesh. This was known to other and older religions than Christianity—to the great Hindu religion as well as to that of ancient Egypt. Indeed, it will be found to be implied, if not expressed, in all the great religions of the past.

Just as the Second Person of the Trinity descends lower than the First, so does the Third Person—God the Holy Ghost, the Flame of God—pour Himself out upon His people at a still lower level. And we find this arrangement repeated also in the soul of man. For the soul of man (as has been said before) is triple, made up of *atma*, the Breath or Spirit of God; *buddhi*, Intuitional Wisdom; and *manas*, intelligence. These, taken together, make what is called the incarnating Ego which goes on from life to life. We have all had many of these earth lives in the past (although most of us do not remember them), and we shall have many more in the future.

That is the method of the soul's evolution. It descends into this earthly life, where it gains certain experiences and develops certain faculties and returns to its own plane for a time of rest and of assimilation.

It is in his threefold constitution that man is made "in the image of God." And this threefold manifestation is more than mere symbolism; it is the representation of the Trinity in the Godhead, which manifests itself through man just insofar as he will allow it to do so.

When the soul "puts itself down" into incarnation, it takes not only a physical body but a mental one, which is commonly called the mind, and an emotional body, through which the emotions function. The latter is sometimes called the "astral" body because it shines and is luminous when it is seen by means of higher sight. In each life these bodies are taken anew.

Only after having assumed these intermediate vehicles can the soul come into touch with an embryo and be born into the physical world. When, at the end of that life, the physical body is worn out, the process is reversed and the soul lays aside one by one the temporary vehicles which it had assumed. So it is that the soul, during incarnation, is temporarily reflected in its three lower vehicles, which collectively constitute the personality of man.

The Causal Body

The causal body is the permanent vehicle of the soul or Ego in the higher mental world and consists of matter of the first, second, and third subdivisions of that world. In most people it is not yet fully active, only the matter belonging to the third subdivision being vivified. As the soul develops its latent possibilities through its long course of evolution, the higher matter is gradually brought into action, but it is only in the perfected man—the adept—that it is developed to its fullest capacity.

When a man reaches the stage where he is capable of abstract thought and unselfish emotions, the matter of the causal body is aroused in response. Its vibrations show themselves to the clairvoyant observer as colors and instead of being, as heretofore, merely a transparent ovoid, it gradually becomes a sphere filled with matter of the most lovely and delicate hues indicative of the spiritual development of the soul.

In the course of evolution in the lower worlds, the soul introduces into its vehicles qualities which are undesirable for its development—qualities such as pride, irritability, and sensuality. These show themselves as vibrations in the various bodies, but since they are vibrations in the lower subdivisions of their respective worlds, they cannot reproduce themselves in the causal body, which is built exclusively of the matter of the three higher subdivisions of the mental world. Each section of the astral body, for instance, acts strongly upon the corresponding section of the mental body, but only upon that. The causal body can be affected only by the three higher sections of the astral body, and the vibrations of those parts represent only good qualities.

The practical effect of this is that the individual can build into the Ego or soul nothing but good qualities. Any evil qualities he may develop in his personality are transitory in nature and are discarded as he advances, because his causal body has no matter within it which can express such qualities.

The Mental Body

The mental body, expressing the concrete thought of the individual, is ovoid in shape and built of matter of the four lower subdivisions of the mental world. We find here the same color scheme as in the causal body. There are in it certain segments which correspond to particular departments in the physical brain. The mental body is, in general, so imperfectly developed in most people that great numbers of these special departments have not yet been brought into activity, or only very slightly so. This is why, for instance, only some people have a head for mathematics, while others can appreciate music but not poetry, and so on. The matter of the mental body should be circulating freely, but sometimes thoughts on certain subjects are allowed to become set and they solidify and harden into a kind of wart. Such a "wart" manifests itself as a prejudice, and until free circulation is restored it is impossible for the person to think clearly in regard to that subject.

Good thoughts produce vibrations in the finer matter of the mental body, which tends to flow in the upper part of the ovoid, whereas bad thoughts such as those of selfishness or jealousy gravitate towards the lower part. Vague, ill-defined thoughts float for a while in space and then slowly disintegrate. Every thought builds a form. A man can make a thought-form and aim it at another with the object of helping him. This is one of the lines of activity adopted by those who wish to serve humanity. Such a thought-form may act like a "guardian angel." Any person who habitually thinks pure and strong thoughts is a great power for good in the world.

The Astral Body

The astral body is the expression of the soul on the astral plane and is the vehicle of passion and emotion. The name "astral" originated with the medieval alchemists. It means "starry" and was probably used because of the luminous appearance of the astral body. This body exhibits many colors expressing the great variety of human feelings and emotions.

When the astral body is comparatively quiet, its colors indicate those emotions which the person habitually entertains. When there is a rush of a particular feeling, the rate of vibration which expresses that feeling dominates the entire astral body for a time. If it be, for example, devotion, the whole of the astral body is tinged with blue.

The permanent colors of the astral react upon the mental body. They produce in it the corresponding colors, but several octaves higher, in the same way that a musical note produces overtones. The mental body, in its turn, influences the causal body in the same way, and thus all the good qualities expressed in the lower vehicles establish themselves by degrees in the soul. The negative qualities are unable to do this, as their rates of vibration find no corresponding vibrations in the higher mental matter of which the casual body is built.

The Physical Body

We have described the vehicles which are the expressions of the soul in the mental world and in the world of emotions. They are vehicles which the soul provides for itself. But in the physical world, the vehicle is provided for it by nature under certain laws. Although also, in a sense, an expression of the soul, this vehicle is far from being a perfect manifestation.

The physical body of man is a wonderful instrument and one of great complexity. Besides the part which is dense enough to be visible to the eye, there is the part we call the etheric body. In this part of the body there are certain force centers through which energy flows from one vehicle or body to the other.

Three principal forces flow through the seven chakras or force centers in the etheric body, and we may think of them as representing the three aspects of the Logos. One is the expression of the Second Outpouring, from the Second Aspect of the Logos—that stream of life which is sent into the matter already vitalized by the action of the Third Aspect in the First Outpouring. This, the primary or life force, is reflected in the incarnation of Christ, who was born "of the Holy Ghost and the Virgin Mary."

The second force is the Serpent Fire which comes forth from God the Holy Ghost. It rests in the chakra at the base of the spine. The third is what we call vitality.

Vitality

We keep our physical bodies alive not only by food and drink and by breathing good air, but also by drawing into ourselves vitality, called in the East *prana*. *Prana* is a fluid, or perhaps we should rather call it a kind of element which comes to us from the sun. Those who have clairvoyant sight are able to see it as tiny particles, and even slightly sensitive people when looking at a clear sky can see myriads of tiny shining points dancing about in constant and rapid motion. They can more easily be seen on a fine day, because when there is bright sunlight they are generated in immense numbers and are especially active. We draw these vitality globules into our physical bodies, and currents of them flow along our nerves and through our whole system.

When a person makes magnetic passes over another and tries to give him strength, what he really does is to pour into him more prana. When we take food into our bodies, before it can be assimilated it must go through the process of digestion. In the same way when we draw these vitality globules[8] into ourselves they must be broken up into their component parts before the body is able to assimilate them. A person who is ill has lost for the time being the power of breaking up these atoms of life and distributing them through his body, therefore he can be very much helped by someone else drawing the "predigested" atoms from his own body and pouring them into him. The patient feels stronger and better after that is done because life is coursing once more through his veins.

Those who are clairvoyant enough to see the health aura which radiates from the body will notice, in the case of a person who is ill, that the radiation is far less strong than in a man in good health and that, instead of shooting straight out in all directions from the body, the lines of radiation fall droopingly like the waters of a fountain which has been turned low.

The vitality globules are a manifestation of God the Father who, by pouring out this stream of vitality, is in a very real sense giver of life to us and to His system.

This, then, is the constitution of man. In the first place he is a Spirit, a Monad, a spark of the Divine.

For the purposes of human evolution, the monad manifests itself in lower worlds. When it descends one stage into the spiritual world it shows itself as a triple spirit, just as the Deity in worlds infinitely higher has three aspects. One of these aspects remains always in that world, and we call that the spirit in man. The second aspect manifests itself in the intuitional world, and we speak of it as the intuition in man. The third manifests itself in the higher mental world, and we call it the intelligence in man.

The soul or Ego is a partial expression of the monad, formed in order that he may enter evolution and may return eventually to the Spirit with qualities developed by experience. The soul in its turn puts down a part of itself for the same purpose into yet lower worlds, and we call that the personality. Just as the soul is a small and imperfect expression of the Monad, so is the personality an imperfect expression of the soul, so that what we usually think of as a person is in truth only a fragment of a fragment.

We find, then, that man is the result of an elaborate evolutionary scheme, and that in him three streams of divine life converge. The idea of God having made man in His own image, when properly understood, is seen to embody a great truth.

WORLD OR PLANE	PRINCIPLES OF MAN			DIVINE PRINCIPLES
	TERMS USED BY ST. PAUL	LIBERAL CATHOLIC TERMS	RELATIONSHIP OF PRINCIPLES	
DIVINE				FATHER A · B C
MONADIC	Spirit	Monad	1	SON D E
SPIRITUAL		Triple Spirit Functioning in Spiritual Body	2 3 4	HOLY GHOST F
INTUITIONAL		Intuition Functioning in Intuitional Body	5 6	
HIGHER MENTAL	Soul	Intelligence Functioning in Causal Body	(The Ego Is 2, 5, & 7 Manifested in the Causal Body) 7 8	
LOWER		Mind Functioning in Mental Body	9	
ASTRAL OR EMOTIONAL	Spiritual Body	Emotional Nature Functioning in Astral Body	10	
PHYSICAL ULTIMATE PHYSICAL ATOMS SUBATOMIC SUPERETHERIC ETHERIC GASEOUS LIQUID SOLID	Natural Body	Waking Consciousness Functioning in Physical Body	11	

Diagram 2. The Principles of Man

28

In the diagram on the opposite page, an attempt has been made to show the relationship between the Persons of the Holy Trinity in manifestation and how this relationship is mirrored in the principles of man. We do not know in what form the Logos exists outside the limits of His system; all that can be said with certainty is that when His life appears in the highest world of the solar system, it pours down in three mighty streams to give rise to the Triple Spirit or, what we call in Christianity, the Three Persons of the Trinity. They are here represented by three circles (A, B, and C). The First Person, the Father (A), does not descend below the divine plane. The Second Person, the Son, descends to the monadic plane, where He is represented as dual (D). The Third Person, the Holy Ghost, passing through the monadic plane, descends to the spiritual plane (F). The symbols used for the three aspects of the Trinity are the same as in diagram 1.

The consciousness of man is a unity, not a multiplicity; but as it manifests itself in the different bodies or vehicles, it presents different aspects. These aspects of consciousness are here termed "principles." A principle is not a body, but the expression of consciousness in a body. The Monad (1), termed by St. Paul the Spirit, is the divine spark in man, the divine source of human consciousness. When the Monad manifests itself a plane lower—the spiritual plane—it is always as a triplicity (2, 3, and 4). Principle 2, the Spirit, does not descend below that level. The other two principles manifest in the next lower world—the intuitional—giving rise to the dual intuitive nature. Principle 5 does not manifest below that level. Principle 6 pours itself down into the next world—the higher mental—and manifests as the intelligence in man. Principles 2, 5, and 7 together constitute the soul or Ego in man, the reincarnating center of consciousness which persists through the whole series of human lives. In the lower worlds, the soul or Ego is reflected in principles 9 (the mind), 10 (the emotions), and 11 (the physical body). These three collectively constitute the transitory personality of one life. The link between the soul and the personality is called the *antahkarana* in Indian philosophy (8). If we think of the Ego as the true man, then the personality is the hand which he dips down into matter in order to work through it, and the *antahkarana* is the arm linking that hand to his body.

4

THE HUMAN SOUL

In a previous chapter I described how the Holy Spirit, in the First Outpouring, descends into and vivifies matter of the various planes, first building their respective atoms and then aggregating those atoms into elements.

Into the matter so vivified the Second Outpouring comes down from God the Son, and the Divine Life, of which that outpouring consists, incarnates or draws the matter together into bodies or vehicles which it can inhabit. At the lowest level of materiality that Life ensouls the mineral kingdom. As it evolves, it becomes definite enough to ensoul the vegetable kingdom and still later, the animal. When it has risen to the highest level of the animal kingdom a remarkable change takes place and an entirely new factor is introduced—that of the Third Outpouring, which comes from the First Aspect of the Logos, commonly called God the Father.

That force which has hitherto been the ensouler now becomes, in its turn, the ensouled, and the force from the First Person seizes upon what has heretofore been the soul of the animal and of it makes for itself a body of matter so exceedingly fine as to be utterly imperceptible to our physical senses.

Thus is born the Ego or soul in its causal body. At once it draws into itself the result of all the experience that has been gained by the animal soul during all the aeons of its previous development, so that nothing of the qualities which have been acquired in the course of its evolution is lost.

The wonderful force that rushes from the highest aspect known to us of the Solar Logos is, in very truth, the actual life of God Himself. So are also the First and Second Outpourings, but they have come down slowly and gradually through all the subplanes, drawing round themselves the matter of each of these and enmeshing themselves in it so thoroughly that it is scarcely possible to discern them for what they are, or to recognize them as divine life at all. But the Third Outpouring flashes straight down from its source without involving itself in any way in the intermediate matter. It is pure white light, uncontaminated by anything through which it has passed.

The Monad

This third stream of the Divine Life has, in fact, issued forth from the Logos long ages ago and is hovering at an intermediate point in the second of our planes. When hovering at that level it is called the Monad, which we may think of as a part of that which cannot be divided—a spark thrown off from the divine fire, yet ever united to it. A paradox, truly, to our mortal intellect, yet enshrining an eternal truth which is far beyond our comprehension.

The general method of the descent of spirit into matter seems to be always the same, though the diverse conditions of the different planes naturally produce many variations in detail. The Logos Himself puts down the Monad—a tiny fragment of Himself—into a level far below His own. Of course, such a descent must mean a most severe limitation, though it is all too far above the utmost reach of our consciousness to be described or understood. In exactly the same way, the Monad puts down a fragment of himself, which becomes the Ego or soul, and the limitation is enormously increased. The same thing happens once more when the Ego repeats the operation and projects a minute fragment which we call the personality into the mental, emotional, and physical bodies of man.

The last tiny fragment is the point of consciousness, which those who are clairvoyant can see moving about within man. According to one system of symbology it is seen as a "golden man the size of a thumb,"[9] who dwells in the heart; and to another it is seen as a brilliant star of light. A man may keep this star of consciousness where he will, that is to say, in any one of the seven principal centers of his body. Which of these is most natural to a man depends largely upon his Ray, and I think also upon his race and subrace. Those of us who belong to the fifth subrace of the fifth root race nearly always keep that consciousness in the brain, in the center dependent upon the pituitary body. There are, however, men of other races to whom it comes more natural to keep it habitually in the heart, the throat, or the solar plexus.

The Personality

This star of consciousness is the representative of the soul in these lower planes, and as it manifests through those vehicles we call it the personality; this is the man as he is known to his friends down here.

But though the personality is absolutely part of the Ego or soul—though the only life and power in it are those of the Ego—it nevertheless often forgets this fact and, coming to regard itself as an entirely separate entity, works down here for its own ends. It has always a line of communication with the Ego (sometimes referred to as the *antahkarana*), but it usually makes no effort to use it. In the case of those who have never studied these matters, the personality is, to all intents and purposes, the man, and the Ego manifests itself only very rarely and partially.

Man's evolution in its earlier stages consists in the opening up of his line of communication, so that the Ego may be increasingly able to assert itself through it, and finally entirely to dominate the personality, so that it may have no separate thought or will, but merely (as it should be) an expression of the Ego on these lower planes. It must, of course, be understood that the Ego, belonging as it does to an altogether higher plane, can never fully express itself down here; the most we can hope for is that the personality will contain nothing which is not intended by the Ego—that it will express as much of it as can be expressed in this lower world.

The Evolution of the Soul

The spiritually untrained man has practically no communication with the Ego; the Initiate has full communication; consequently we find (as we should expect) that there are men among us at all stages between these two extremes. It must be remembered that the Ego itself is only in process of development, and that we have therefore to deal with Egos at very different stages of advancement. In any case, an Ego is in a great many ways enormously more developed than a personality can ever be.

Life on this level is infinitely larger and more vivid than what we know as life down here. Just as it is evolution for the personality to learn to express the Ego more fully, so is it evolution for the Ego to learn to express the monad more fully.

Some Egos are more awake to the necessities of their evolution than others, which is only another way of saying that there are older and younger Egos and that the older are striving more earnestly than the younger to unfold their latent possibilities.

We are apt to think that the only development possible for an Ego is through the personality, but that is not so—or rather it is only in connection with one small set of qualities. As I have explained at length in my book *Man Visible and Invisible*, the causal body of a primitive man is almost colorless. In the process of evolution he develops good qualities, which are able to find corresponding vibrations in the matter of the causal body; the colors expressive of these qualities begin to show themselves and, presently, the causal body, instead of being empty, is full of active, pulsating life. So much more of the Ego can now manifest through it that it has to increase enormously in size; it extends further and further from its physical center until the man is able to enfold hundreds and even thousands of persons within it and so exercise a vast influence for good.

But all this, wonderful though it be, is only one side of this development. There are other lines of progress of which we know nothing; the soul is living a life of its own among its peers, among the great *arupadevas*,[10] among all kinds of splendid angels in a world far beyond our ken. The young Ego is but little awake as yet to that glorious life, just as a baby in arms knows little of the world surrounding him; but as its consciousness gradually unfolds, it awakens to all this magnificence and becomes fascinated by its vividness and its beauty. Can we wonder that this seems immensely more important than the faint far-distant struggle of a cramped and half-formed personality veiled in the dense obscurity of a lower world? The soul knows that certain necessary parts of its evolution can be achieved only through a personality and its mental, astral, and physical bodies. But we can well understand that the task may often seem uninviting, that a given personality may appear anything but attractive or hopeful. If we look at many of the personalities around us, their physical bodies poisoned with meat, alcohol, and tobacco, their astral bodies reeking with greed and sensuality, and their mental bodies having no interest beyond business, or perhaps horse racing and prizefighting, it is not difficult to see why an Ego, surveying them from its lofty height, might decide to postpone any serious effort to another incarnation, in the hope that the next set of vehicles might be more amenable to its influence.

Personality Development

When the soul at last decides to turn the full force of its energy upon the personality, the change produced is marvelous. No one who has not himself investigated the matter can imagine how wonderful, how rapid, how radical such a change can be when conditions are favorable, that is, when the Ego is reasonably strong and the personality not incurably vicious. It is not easy to explain in physical words the differences which exist between Egos, since all of them are in many ways much greater than anything to which we are accustomed down here.

Analogies are notoriously misleading if pressed too far or taken too literally; but I may perhaps convey some faint reflection of the impression produced upon me by intercourse with them, if I say that an advanced Ego reminds me of a dignified, stately, and most courteous ambassador, full of wisdom and kindliness, while the less developed man is more like the bluff, hearty country squire. An Ego who is already on the Path, and is nearing adeptship, has much in common with the great angels and radiates spiritual influences of prodigious power; to come into contact with such a one is indeed a privilege and a blessing.

The difficulty of this subject is greatly enhanced by the fact that it is necessary for us to regard it simultaneously from two points of view. Most of us down here are very emphatically personalities and think and act almost exclusively as such; yet we know all the time that in reality we are Egos, and those of us who, by many years of meditation, have rendered ourselves more sensitive to finer influences are often conscious of the intervention of this higher Self. The more we can make a habit of identifying ourselves with the Ego, the more clearly and sanely shall we view the problems of life; but insofar as we feel ourselves to be still personalities, looking up to our higher Selves, it is obviously our duty and our interest to open ourselves to them, to reach up towards them, and persistently to set up within ourselves such vibrations as will be of use to them.

Since selfishness is the intensification of the personality, our first step should be to get rid of that. Then we must keep our minds filled with high thoughts; for if they are continually occupied with lower matters (even though those lower matters may be quite estimable in their way) the Ego cannot readily use them as channels of expression.

Intuition

We bring over our capacities from one life to another. But sometimes something definite can be brought through from the mind to the physical brain, and we call that an intuition. As far as we are concerned down here, what we should do in some crisis or the solution to some particular difficulty will suddenly flash upon the mind. A very good example of this is found in our attitude towards any new teaching which may come before us. I can remember very well in my own case, when I first came across this great body of oriental teaching on all these subjects, the moment it was presented to me I knew it must be true. Something flashed into me from above which convinced me of its truth so that at once I accepted it, because I could not doubt it. Since then I have learnt how to prove it for myself in many different ways, but even now, when I have done all that, I do not believe it any more strongly than I believed it in that first moment. I was just as certain then as I am now, only then I could not have told you why I was certain, whereas now I can, because I have tried the experiments, I have myself gone through the experience. I have watched the phenomena and now I can say, "I know," whereas before I could only say, "I believe," and yet the belief was just as certain, because it was the result of the fact that I myself had been studying these things in other lives. This same philosophy was taught to us by Pythagoras in Greece 2300 years ago and more. I learnt then how to see the truth of some of it for myself, and therefore in my soul or Ego was the certain knowledge of this teaching. But this knowledge was not in the physical brain at all, and, so far as I can see, it might never have come through into my new mind unless the facts had been put before me from the outside. It needed that stimulus apparently to awaken the old recollection, which enabled the soul to impress upon the brain the fact that this is true. For that moment the soul and the lower mind became one to the extent that the conviction from the soul came through into the lower mind. That is one kind of intuition, and you will see at once that that also is only knowledge based on experience. We call it intuition because, so far as we are concerned, it comes into this lower mind from above.

Now besides intuition there is such a thing as impulse. Impulse is the result of feelings, of likes and dislikes, which come from the emotional body. But so far as the physical brain is concerned, an impulse is an impression from above just as intuition is, and the difficulty is to know the intuition from the impulse. We all know that likes and dislikes often come to us without any particular reason. We do not know definitely why we have a liking for certain people. We know that the first time we meet certain people the soul seems to leap out to them, and we feel at once that they are old friends. Why? Almost certainly because we have known those souls when both of us wore different vestures and were in other bodies and in other races. We have known those people before in other lives, and when we meet them again, though neither of us remembers it, still the old affection leaps out from soul to soul and we make friends with them very quickly.

At other times we may meet someone who does not attract us; we may even feel repelled by that person. There, again, in old days you have been together, and one may have harmed the other. In such cases it is wiser not to come into close relations with that person but, while keeping at a distance lest this feeling should grow stronger, to think kindly of him. Continue to think kindly, and then when next time you meet you may find that the kindly feeling has overpowered the old dislike and that you are able to make friends.

All these things are perfectly scientific and, if we counteract one force by another, we presently get a condition of stability just as we should in mechanics on the physical plane. The spiritual world is higher and finer and is vibrating far more rapidly than the physical world, but it obeys the same general laws with only such modifications as are necessary for the change of substances. Generally speaking, when we come into touch in this way with someone whom we have met before, the old feeling is likely to be revived. It is there in the two souls, but the coming through into the physical plane often seems to be practically impossible until some physical plane suggestion revives the old remembrance and brings it through. I cannot say exactly that it reestablishes it, because the two physical bodies have not met before and have had no previous contact with each other, but it is the breaking through of the veil of rebirth, and so the souls are able to regain their communication on this lower level through their physical bodies.

The Larger Consciousness Within

I have spoken of the remembrance of the soul as being the work of the intelligence, which is part of that soul, through the lower mind. But there is another possibility of intuition. Remember that that higher mind which is part of the soul itself may still err, though it is much less likely to do so than the mind down here, because it has had far greater experience, although it is still not perfect. It is not yet fully developed, and certainly it may err, though it is not liable to do so. But there is that higher part of the soul, which in the East is called the *buddhi* or intuitional wisdom. It is possible for that sometimes to press through and to seize upon the subconscious rather than the conscious self.

There is within us a far larger consciousness, which is sometimes called "subliminal" consciousness, from *sub*, "under" or "below," and *limen*, "threshold"—that which is below the threshold, which does not come into ordinary life. The "supraliminal" is that which is above the threshold, and which we sometimes think we know all about. Through this subliminal consciousness we may occasionally receive a flash of real knowledge, which is sure to be right, because it comes from the *atma*, of which the *buddhi* is only the sheath or the vehicle. But even when that comes to us we may misinterpret it, although it comes from the divine within us and is therefore true.

Each man certainly has the germ of an intuitional body. Let us go a stage further, although in so doing I am afraid that it will be somewhat incomprehensible. When one reaches the spiritual consciousness which functions on the spiritual or *atmic* plane, one finds a consciousness which is indeed an atom, and yet at the same time apparently the whole. This is the condition which St. Bonaventure tried to describe when he made the statement that we must think of it as "a circle with its center everywhere and its circumference nowhere"—not very helpful

39

to the mind, and yet somehow marvelously illuminative. One may have a kind of intuitive grasp of his idea. This is the consciousness of Divine Union which, in the East, has been called nirvana.

You can come down from that and imagine that you are yourself, that you yourself include many other selves, that that number is increasing, and that on the highest subplane of the intuitional plane it would be practically coextensive with our worlds. Yet in all that, though you share the consciousness of others, you can yet so hold yourself as to see their consciousness as a separate thing; the normal condition of the plane being that all the consciousnesses are merged into one. Thus we have something which is greatly less than the nirvanic condition and is yet much more than the causal body.

This germ is often quite undeveloped in the ordinary man of the world who has never thought of these matters; but in those of us who have given much time to meditation it has already grown at least to some slight extent, and it is capable of rapid unfoldment when we really turn our attention to it.

5

The Method of Human Progress

A boy went to school. He was very little. All that he knew he had drawn in with his mother's milk. His teacher (who was God) placed him in the lowest class and gave him these lessons to learn: Thou shalt not kill. Thou shalt do no hurt to any living thing. Thou shalt not steal.

So the man did not kill, but he was cruel and he stole. At the end of the day, when his beard was grey, when the night was come, the teacher (who was God) said: "Thou hast learned not to kill. But the other lessons thou hast not learned. Come back tomorrow."

On the morrow he came back, a little boy. And his teacher (who was God) put him in a class a little higher and gave him these lessons to learn: Thou shalt do no hurt to any living thing. Thou shalt not steal. Thou shalt not cheat.

So the man did no hurt to any living thing, but he stole and he cheated. At the end of the day, when his beard was grey, when the night was come, his teacher (who was God) said: "Thou hast learned to be merciful. But the other lessons thou has not learned. Come back tomorrow."

Again on the morrow he came back, a little boy. And his teacher (who was God) put him in a class yet a little higher, and gave him these lessons to learn: "Thou shalt not steal. Thou shalt not cheat. Thou shalt not covet."

So the man did not steal, but he cheated and coveted. And at the end of the day, when his beard was grey, when the night was come, his teacher (who was God) said: "Thou hast learned not to steal. But the other lessons thou hast not learned. Come back, my child, tomorrow."

This is what I have read in the faces of men and women, in the book
of the world, and in the scroll of the heavens, which is writ with the stars
(Berry Benson, *The Century Magazine*, May 1894).

Humanity is part of a gigantic sweep of the divine life into matter. We
have long ago passed the lower level of descent and have risen up to the
other side of the curve, to the human level. We shall pass on higher and
higher to the levels of the angels, the great spirits, levels beyond our
reach as yet, and so back to Him from whom we came.

There is a great deal of work in that climbing, a vast number of little intermediate expeditions, so to speak. There is one mighty curve
of the whole evolution, but human progress along that line consists of
a number of little curves, a number of little dippings down into matter and rising out of it again, each little curve representing a life or
incarnation.

Again and again the soul puts himself down, each time to develop
a new quality in himself, each time to strengthen himself until he can
rise to the fullness of the measure of the stature of the Christ. Man's life
is not merely a matter of seventy or eighty years; it is a matter of many
millions of years, and what we are in the habit of calling a life is only one
day out of that long life. It is not even one whole day; there are twenty-
four hours in our day down here, but we do not spend the whole of it
in active work; part of the time we have to rest and refresh ourselves.
It is exactly the same with these little descents into matter, except that
the periods of rest and refreshment are much longer in proportion to
the period of manifestation. Human evolution is a slow process, and it
takes many days and many of the nights which come in between them
when, though the man has no physical body, he is developing and as-
similating all that he has learnt during these lives. It must always be
remembered that the soul is as yet, even in the best and cleverest of us,
an undeveloped soul. He is indeed a spark of the divine fire, and so has
within himself the most wonderful divine possibilities; but as yet they
are but germs, and they need development.

He is not capable yet of functioning fully at his own level where he lives as a fellow with other souls, having all sorts of wider faculties and greater knowledge than he has down here. He is not fully developed at that level, but he is gradually becoming so.

More Rapid Vibrations

The higher worlds or planes, to the finer movements of which the undeveloped soul cannot yet respond, are material, as is this physical plane, but they are built of a finer kind of matter, whose vibrations are far more rapid than the vibrations of matter down here. We have, of course, always to keep in mind the scientific conception that all material objects are really in a state of rapid vibration all the time. The objects as a whole appear to our rather coarse and clumsy sight to be at rest, but science tells us that there is rapid vibration going on among the particles, and however dense the substance may appear no two particles actually touch one another. There is a fairly wide gamut of vibration, and within certain rates of vibration all matter exists. The matter of the higher planes is, as I have said, vibrating far more rapidly than that of the physical plane, but even the vibrations down here when expressed in numbers and time are tremendously rapid. In any scientific book on the subject there will be found tables showing how certain rates of vibration appeal to the ear and make sound, how certain other rates of vibration appeal to the eye and make sight. Others make what are called Hertzian rays, electrical vibrations, X-rays, and so on. We get a vast number of differentiated rates of vibration. That goes on and on into infinity, getting shorter and more rapid all the while. We do not know what the limit is.

There is a vast difference in the power of response to these vibrations in different individuals. One way of testing this is by listening to the sound of the squeak of the bat, which is just on the border of human audibility. One man may hear the air full of those needlelike cries; another standing close by him will not be able to hear them at all; they

CHAPTER 5

are just a little too high for him to catch. We undoubtedly vary in our power of response, but it is quite feasible for some of us to get beyond the average physical response.

The same thing is true with regard to those higher levels. The Ego or soul lives in a world of vibration, but the undeveloped soul cannot fully respond to those vibrations. He realizes only a small part of them, and so he has to learn how to respond to the rest. How is this to be done? Only by coming down to some level where the vibrations are slower, so that he can first get used to responding to them. Then as his evolution proceeds he learns to respond to vibrations a little faster and still a little faster, until he will eventually get back to his own level with full power to respond to all that is going on there.

That is the mechanical aspect of the soul's periodical descents into matter. He takes on the lower vehicles because at his own level he does not feel fully alive. He puts himself into the lower part of the mental world and draws round him matter of that plane which is not so fine, though very fine still from our point of view. Out of that he constructs for himself a mental body. That is practically what we call the mind; it is a vehicle the vibrations of which are his thoughts. He comes down a little lower and draws round himself astral matter, and that makes the body of his emotions; it is with that he is able to feel. Then he comes down to the physical plane and enters a physical body—he is born as a little baby and gradually takes hold of that body and tries to mold it a little as it is growing.

This is a birth or incarnation—the commencement of a physical life. During that life all kinds of experiences come to him through his physical body, and from them he should learn some lessons and develop some qualities within himself. After a time he begins to withdraw again into himself and puts off by degrees the vestures that he has assumed. The first of these to drop away is the physical body, and his withdrawal from that is what we call death. It is not the end of his activities, as many people suppose; nothing could be further from the fact. He is simply withdrawing from one effort, bearing back with him its results;

he returns, as is said in the Gospel, bearing his sheaves with him;[11] and after a certain period of comparative repose, he will make another effort of the same kind. Each life gives certain results, and these results are assimilated and worked up into faculties and powers during the time that intervenes between the death of a man and his next incarnation. Down here on the physical plane he gets vibrations pouring in from all sides; he gets a fuller, a more vivid life of a kind, but of course it is of a lower kind. Gradually as the soul evolves life after life, he becomes able to respond to more and higher vibrations. So there will come a time when he will return to his own home—to his own soul plane—and find himself fully responsive there, fully alive, as it were.

Needless to say, when he does reach that stage he will have a far more magnificent and splendid life than anything we know about here. Before he has reached that high level, whenever he has the experience of returning to that plane which is his true home between these days at school which we call lives, he finds that, with all its splendor and its glory and its beauty, for him it is unsatisfactory because he is not yet up to that level. He is not fully alive there, and he yearns again for that full response. That yearning is spoken of in the Oriental scriptures as *trishna* (Sanskrit) or *tanha* (Pali), both words meaning thirst—the thirst for fuller life, the thirst to feel himself in full activity—and so the soul puts himself down again in order that he may experience this. It is by virtue of that experience and the use that he makes of it that he is able to carry back with him more and more results of experience—more and more material for working up into powers.

All this life of which we are so full, in which we think we are so busy and so clever, is but a preparation for a very much bigger life. Exactly as the boy's life at school is only a preparation for real life in the world, this physical life of ours is a preparation for the life on higher planes. Down here our efforts are feeble and often seem fruitless and futile. When we are able to reach the levels of the higher life, we shall have tasks to carry out which will be really worth our while. Then we shall have a life that is worth living to an extent we cannot possibly imagine down here—a life of glorious activity and success, a life of helping others, of managing, directing, and guiding systems, worlds, nations—a far higher life than we know anything about down here, but to equip ourselves for that we must go through this school. Thus only can the divine spark which is the soul of man fulfill its glorious destiny and develop into a flame, into a great fire, into a very sun—a sun pouring out light and heat and strength and help on all around it, just as God Himself pours His life through the whole of His universe. In a distant, but nevertheless a quite certain future, we shall have the power of exercising the divinity that is within us, and of working always within it and under its direction, each in his own way.

The Great Ones

It may be asked: "How can we be certain of that?" All I can say is that to myself as well as to other students of occultism these things are unquestionable facts. We have, during our investigation, come into touch with great numbers of people far more highly developed than ourselves. They are so much grander in every way than we that we might well think of them almost as gods, but they themselves disclaim any such idea. They say, "We are men just as you are; but we have gone further on the way than you have yet gone." Every step on that way between us and them is occupied by those who are climbing up towards them. Beyond even them we see greater spirits, mightier ones still, reaching on and on until all is lost for us in a cloud of glory that we cannot penetrate. But on every step of that long ladder are human beings like ourselves—only faultless, whereas we are full of faults; thoroughly developed, whereas as yet we are only partially developed. In just the same way we can look down that ladder on men standing at lower stages than ourselves. We know from studying the subject that those men, now occupying lower steps, will presently climb to where we are, but while they are climbing to this level we will climb onwards and upwards. Those great Masters of the Wisdom who seem so divine to us tell us that they were not long ago at the stage where we are now; that we have only to keep on climbing and we shall become as they are; but in the meantime they will have passed on to greater heights still.

What will be the ultimate end of all this age-long climbing we do not know. We are told that we came forth from God and that we must go back to Him, and I see quite sufficient evidence to convince me that it is so; but there is certainly no end within my power of perception, and the greater people tell us also that they know nothing about an end. But we do see what happens to be an infinity of progress stretching before us, and however great it may be in the ultimate, it is achieved—like all other progress—step by step, little by little. There is no question at all but that each of us can do it, because, as I have said, those glorious perfected beings, our great Masters, stood no long time ago, as time goes with them, where we stand now. We have only to follow in their footsteps, and we also shall attain.

The Laws of Evolution

All this evolution is taking place under never-changing laws. If that were not so, there could be no real progress. We can understand how it would be for a boy at school if he found all the school rules changing every day—sometimes kept and sometimes not kept—he would never know where he was; but in the school of life we are working under natural laws which never change. The first great law is that of evolution, the steady pressure onward and upward, and the next great law is the law of divine justice, the law of cause and effect. There is in the latter no thought of reward or punishment; it does not work that way. It is simply a matter of the effects produced by causes. There is no effect anywhere without a cause, and there is no cause which does not produce some effect somewhere.

Now we know that is so in science; it is so in chemistry and mechanics, because there we can generally see the result immediately. Action and reaction are equal and opposite always, and that is true in

47

the spiritual world just as much as it is in mechanics or chemistry. We cannot see reaction in the higher worlds, because, for one thing, it is not instantaneous. It may come quickly or after a long period, but the reaction always takes place and is always equal and opposite. If we send out evil to others, evil will come back to us; if we send out good, good will come back to us, and so we may be sure that the same great law of cause and effect obtains in the higher worlds as it does down here.

The result of good action, yes, and good speech and good thought too, is always happiness in some way and further opportunity, whereas the result of evil is always eventually sorrow and limitation. If we find ourselves limited in any way in this life, then the limitation is of our own making. If we have suffering or sorrow we alone are responsible for it, because it is the result of something that we did in the past. The manifold and complex destinies of men answer with rigid exactitude to the balance between good and evil in their previous actions. Therefore nothing whatever can come to any man unless he has deserved it, and everything that happens to him (whether it be sorrow or joy) is, on the one hand, the direct result of his own action in the past and, on the other, an opportunity by means of which he can deliberately mold his future.

This great law works both ways; it does not only react upon us from our past, but it also reaches forward from our present into our future. Every thought, word, or action produces its definite result—not a reward or punishment imposed from without, but a result inherent in the action itself, definitely connected with it in the relation of cause and effect, these being really but two inseparable parts of one whole; so that just as our present is the absolute result of what we thought and said and did in the past, so are we absolutely, definitely, and unfailingly building our future for ourselves by what we think and say and do now.

Therefore it is both our duty and our interest to study this divine law of cause and effect very closely, so that we shall be able to adapt ourselves to it and to use it, as we use other great laws of nature.

We are all moving steadily forward under the divine order towards a final consummation of good, but we are working our way towards it under the great laws of nature which we may quite rightly call the laws of God. For it is God's will that we should evolve; and that we should do so by ordering our lives intelligently in accordance with His laws.

The Future of Man

It may be of interest to see what light is thrown upon the problem of the future by the higher extensions of human consciousness of which we have spoken elsewhere. We find that from this point of view the future divides itself into three parts—the immediate, the remote, and the ultimate; and, oddly enough, it is of that which is furthest from us that we are able to speak with the greatest certainly, because the plan of evolution is visible to the higher sight and its goal is clear. Nothing can interfere with the attainment of that goal, but the stages that lead up to it may be largely modified by the free will of the individuals concerned and can therefore be foreseen only in their general outline.

The end, so far as this cycle is concerned, is the accomplishment of the perfection of man. Each individual is to become something very much more than what we now mean by a great and good man, for he is to be perfect in intellect and capacity as well as spirituality. All the intellect of the greatest philosopher or man of science, and far more; all the devotion and spirituality of the greatest of saints, and far more; these are to be possessions of every unit of humanity before our cycle ends.

To understand how such a stupendous result can be possible, we must grasp the plan by which evolution works. Obviously, on the ordinary theory of one poor little life of seventy years, followed by an eternity of purposeless joy or suffering, nothing of this sort could ever be achieved; but when once we realize that what we commonly call our life is only one day in the real life, and that we may have just as many of such days as are necessary for our development, we see that the command of Christ, "Be ye perfect even as your Father in heaven is perfect" [Matt. 5:48], is no vain hyperbole, but a plain direction which we may reasonably expect to be able in due time to obey.

The ultimate future, then, is perfection for every human being, no matter how low or undeveloped he may now be. Man will become more than man. This is what was meant in the early Church by the doctrine of "deification,"[12] to which many of the Fathers refer. It is a matter, not of pious opinion but of utter certainty to those who see the working of the scheme.

Obviously, however, we are yet very far from this attainment; a long upward path lies before us before we can reach that far-distant summit, and though on the whole it rises steadily, there must necessarily be many minor ups and downs in the future, as there have been in the past. History shows us that hitherto the advancement of mankind has been cyclic in character. Each unit lives his long series of progressive lives not in one race, but in many successive races, in order that he may learn the special lessons which each has to teach. One can imagine a soul incarnating in ancient India to develop religious fervor, in classical Greece to gain artistic capacity, in the Rome of the Caesars to learn the immense power of discipline and order, among ourselves at the present day to acquire the scientific habit of mind, and so on.

The same great host of souls sweeps on through all the ages animating all these races in turn and learning from all; but the races themselves arise, grow, decay, and fall as they are needed. So when a nation loses its former glory and falls behind in the race (as, for example, modern Greece seems to have done in comparison with ancient Greece), it does not mean that a certain group of men is decadent, but that there are at the moment no souls who need precisely the type of training which that race at its best used to give. Consequently, the physical bodies of the descendants of those great men of old are now animated by souls of a lower type, while the great men themselves are now as ever in the forefront of evolution, but incarnated in some other race in order to grow still greater by developing in new directions. A race dies precisely as a class at a university might die if there were no longer any students taking up that particular subject.

50

Clairvoyance enables us to examine a much larger section of the earth's past history than can be reached along ordinary lines; and this fuller study of the past makes it possible to some extent to forecast by analogy some of the steps in the more immediate future. From such a study of the records it appears fairly certain that we are at the moment passing through a transition period, and that instead of representing, as we often fondly imagine, the very highest development yet seen on earth, we are in reality in the trough between two waves of progress. The democratic tendency of which some of us are so proud does not represent, as is generally supposed, the ultimate achievement of human wisdom, but is an experiment which was tried very thoroughly and carried out to its logical conclusion thousands of years ago and then abandoned as irrational, unworkable, and leading to endless confusion.[13] If we are to repeat the course of that last experiment, it seems unpleasantly certain that we shall have to pass through a good deal of this confusion and suffering once again.

But when that is over and reason begins to reassert itself, there will be before us a period of far more rapid progress in which we shall be able to avail ourselves of many aids which are not now at our disposal. The mere fact that the use of the higher faculties is slowly spreading among humanity will presently make an almost incalculable difference in many directions.

Imagine a state of affairs in which all deception or fraud will be impossible, in which misunderstandings can no longer occur, because each man can read the thoughts of the other; in which no one will ever again be set to do work for which he is unfitted because, from the first, parents and tutors will be able to see exactly the capabilities of those committed to their care; in which a doctor cannot make mistakes because he will see for himself exactly what is the matter with his patient and can watch in detail the action of his remedies. Think what a difference it will make in our lives when death no longer separates us from those whom we love, because the astral world lies open to us just as does the physical; when it will be impossible for men any longer to doubt the reality of the divine scheme, because its lower stages are visible before their eyes. Art and music will be far grander then, for astral colors and harmonies will be at our command as well as those which we now know. Every feature of life will be wider and fuller because we shall see so much more than we do now of the wonderful and beautiful world in which our lot is cast; understanding more, we cannot but admire and love more, and so we shall be infinitely happier, as we draw steadily nearer to that ultimate perfection which is absolute happiness, because it is union with the Eternal Love.

6

REINCARNATION

The doctrine of reincarnation or rebirth was widely known in ancient civilizations and is even today held by the majority of the human race. For instance, it is held by the Hindus, the Buddhists, and by a certain section of the followers of Islam, some of the Sufis, who study the esoteric side of their religion. It appears in some private books of the Jewish religion, and there are certain definite statements of the Christ which seem to prove that this belief was both held and taught by Him.[14] Modern as well as ancient philosophers recognize this hypothesis as one deserving the most serious consideration. Lessing taught it; it is advocated in Schopenhauer's works, and Hume in his *Essay on Immortality* wrote: "What is incorruptible must be ungenerable. The soul, therefore, if it is immortal, existed before our birth. Metempsychosis, therefore, is the only system of this kind to which philosophy can hearken."

That is to say, the common idea that the soul began with our birth and is eternal is philosophically impossible. If it began with our birth, it will end with our death; if it had a beginning, it will have an ending. If it comes forth from eternity then it must at last go back to eternity, but we cannot philosophically hold the idea that a thing begins in time and does not end in time.

Again, Huxley writes in his *Evolution and Ethics*: "Like the doctrine of evolution itself, that of transmigration has its roots in the world of reality; and it may claim such support as the great argument from analogy is capable of supplying."[15]

53

Max Müller, the great orientalist, began by writing of this theory as a superstition, but at the end of his life, in a work which was published after his death, he admitted that he himself believed in it. So it is clear that many of the greatest minds have held this idea, and for that reason alone it is not to be dismissed as a mere superstition.

Some Misconceptions

Like other teachings, the doctrine of reincarnation has been very much corrupted and misunderstood. There has been a great deal of misconception due to the idea of metempsychosis[16] which was held in later days in Greece and Rome and also in India. Those who held this idea taught that it was possible for a very wicked man to be reborn in an animal body as a punishment for his sins. There is no foundation for that idea, and it has never been taught in the Mysteries or in the inner teaching of any religion.

It is perhaps not unnatural that it should have arisen. There are various indications that might be taken to suggest it; for instance, we very often see a person whose face recalls some kind of animal. It is not unnatural that uninstructed people should have imagined that such a one had been born in an animal body previously and had brought over some trace of it into his life. Then also some of the lower types of man distinctly show animal characteristics; cunning such as is attributed to the fox, ferocity such as is credited to the wolf, in fact, many qualities that are supposed to be typical of animals. It is not surprising that people should have thought that if a man showed such distinctly animal characteristics during his present life, he might find himself hereafter in a body more suitable for their expression. But there is no truth in that idea.

It is true that each man in one life reaps the result not only of his last life but of all his previous ones. They mold him in certain ways, and he receives a physical body capable of expressing the type of man that he is. It is therefore possible for a man by a very foolish or sensual, or perhaps by a very wicked, life to fall back somewhat, though not very much, even at the worst; a man who is capable of a very coarse, animal life is not in any case a highly evolved person, and therefore he does not throw himself very far back by living such a life. He does thereby reduce his chances of progress but, since the current of evolution always tends to help and not to hinder us, it is difficult for a man to behave so badly as to throw himself back to a much lower level of human life.

So far as we have seen in the investigations we have made (and altogether we have examined many thousands of cases), it is absolutely impossible for any human being to throw himself back into a lower kingdom from which he came up thousands of years ago. But, it might be objected, a man who has just emerged from the animal kingdom might possibly throw himself back again. Not so, because the man who has just come out could not have the strength of will to be wicked enough to produce any such results, and the animal and human kingdoms are very definitely divided. Certainly there is a great deal of overlapping, but when an individual reaches the human kingdom, he receives a divine spark and cannot again relinquish it. A man belonging to a highly evolved race who lives an exceptionally evil life might be reborn in some less-evolved race; he might possibly throw himself back far enough to deserve birth in some primitive tribe, though such a man has already so many more interests, so much more capacity than the primitive man that it is doubtful if he could throw himself back into such an incarnation as that. But he certainly might, in exceptional circumstances, be reborn into surroundings where he would have not so good an opportunity of progress as he has now.

The old theory of falling back into animal life is an impossibility; we cannot do that because life is a continual progress and when once a man comes into existence as a human soul inhabiting a causal body, he can never again fall back into a lower kingdom of nature, whatever mistakes he may make, or however he may fail to take advantage of his opportunities. If he is idle in the school of life, he may need to take the same lesson over and over again before he has really learnt it; but still, on the whole, progress is steady, even though it may often be slow.

Reincarnation Solves Many Problems

There are many problems in life which can be solved if we accept the idea of reincarnation, while they remain hopeless puzzles in any other theory. First of all, there is the awful problem of the different destinies of men. We talk about men being born free and equal. Are they? If we really think of it, we shall see very soon that they are not.

We must try to realize that the world is a school and that the savage is a young soul in a lower class of this world-school, whereas the civilized man is an older soul in a much higher class, and each is getting what he can appreciate and assimilate. One has passed through the lower stage long ago, and it is not unfair that he should have the higher chance now because he has earned it by working through the lower classes. It is not unfair that the savage should be in the lower class. It is no more unfair than that one child should be six and another twelve or sixteen. One is younger than the other, but he will one day grow up to be something comparable to what the other is now. We would not say a school is unjustly ruled because the small children are in one class and the bigger children are in another. That is exactly how it must be and how it ought to be.

Again, if we are to believe that there is only one life and that all eternity depends on that one life, it is utterly useless to talk about divine justice or to suppose that there is a beneficent Deity. That is the truth about it, if we face the facts; but people do not think of these things. The belief in reincarnation alone makes it possible for us to see things as they are and yet to hold the theory of absolute divine justice.

Then take the question of the innate qualities of men. There is no doubt that some people are born cleverer than others. Those who have had anything to do with education know that in a school there are clever boys and stupid boys. It is not a question there of the age of the body.

Some learn eagerly and quickly, others find it practically impossible to get along at all, and then, on the other hand, and perhaps as a sort of corollary to that, you also find that some are very quick along one line and exceedingly stupid along another.

Why? A man has practiced one of these things, and so he does it perfectly. The other thing he is attempting for the first time, and so he does it clumsily. It is quite natural when we grant that there are many lives.

Takes the case of a genius. Mozart as a little boy of four years old could play beautifully and compose really splendid and difficult music. Haydn was also a composer at the age of ten. Now the business of making harmonies is to a certain extent a complicated matter. The ordinary man has to study for some years in order to do it perfectly, but Mozart as a little child four years of age composes, offhand, harmonies to which no one can take exception. How could that little child do that? Why should not every child be equally capable? The common explanation is that he came of a musical family. But some hundreds of people must have come from the same line of descent, and yet we do not get hundreds of famous musicians.

The reason is perfectly clear. The man who is a genius along one line has worked along that line before. He knows how to compose music just precisely for the same reason that you and I know certain things. I know something about occultism and theology. Why? Because I have spent a great many years in the study of these things. It may be that you have meanwhile been immersed in business. It is not unfair that I know more about occultism and theology than you do. If it came to the question of business you would probably know more than I do, but that is not unfair because you have spent your life in business and you have acquired that faculty, whereas I have been acquiring others. In each case, we have the straightforward result of what we have done. A man is born with certain qualities and faculties because in other lives he has done certain things, and so he brings over a general familiarity with them, and interest in them, and a talent for them. That accounts for precocious children.

Then there is the way in which we at once recognize certain things. I can remember quite well when the mystic teaching which is often called Theosophy first came to me; it was absolutely new to me, and yet as I read, I recognized point after point as the truth. I could not then have explained by argument how I knew it to be true, but I did know it. Many others probably have had similar experiences. Why? Because they too have studied these things in other lives, and the soul within them knows it. Again we meet a person and suddenly are strongly drawn to him. We know at once that we are going to like him and get on with him. Why? Because we have met that person before and he is a friend of old. And we have met other persons from whom we have instinctively recoiled. Why? Because we have met them before and perhaps they did us some injury or we ourselves did them some harm, and that is why we feel instinctively that we shall not get on with them.

There is another point which this theory explains. Why do great races die out in the world? Why did the glory that was Greece die out as well as the grandeur that was Rome? Why are some races apparently on the downward arc, their birth rate decreasing and fewer and fewer people appearing among them? There is a good reason for it. As I have said before, each race represents a class—a class in which certain lessons are taught. Some of the souls going to school in this world have already learnt all the lessons that a particular race has to teach, therefore they will not go back into it, and when all the Egos who need these lessons have passed through it, it is no longer required. Each soul goes where he can best acquire the teaching he especially needs. That is the scheme of evolution, therefore when its special lesson to the world has been given by a race, it begins to die out, but so long as there still remain souls who require that particular lesson that race will persist.

Various objections are made to the theory of reincarnation. People often say: "I could not possibly think of having another life. I have had such a lot of misery and suffering, I could not possibly endure another; it cannot be true." But the universe is not arranged to suit our personal wishes, but to give us whatever is good for us in the way of evolution; so the mere fact that man thinks he could not possibly endure another life is no proof that he may not eventually have to take another. True, his strong desire in the matter would be a factor in holding him back from another incarnation for some time, but it would only be holding him back from the opportunity of learning the lessons he needs. The mere fact that he does not want to live again does not affect the case at all.

Why We Do Not Remember Our Previous Lives

People often say: "Why do we not remember those other lives?" Why do we not remember, now, in this life, every day we spent in learning to read? We do not remember every stroke we made in learning to write, but we can write. We have acquired the faculty, but we have forgotten the details through which we learnt it. Now exactly the same thing is true with regard to reincarnation.

That with which we remember is our mind. It is not the same mind that learnt those lessons of the past, because at every birth the soul puts itself down afresh and draws round it new astral matter, new mental matter, and a new physical body. Therefore, just as the body a man has now cannot recall the feelings of another body he had many hundreds of years ago, so his present mind cannot remember the detailed experiences of a life long ago when it did not exist; but the soul behind—the real man—remembers at his own level. He cannot make this physical brain of his remember down here, but he knows well enough at his own level what he can do. He can throw down into these lower vehicles the powers which he acquired in that previous life because these powers are drawn up into him, and when he puts himself down again he puts down the powers which he acquired as the result of all these lives, but he does not remember the details.

At the same time there are a great many people who do remember. I am not referring to those who have been taught how to do it (as I was long ago in India), but I am thinking of people who do it naturally. Now and then we find children who do remember, chiefly when they have died in early childhood and have been reborn almost immediately. They will say, "I had another mother once." They will describe this former mother and perhaps even remember her name.

In Eastern countries like Burma, it is not uncommon for children to remember their immediate past. I have investigated several cases of this sort where a child asserted that he had been born previously in such and such a village, perhaps fifty miles away. I have had the child taken to that village to see whether going to the spot would stimulate his memory, and it has done so very often. He has been able to point out the people whom he used to know and to call to memory things which proved he had lived there before.

One should attach but little importance to claims by people to have been somebody of great power and influence in the past. For one reason because the person who was in a position of power in any incarnation must have made a very widespread karma—karma which acted on many hundreds of people and they must have reacted on him—and therefore such a person could never have an ordinary obscure life such as most of us have, because it would be useless to him. He (or she) would not be able to work out the karma which he had already made under such conditions. It is almost certain that he would be in some prominent position again, because only in that prominent position could such a tremendously mixed karma work itself out. We find that people of great distinction in the past were usually people of prominence in other lives.

Intervals between Lives

There are two great groups of people among those who are likely to incarnate in the more advanced races, one of them taking an interval of about 1000 to 1200 years between births and the other about 700 years. But those are averages, and a great many take very much shorter periods than that. It depends upon a very large number of different factors. Our examination of the subject has shown us that, and there may well be other factors we have not yet discovered. But it is quite certain that there can be very large variations.

Those who are less developed come back very much sooner because it is the wearing out first of the astral vehicle and secondly of the mental vehicle that takes up the interval between lives. The people who have very little mentality come back very quickly because there is little or no time spent in using up their mental processes. That is why, although their number is actually not as large as it appears to be, there seems to be such an enormous preponderance of undeveloped people in the world. There are, in fact, many more highly developed Egos than one would suppose, but they come back at longer intervals.

For myself, I believe in reincarnation, or rather I *know* it is true, because I have been taught to look back into previous lives of my own. I have proved to myself that I was not hallucinating, or dreaming, or imagining things by having been able to verify certain facts. I have been able, for example, to complete certain inscriptions, parts of which were missing, and I have been able, in a number of instances, to supply certain details with regard to early times which could only have been explained by personal memory of the case.

7

THE JUST LAW

It is a fundamental article in our Liberal Catholic teaching that perfect justice rules the world. We have heard a great deal about "God's holy law that changes not," the law of karma, of cause and effect, of action and reaction, or of readjustment; and those who have succeeded to some extent in opening the faculties of the soul (and have thereby obtained the power to see upon other planes than the physical) have seen enough to convince them of its existence and of the perfection of its working.

Those who do not yet see on higher planes will realize, if they will follow the argument out logically and carefully, that this law is a necessity. It is a great truth that "God is not mocked" and that "as a man soweth so shall he also reap" [Gal. 6:7]. Even without the inner sight one may arrive at a reasonable certainty with regard to the fact of this law. But as to the method of its working little is known, and it is not easy for us to form even a rudimentary conception upon the subject.

We know that its administration is in the hands of the four great beings who in India are called the four *devarajas* (or Angel Kings). Sometimes they are spoken of as the Four Regents of the earth or of the elements, or sometimes of the four quarters of the globe. Sir Edwin Arnold speaks of them in that way in *The Light of Asia*.[17] A poetical oriental description, you may say; yet it has a definite foundation in fact. The form in which it is cast is obviously traditional—a sort of fairy tale; but there is a fact behind it.

Both the prophet Ezekiel and the evangelist St. John speak of these *lipika*[18] as living wheels of fire full of eyes within, or as the Four Creatures round the throne of God [Ezek. 1:18; Rev. 4:6, 8]. They are the Holy Ones for whom, and for their armies, *fohat*[19] builds the four winged wheels. Madame Blavatsky writes of them in *The Secret Doctrine*:

> These are the "Four Maharajas," or great Kings, of the Dhyan Chohans, the Devas, who preside each over one of the four cardinal points. They are the Regents, or Angels, who rule over the Cosmical Forces of North, South, East and West, Forces having each a distinct occult property. These beings are also connected with Karma, as the latter needs physical and material agents to carry out its degree, such as the four kinds of winds, for instance, professedly admitted by science to have their respective evil and beneficent influences upon the health of mankind and every living thing.

Vossius[20] writes to the same effect:

> Though St. Augustine has said that every visible thing in this world has an angelic virtue as an overseer near it, it is not individuals but entire species of things that must be understood, each such species having indeed its particular Angel to watch it.

All these descriptions are incomprehensible to many, and yet no one who has seen these strange and wondrous potencies can doubt for a moment, reading these accounts, that those men of old had seen them too. But even this vivid description gives us no hint of the manner of their actions, of the way in which they do their wonderful work.

They are "full of eyes within," typifying unceasing watchfulness on all planes and in all dimensions; yet they never see the millions of human beings for whom they legislate with such amazing accuracy—never see them, I mean, as beings, as individuals, as entities of any kind. How, then do they see them, and how do they carry out their work?

A Stupendous Mathematical Problem

Perhaps the nearest that we can come to the truth is to say that to the *lipika* the whole of our evolution is a stupendous mathematical problem, a vast equation to be solved, a sum so immense that all heaven and earth are but the slate upon which it is written; and that in that vast sum each man is a little subsidiary calculation, a tiny yet quite necessary part of that inconceivable whole, a single item in a colossal celestial account—infinitesimal in itself and yet indispensable to the balance and symmetry of that tremendous total, and therefore to be treated with the uttermost care and respect and worked out with meticulous accuracy.

That is no doubt a somewhat mechanical view, but we must observe that this law of karma is one of the great laws of nature, that it does thus act mechanically, and that there is a close and real analogy between it and the mathematical idea. When the One becomes many, when the Logos puts Himself down into matter, He may be said to state that prodigious problem. Indeed, He makes an almost infinite number of separate statements which He throws forth in ever greater and greater quantity as the universe passes onward; and all these influence one another, borrow factors one from another, act and react upon one another creating ever-increasing complexities until all possible combinations and permutations have been made, until the fullest expression has been attained. This is the *pravritti marga*, the Path of Outgoing.

When this has been trodden, when its results have been fully achieved, then commences the *nivritti marga*, the Path of Return—the process of simplification and solution. Each minor equation balances itself, cancels itself out; one by one these are withdrawn as men attain adeptship, until finally *all* is withdrawn; the great effort is over, the Hidden Work is done, and nothing is left upon the lower planes. Each one who achieves adeptship reduces the complexity and lessens the pressure for all the others until finally all is balanced; the operation has succeeded, the harvest is garnered, the victory is won, the purpose of the Logos is accomplished in the consummation of the ages.

That statement of karma may be new to some, but I think it will be found an illuminative statement; and if we follow it out carefully and fully it will be seen that the analogy is a close and real one. I do not know the higher mathematics sufficiently well to trace it fully, but I am sure that along that line there is illumination to be attained. As Pythagoras said long ago, "God geometrizes," and he will surely get some hint who thinks of man the variable, always drawing nearer and nearer to the limit, but never fully touching it—if he thinks of the different variables and of the constantly changing relation between them which in mathematics is called the differential, which has to be calculated at every moment by these great Lords of Karma.

Meantime we are in the midst of all this intricate calculation and far as yet from that great fulfillment. Each man is still striving to find expression for himself—that full expression of what the Logos means him to be which is needed for the realization of the Divine Plan. And because as yet we are so far from the goal, man finds his expression often in unbalanced forms, in incomplete statements, leaving many reactions for the present unsatisfied, putting aside one part of the sum until another has been worked out.

The whole problem with all its manifold ramifications is before the *lipika*; that is their work, and they are fully competent to deal with it. But they can give it to us only bit by bit as we come to it and as we are capable of handling it.

As each man ends his life in the heaven-world, they glance over the state of his account and its relation to scores—perhaps hundreds—of other accounts around it; and they at once decide for him two things—the kind of physical body which he has earned for his next birth and the amount of karma that he can work out during the forthcoming incarnation. This latter is his *prarabdha karma*, the destiny which he has to work out during that life.

The design of the future body is thrown out in the shape of a thought-form into which, as into a mold, the matter of his etheric body will be poured; the prescribed karma presents itself as a mathematical problem to be solved by the legion of agents of the *lipika* on the various planes who have to find suitable methods for its application. In each birth some advancement is made towards the working out of the greater problem, and some of its factors are resolved; but necessarily in this process fresh karma is generated and certain new factors are introduced which have to be resolved or adjusted in turn. Often some sort of surd or apparently irreducible quantity will be left over and will have to be handed on from life to life until some factor turns up which will balance or absorb it. Sometimes quite a large amount of entirely fresh, but reducible, karma has to be introduced in order to get rid of that surd—thus creating fresh complications in order to solve others, but always bringing the whole nearer to the final solution.

Thus it is that these great Lords of Karma envisage the magnificent task which is entrusted to them; complexity which no human mind could grasp is simplicity to them. All is absolutely impersonal, for they see men only as equations, and the law which they administer works with flawless accuracy. Remember how it is said in *The Light of Asia*:

> It knows not wrath nor pardon; utter-true
> Its measures mete, its faultless balance weighs;
> Times are as nought, to-morrow it will judge,
> Or after many days.

Their ingenuity is taxed, if we can reverently put it in that way, to find the readiest solution for each man's problem, giving due consideration to all the myriad influences involved and ever taking heed that the weight of long-past evil shall not press too hardly in any one incarnation and so defeat the ultimate object of human evolution.

When the end is reached, perfect justice has been done to all even in the most minute particular. But that very fact implies that to our consciousness, limited as it is by our illusion of space and time, there must be intermediate points at which justice is not yet complete, at which we still have many debts to pay to others and many compensations to receive

from them. Observing this, as sometimes we must, let us not allow ourselves to be misled by the appearance of the moment into doubting the
perfect working of the Divine Law. Be sure that it is there. "Though the
mills of God grind slowly, yet they grind exceeding small."[21]

But it is only at the end that the perfect consummation shall be seen.
Yet all the way through, at every point, unsleeping vigilance is being
exercised. Every man has his little quota to contribute to this great sum;
every man is a necessary part of that august and sacred plan. Therefore
it is that we lean upon His justice as upon a pillar of His throne; therefore we know that all is well even when roads are rough and skies seem
dark; for behind all clouds shines always the Sun of Righteousness and
above our heads gleams ever the Star of the King.

God's Justice Surest Proof of His Love

God's eternal justice, working through His mighty law of cause and effect, is one of the surest proofs of His love, because without that law of
eternal justice we should never know what would be the result of any
of our thoughts and words and actions. We should live in a chaos of ignorance and misery. It is the inevitability of that great law of cause and
effect, that "whatsoever a man soweth that shall he also reap," which enables us to plan our own future with absolute certainty and so to obey
His command that we shall presently become "perfect even as [our] Father in heaven is perfect" [Matt. 5:48]. That is a high ideal for any man
to set before himself, but the Christ Himself has said it, and He never
told His people to do that which was impossible for them. It would
indeed be impossible if we had only this single life and had to achieve
this ideal in a limited and circumscribed time; but when we realize that
we have all time before us and that all things work together for good to
them that love God; when we learn that we may come back into earth
life again and again so that the temptation which has been too much for
us in one life may be vanquished in another, we understand how it is
possible for man at last to become perfect. We see how every man will

finally attain what God means him to attain, no matter how far away he may seem to be straying from the path.

Those who are called the wicked are young souls who do things they should not do because they are young and ignorant. They make mistakes because they know no better. When these souls grow up, they will know more, so that those who are now wicked or careless men will be the good men of the future. No man is forced, no man is driven, except insofar as the eternal law of cause and effect brings inconvenience and suffering as the result of deviation from the path; and so at last by slow degrees the soul learns that he must control his bodies and prevent them from controlling him, from doing such things as will bring him into difficulties in the future. To that extent he is driven by the action of the universal law, but otherwise God interferes with no man. Our choice is free; we have more and more free will given to us as we grow better and stronger. As we ascend higher and higher on the ladder of evolution, more and more power is given to us. Only a little power is given at first, lest if we misuse it we should wreck ourselves altogether. It is like a little child learning to walk. The mother must let it try; she knows it will fall, but she takes care that it may fall softly. In the same way, the young soul will inevitably make mistakes, but the amount of free will given is not enough to allow him to wreck himself, but just enough for him to learn by experience what he should do and what he should not do.

Karma and Divine Grace

Karma is the effect of what we have done. It is not a cold, lifeless destiny or fate. It is the effect, the very pliable and adaptable effect, of what we have done in this or in past lives. How can it be reconciled with divine grace? It depends on what we mean by divine grace. If we are thinking of it as some scheme by which we can escape results of what we have done then, certainly, the two cannot be reconciled. If we have set certain forces in motion, then the result will come to us. Not only that we cannot escape it, but if we know anything at all about the divine law we would not even wish to escape it. Cause and effect are simply two sides of the same thing.

Divine grace is divine power and divine help poured down upon us. It flows out over the world like sunlight. We can take advantage of the sunlight, or we can shut ourselves away and not take advantage of it. In the same way divine grace is the power with which God floods His world. If we do not take advantage of it that is not His fault. It is the same with that great outpouring of grace, the Sacrament of the Altar. No one is compelled to come and partake of it, but there it is ready for those who will take it.

Those two, karma and divine grace, do not contradict each other. Whatever we have done, the result comes to us. But we can modify the action of karma by setting up fresh causes, by applying a new force which counteracts the old. Karma is very adaptable, and it will work itself out in one way or another.

All things are arranged for our helping and not for our hindrance, so if we cry out when things go wrong with us that God has forgotten us or that He is not a God of love, we are only betraying our ignorance and showing that we do not understand the experiences through which we are passing. Under this most marvelous law of cause and effect, nothing can fall upon us unless we have deserved it in the past; and because we have deserved it, and we owe that much of debt, the sooner we can clear it off, the better for us in every way. It is in love that this evil comes to us, and we must receive it understandingly and not rebelliously and ignorantly, knowing that it comes because it has to come, and the sooner we get rid of it the sooner we shall be free for further evolution.

Sometimes, looking at things from the physical point of view only, we find it hard to see how the love is working. He who is clairvoyant and can see what happens on higher planes can also see much more of the working of this great Law. We cannot pretend to explain everything as yet by any clairvoyant sight to which we have attained, but we can at least tell our people with absolute certainty that the utter love of God has been proved over and over again beyond all possibility of mistake or error, and that when we see what we think to be failures in the working of that mighty law, it is because we see only in part and therefore cannot understand what is being done. All that happens is being guided and used for our benefit, and the best that under all the circumstances is possible is being done for all; when we can see from the higher level we are utterly certain of that.

For the moment, most of us have to take it to some extent on faith, though I believe that even on the physical plane there is abundant proof of the love of God and of the evolution which is His plan for men. It is only because we are short-sighted, because we are only just beginning to climb the Path of Return to Him from whom we came, that we seem to see so much of evil and cannot understand the ever underlying good, though there is indeed overwhelming proof of it. We must never forget, if we wish to understand, that God's arrangements are always for the evolution of the man himself, the soul; so we must look at what happens always from the point of view of the soul, not of the body.

This certainty of the utter love of God permeates the whole of our Liberal Catholic theology. It is all based on that great fact; and he who wishes to comprehend the truth of things as we see it must always have that idea in mind and never allow himself to be turned aside from it or lose sight of it for a moment. That is the fundamental rock upon which the structure of true religion is built, that God is Love and Light and that in Him there is no darkness at all; and if we wish to serve God as He wishes to be served, we must show that Love and that Light in ourselves as far as we can. We must imitate Him, and in us also there must be no doubt of the Love or the Light, no failure in love towards our brethren, because by showing love to others we may truly follow our Master the Christ, who is the Lord of Love.

8

SALVATION

We are now in a position to understand something of the real truths which lie behind the idea of salvation. The idea of salvation from an imagined hell is entirely out of touch with the facts, because that from which men are supposed to be saved simply does not exist. None of the texts which are supposed to justify this idea can in reality bear the meaning popularly attached to them. "Eternal hell" is a figment of the imagination and has nothing whatever at the back of it which is worthy of the attention of a thinking man.

There are various uses of the word "saved," and we find at least one or two texts in which its use not only does not fit in with the popular idea but even indicates something of the real truth.

Let us, to begin with, examine some exceedingly significant texts. In Luke 23:13, someone asks the Christ: "Lord, are there few that be saved?" In His answer He makes a very remarkable statement. He says: "Strive to enter in at the strait gate; for many . . . will seek to enter in, and shall not be able." In Matt. 7:13, 14, we find the same statement in another form: "Enter ye in at the strait gate: for wide is the gate, and broad is the way, that leadeth to destruction, and many there be which go in thereat: because strait is the gate, and narrow is the way, which leadeth unto life, and few there be that find it." There are actually some exponents of scripture who apply these texts to the gates of heaven after death. But the meaning of these texts, when properly understood, is something entirely different and something quite reasonable, as we shall see further on.

As has been pointed out before, we must take words written at a certain time in the world's history in the sense in which people, in that country and at that time, used them and understood them. If a writer uses a word, we may be sure he uses it as other authors of his period use it, and therefore it is useful to examine other literature written at the same time and see how those words were used then.

The word *saved* (from Latin *salvus*, "safe") has a technical meaning which was just as well known to students then as it is now to those who have studied the literature of that period. In order that I may make its exact meaning clear, I must ask the reader to bear in mind the conception of evolution outlined in the preceding chapters. We have seen that man is the resultant of a great evolutionary scheme. The true man within is royal and divine, and the object of evolution is to let that divine man manifest through his lower vehicles which are constantly evolving and learning to express more and more of his divine nature, until at last the man becomes a perfect channel for the life and power of the Logos. This is the glorious goal which every man must some day reach.

But we must not think of this development as happening simultaneously for everyone. Not all men now on earth are at the same level of development; we know that as a matter of everyday experience. How is that to be accounted for? If we were to suppose that all mankind started even and equal at some remote period in the past, some must have gone ahead more rapidly and others have fallen back in the most amazing manner. That is not at all the explanation. What we find to be the fact in investigating it is that constantly waves of divine life come pouring down in succession into this universe. That fact is exactly in harmony with all that we see round us in this world.

Take as an example any human family. Its members are not all the same age; they did not all start in life at the same moment. They represent a number of successive generations, and therefore some are children still, some are young people, some are middle-aged, some growing old. It is a fact in nature which we have to recognize, and just as several generations follow one another so do successive waves of evolution follow one another.

A better illustration still is to think of classes in a school. In any school there are a number of classes. It is not the fault of one particular boy that he is ten years old, while another boy is fifteen. It is not the fault of the more primitive races that they are not highly developed. It is simply that they are generally younger souls, and they have not yet had the teaching and experience which some of us have had in the past. Of course, it is perfectly possible for those in the same class to advance, or to slip back, to take advantage or not of the teaching which is given to them. That makes a comparatively small variation, whereas the big variation of age decides the "class" in which the people begin their lives, and it is only rarely that one here and there gets very far ahead of his contemporaries.

We, all of us, represent a certain stage in development. We are, let us say, a class in God's mighty school. We are supposed to be learning certain lessons. Some of us are learning those lessons quickly, and some are slow learners.

Souls differ, just as boys in a school differ. Some boys are clever and some are stupid; some take the trouble to learn the rules of the school and conform to them; others are ignorant and careless.

Just like that are the souls that come down into incarnation. Some of them at once try to learn the rules of life and live according to them. They are like the good boys of the school; they get on quickly, and their way is comparatively easy. Those who are dull and ignorant, who do not understand the rules, or even if they do, will not take the trouble to follow them, are the less developed people, and they have a great deal of trouble with their progress. They do not learn rapidly; they have to keep on coming back time after time to learn the same lesson all over again.

The people who are earnestly trying to improve certainly do improve, even though they may not be able to see much fruit of their effort in a few years' time. As they pass from life to life, they do very certainly show great advancement. But those other people, who are not really trying to evolve, only make very gradual progress. Some advance they must make, because everything round us is very slowly moving onward and upward and they are swept along with the current, but it will be so slow as to be scarcely perceptible.

The Day of Judgment

Each successive age or aeon has its special form of life, its own special virtues to develop, its own evil qualities to overcome, and so on, and represents a class in the divine school. There have been other ages before our own; they were higher classes or classes, at any rate, where the people had been longer in the school. There are others coming on behind us, younger souls than we; they will belong to their own separate class. We are expected, by the end of our particular aeon, to reach a certain level. Long before that, a great examination, a great testing, will take place, and a decision will be made as to which of the people will be able to reach the required level in the time allotted.

It is that examination which is symbolized in our scriptures by the Day of Judgment. The Christ is simply examining His people on that occasion; He is not condemning them for evil done or rewarding them in a material way for the good they may have done, but He is testing them to see whether they are fit for certain progress, or whether they are not. Those who are fit for that progress He moves on. Those who would be lagging behind and be a hindrance to the more advanced, would, by dropping back, themselves become the more advanced members of the next wave of souls. So that would be an excellent arrangement for all concerned. That is a rough analogy of what the Logos of the system does with us. His Day of Judgment is still a long way off, but it will certainly come.

At that critical period, a considerable portion of humanity will have to drop out from our scheme of evolution simply because they have not yet developed themselves enough to be able to take advantage of the opportunities which will then be opening before mankind. This is the separation of the "sheep" from the "goats." The sheep will pass on into aeonian (age-long) life;[22] the goats into temporary aeonian death—or, more correctly, into a condition of comparatively suspended evolution, but not for a moment to be looked upon as eternal. Those who thus fall out of the current of progress for a period of time will take up the work again in the next scheme of evolution.

He who is *salvus*, or saved, is the man who is even now already quite sure to pass that examination and is certain to go on with the present wave of evolution. The man who is not saved is the one who may not be ready when the time comes to go on and will have to drop back and learn some of his lessons all over again. There is merely a decision against him as far as that aeon or age is concerned.

What the occult student understands by salvation is thus being safe from this adverse decision and absolutely certain to go on with the particular life wave into which God has put us from the beginning. Those who are able to do that, to use the Buddhist term, "enter the stream," which means that they take what is called the first great initiation. The man who enters the stream is swept on by that stream and will quickly reach the further shore; that is to say, he will reach adeptship in a few lives.

All Will Eventually Be "Saved"

None can fail eventually. Failure is absolutely impossible because all the time required is given to us. We cannot remove ourselves from the stream of evolution; we can delay on the way, and to delay means further lives on earth. To get away from these repeated incarnations is to escape, as it is put in the Buddhist religion, "from the wheel of birth and death." This is what the Christ meant when He spoke of the broad way that leads to destruction and how many there be that follow it and of the narrow and difficult path that leads to life and how comparatively few there are who follow it [Matt. 7:13].

He said again and again that the broad way leads to death. So it does; it leads to death and birth; it leads, in fact, to a continuation of what we have been doing for many thousands of years—being born over and over again and making just a little progress each time. The other way—the narrow, steep, upward path—leads to escape from rebirth and to an endless life outside these physical conditions. It is just that—the broad road is a slow way, the steep, rocky, rugged upward path is a swift way; the goal in the end is the same.

But when the Christ said that there are few who take the swift but steep and rugged path, He did not mean in the least that there were few who enter into the heaven-world after death; that is a misrepresentation of the facts. Moreover, it absolutely contradicts a number of other texts in which the heaven-world is clearly indicated. For instance, when the apostle John is attempting to describe the heaven-world, he speaks of a great multitude which no man could number, of all nations and kindreds and people and tongues, clothed with white robes and with palms in their hands (Rev. 7:9).

When Christ speaks of the "kingdom of God" or the "kingdom of heaven," He is really using a technical term belonging to the Mysteries. He thereby means the Great White Brotherhood—the great Initiates, the great Saints, as they are generally called in the Church. They are the "safe" or "saved" ones, and the man who joins their ranks rises to a higher level altogether; he becomes a superman, and to attain that, certainly "strait is the gate and narrow is the way and few there be that find it." Few choose that difficult path; the majority of mankind will certainly travel along the broad and easy road and will take innumerable lives to reach the goal. But, eventually, as Sir Edwin Arnold has put it, "All will reach the sunlit snows."

Though all will be gradually shepherded along the path of progress, whether they understand it or not, it is obvious that the slower we go, the more we delay ourselves on the way, the more trouble we shall have and the more difficulties we shall find.

If we apply our intelligence to try to understand God's plan and our will to work with it, we shall save ourselves a vast amount not only of time and trouble but of the suffering which is inseparable from all these physical lives. But to say that those who take the broad road will not be saved is to make a mockery of the Savior of the world; it is to say that He does not save the enormous majority of human beings. Of course He does, but only in His own time and in His own way. It is perfectly true to say that Christ is the Savior of the world. It is the Christ in every man that is our hope of glory and, without that Christ within, indeed our chances of evolution would be very poor; it would be practically impossible for us to rise "to the measure of the stature of the fullness of Christ."

PART TWO

THE INNER TEACHING OF EARLY CHRISTIANITY

9

THE ORIGINAL TEACHING

With the passage of time all religions gradually depart from the original form in which they were cast by their founders. Nearly always this change is for the worse. There is a certain lessening of the first enthusiasm and a certain effort to adapt the religion to the laxity of the times. Also, when a Church of any account becomes established, it usually acquires property of some sort and then, inevitably, the original purity is affected and there arises orthodoxy, narrowness, bigotry. All this is true of Christianity as well as of other religions.

In all cases there is some change. In the case of Christianity there has been an almost absolute reversal—a most extraordinary change, so that the very foundations are different now from what they were in the beginning.

Originally, Christianity was a magnificently elaborate doctrine—the one doctrine which lies at the foundation of all religions. When the Gospel story, which was meant allegorically, was degraded to a pseudo-historical report of the life of a man, the religion became confused. Hence all texts relating to higher things have become distorted and therefore do not any more correspond with the truth lying behind the thought. Because Christianity has forgotten much of its original teaching, it is customary nowadays to deny that it ever possessed any esoteric teaching.

In that original teaching of Christianity there was an aspect deeper than that which is commonly presented to us in its name today. Very much of what originally formed part of the Christian faith has been neglected and almost forgotten.

Modern orthodox teaching is based largely on a few texts which have been badly mistranslated and are, in consequence, in opposition to many others that contain the liberal and generous spirit of Christ's own teaching. On these few texts has been built an insecure edifice of unreasonable doctrine which, when assailed by the light of reason, immediately proves indefensible. The true and noble teaching of the Christ, which, if Christianity is to live on into the future, must sooner or later take its place, is indicated quite clearly in the very scriptures themselves. They constantly tell us of a hidden doctrine which was not given to the public. It has long been the custom to deny this and to boast that Christianity contains nothing which is beyond the reach of the meanest intellect. It is surely a very serious reproach to Christianity to say that there is nothing in it for the thinking man.

It is evident that all religions have to provide for different classes of men and all grades of intellect. There is a vast host of simple people who would be entirely unable to appreciate metaphysics or to follow abstruse philosophical arguments. They must have plain, definite, ethical teaching; they must be told how to live. They must have it clearly put before them that their happiness or their suffering depends entirely upon the life which they choose to live. In every religion there is always such simple teaching which is necessary for their progress and is suited to them at the stage where they are.

There are others who need the philosophy and the metaphysics, who would be entirely unsatisfied unless they were able to fit their ideas in with some definite scheme. They want to know whence man came and whither he is going; how this universe began and what is the object of it. Therefore a philosophy has been given by every religion worthy of its name.

Since in every other great world-religion there have been these higher teachings, if we are to regard Christianity as the only exception to the rule, it stands self-convicted as an imperfect religion; but that is not true at all. The inner teaching is found in Christianity as in all the other religions; it could not be otherwise, since all are endeavors to state, from different points of view, the truth which lies behind all of them alike.

In his *Retractions* (Book 1, chapter 13, verse 3), St. Augustine, one of the greatest of the Christian Fathers, in a remarkable passage, says: "This which we now call the Christian religion existed among the ancients and was from the beginning of the human race until Christ himself came in the flesh, from which time the already existing true religion began to be styled Christianity." One could not have a plainer statement than that from a Father of the Church, that the true religion had existed all the time; since Christ came, people began to call it Christianity because they were now putting forth the form of it which He had taught, which was only a new statement of the truth that had always been known.

The Mysteries of the Kingdom

In the Gospels we find that Christ frequently told His disciples that He explained only to them the full meaning of what He wanted to teach and that He spoke to the public at large in parables. If we want to understand what that means we must first observe what Christ Himself declared, then what His apostles taught, and finally what was said by the Fathers of the Church who followed the apostles. In Mark 4:11 Christ says to His disciples: "Unto you it is given to know the mystery of the kingdom of God; but unto them that are without, all these things are done in parables." Then a few verses lower down we read, with reference to His public teaching: "Without a parable spake he not to them," but when He was alone with His disciples He explained all these things to them. It is a matter of common knowledge to students that in old traditions it is always stated that there was a triple meaning in all parables. First of all, there was the story just as it was told—a story for simple souls, an illustrative story; secondly, there was the intellectual meaning.

For example, take the parable of the sower. It tells that a sower went forth to sow his seed, and some fell on good ground, some on rocky ground, some in sandy soil, and some among thorns. That is a story which we might tell to a child or to any simple person. Then comes the intellectual interpretation: Christ explained that the seed is the word of God and the different kinds of soil are the different types of hearts into which the seed falls. Behind that again, according to universal tradition, there was the deep, mystic, spiritual meaning, which was never written down at all, but was always conveyed from mouth to ear. In the secret teaching given only to those proved and tried members who showed that they were worthy of it, the inner meaning of that parable refers to the outpouring of the divine life into nature, and the different strata which it touches as it pours down, and the results which it is able to produce at those different levels.

Then again, according to John 16:12, Christ said, on the night before His death: "I have yet many things to say unto you, but ye cannot bear them now." When was He to say these "many things" to them, and when was it that they would be able to bear them? Obviously, it must have been in that time after the Resurrection when, we are informed, He taught them all things concerning the kingdom of God. But where is the record of that teaching? It is impossible to suppose that it was forgotten. It must have been treasured with the rest of the disciples' memories.

There are many gospels besides those generally known, and in some of them are traces of these secret teachings. One of those is the great Gnostic gospel called the *Pistis Sophia*—the "Faith Wisdom"—and in that it is stated that Christ communicated with His disciples and taught them after His death; not for forty days only, until the time of the Ascension, but for eleven years after His resurrection He continued to teach them. Some of His instruction is given in that very book, but much of it is obscure and very hard to understand because it has passed through three translations before we read it. If ever an original copy is found, we shall probably obtain from it a very much better idea of the teachings of the Gnostics than is available at present.[23]

86

Christ Himself, throughout the New Testament, constantly uses technical terms which were employed in what used to be called the "heathen" Mysteries. One of those terms, "the kingdom of heaven," I have already explained elsewhere. Then there is the text which relates that when the young man came and asked how he could reach aeonian life—the life proper to that aeon—Christ said: "If thou wilt be perfect [a term used in the Mysteries to indicate a certain degree—the fourth initiation], go and sell that thou hast, and give to the poor, . . . and come and follow me" (Matt. 19:21). That meant: "If you wish to reach the level of the perfect you will have to give a great deal of time to the work, therefore you must get rid of all your worldly encumbrances." We are told that the young man went away sorrowful because he had great possessions. Then follows the statement by Christ that it is easier for a camel to go through the eye of a needle than for a rich man to enter the Kingdom of God.

In all religions it has been held that poverty, chastity, and obedience were necessary for the highest form of development, and Christ here repeats the teaching of the Eastern sages: "It is exceedingly difficult for a rich man to become a great initiate" because, to reach that level, a man must devote most of his time to study and work, and if he be a rich man cumbered with all sorts of business cares and worldly duties, he cannot very well do that. Worldly wealth is a great privilege, and it is given to a man as an opportunity, as a test, to see whether he will use it rightly. But besides being a test and an opportunity it implies very serious responsibility. The man who has great wealth must surely administer it for Christ and for His work, and that will mean that he must devote much time and attention to it, and while he is fulfilling that duty it would be very difficult for him to have time to devote to meditation and spiritual advancement.

Again, the Christ speaks about not giving that which is holy to the dogs, or casting pearls before swine (Matt. 7:6). We should not consider it polite to call people dogs and swine in these days, but those are technical terms in the Mysteries. One of them is used in a great secret society of the present day, though many of its members are not aware of its origin. Probably those words were used in the Mysteries to indicate outsiders, and because no one outside the Mysteries knew about it there was no misunderstanding.

St. Paul

The writings of St. Paul are also full of references to occult teaching. He speaks of the Mysteries, and he uses technical terms, even as Christ does, very freely. In the first Epistle to the Corinthians he says: "We speak wisdom among them that are perfect" (1 Cor. 2:6–7). If it meant "perfect" in the ordinary sense of the word, what would be the use of teaching them at all? What he means is, "We give that higher teaching to the people to whose degree it belongs." There were different degrees in the Mysteries just as there are in other organizations; to each degree belonged the teaching of the degree, and it was never given to any one in a lower stage. So to the "perfect" was given the "wisdom" or gnosis.

Gnosis, or "wisdom," was another technical term.[24] It did not mean ordinary wisdom, but the special religious teaching given to those who are at the stage of the perfect. The whole passage to which I am referring is full of significance. It runs: "Howbeit we speak wisdom among them that are perfect; yet not the wisdom of this world, nor of the princes of this world, that come to nought. But we speak the wisdom of God in a mystery, even the hidden wisdom, which God ordained before the world unto our glory." If St. Paul meant any ordinary Christian teaching, that statement is flagrantly untrue. It has often been asserted that all these references to Mysteries were to the Holy Eucharist. It is true that only those who had reached a certain level were permitted to be present at it, but it was not a Mystery in that sense.

It could not have been the Holy Eucharist, because the apostle was writing to the Corinthian Church and, from what he says in other parts of the epistle (as where he speaks of certain rites which attended their celebrations of the Holy Communion), it is evident that those Corinthians were full communicants, fit only for the earlier wisdom; so certainly the Mysteries which were not taught to them were not the Eucharist. Continuing, St. Paul speaks of the teaching known of God which the Holy Ghost teaches. Again, he uses also other technical terms, calling himself a master builder and a steward of the Mysteries of Christ. He also speaks of striving if by any means he "might attain to the resurrection of the dead" (Phil. 3:11). People generally take that to mean that he, the great apostle, was not sure whether he would rise again at the last day. But all are to rise again according to the teaching—the good and the bad alike. There is no effort needed for that. What was it he was striving so earnestly to attain? Of course, he was aiming to reach the great initiation which liberates men, which sets them free from the earth. He says: "I press toward the mark for the prize of the high calling of God in Christ Jesus"; and in a verse or two later on he urges "as many as be perfect" to strive, as he is striving, to attain the resurrection from death—the escape from the wheel of birth and death—but he does not recommend the ordinary church members to do it because he knows it is out of their reach as yet. He concludes his exhortation to the "perfect" with the significant words: "For our conversation is in heaven; from whence also we look for the Savior, the Lord Jesus Christ, who shall change our vile body, that it may be fashioned like unto his glorious body, according to the working whereby he is able to subdue all things unto himself" (Phil. 3:20–21).

Clement of Alexandria

The Christian Fathers also constantly use the technical terms of the Mysteries. St. Clement of Alexandria borrows a whole sentence from neo-Pythagorean documents when he says, "It is not lawful to reveal to the profane the mysteries of the Word." The profane are those outside the temple. The last term is a translation of the Greek *logos*. In this sentence he inserts that word in the place of the Eleusinian goddesses who are mentioned in the original document.

Nowadays Christianity considers it to be its highest glory that it has produced great saints, though it does not profess to be producing them at the present day. In earlier times it had the three degrees, purification, illumination, and perfection or deification. Then, purification meant what we now call saintship. The man who was purified was the man of high and holy living; the second degree gave him a knowledge of the Mysteries, and the third degree gave him unity with the Divine at a certain stage. We find the same three stages under other names in the oriental religions. In later days, all that was laid aside when the more ignorant section of the Church gained the upper hand, so we now have a maimed form of Christianity which is by no means as satisfactory a presentation of the eternal verities as are some of the other great religions of the world. The Church now contents herself with the preliminary purification; she has no illumination or perfection to give.

Let us read what St. Clement of Alexandria has to say on this subject. Speaking of purification he writes: "Purity is only a negative state, valuable chiefly as the condition of insight"; that is to say, one cannot gain the higher levels through purity alone. He continues: "He who has been purified in baptism, and then initiated into the little Mysteries [has acquired the habit of self-control and reflection], becomes ripe for the greater Mysteries, for Epopteia or Gnosis, the scientific knowledge of God."[25]

This latter, from the modern orthodox point of view, is a startling claim to make. Few preachers at the present day would claim to have scientific knowledge of God or ever to know in the least what such an expression meant. Yet there it stands in the writing of one of the earliest and greatest of the Church Fathers. Of course, there have always been doctors of the Church—men who have studied philosophy and theology, but generally only in a narrow and partisan spirit. Since the days of the great Gnostic teachers who were expelled for heresy, they have produced nothing at all to compare with the splendid metaphysics and philosophy of the Hindus or the Buddhists.

As to the third stage, that of perfection, they have simply forgotten all about it; yet it was clearly held by the early Fathers that man was capable of attaining "deification," as that degree is often called in their writings.

What has become of this magnificent heritage of Christianity? Why was this wonderful wisdom lost, and how can it be regained? Happily it has not been lost. Though the ignorant majority endeavored with pious fury to destroy all traces of it, yet here and there a book has been discovered where something of the Gnostic teaching has been preserved. Moreover, as will be shown in the following chapters, an attempt has at least been made by some of the higher powers to guide those who have compiled those great symbols called the creeds, so that, whatever they themselves may have known, their language still clearly conveys the grand truths of the original teachings to all who have ears to hear; for much now incomprehensible in those formulae becomes at once luminous and full of meaning when understood in that inner sense which exalts it, from a fragment of unreliable biography into a declaration of eternal truth.

10

The Origin of the Creeds

The Christian Church uses three creeds: [26] the Apostles', the Nicene, and the Athanasian. I shall not deal with the last here since it is of much later origin than the first two. As at present found in the Prayer Book of the Church of England, these two creeds are as follows:

The Apostles' Creed

I believe in God the Father Almighty, Maker of heaven and earth:
And in Jesus Christ, his only Son our Lord, Who was conceived by the Holy Ghost, born of the Virgin Mary, suffered under Pontius Pilate, was crucified, dead and buried, He descended into hell. The third day he rose again from the dead, He ascended into heaven, and sitteth on the right hand of God the Father Almighty; from thence he shall come to judge the quick and the dead.
I believe in the Holy Ghost; the holy Catholick [*sic*] Church; the Communion of Saints; the Forgiveness of sins; The Resurrection of the body, and the life everlasting. Amen.

The Nicene Creed

I believe in one God, the Father Almighty, Maker of heaven and earth, and of all things, visible and invisible:

And in one Lord Jesus Christ, the only-begotten Son of God, begotten of his Father before all worlds, God of God; Light of Light, very God of very God, begotten, not made, being of one substance with the Father, by whom all things were made: Who for us men, and for our salvation came down from heaven, and was incarnate by the Holy Ghost of the Virgin Mary, and was made man, and was crucified also for us under Pontius Pilate. He suffered and was buried, and the third day he rose again according to the Scriptures, and ascended into heaven, and sitteth on the right hand of the Father. And he shall come again with glory to judge both the quick and dead: Whose kingdom shall have no end.

And I believe in the Holy Ghost; the Lord and giver of life, Who proceedeth from the Father and the Son, who with the Father and the Son together is worshipped and glorified, who spake by the Prophets. And I believe in one Catholick and Apostolic Church. I acknowledge one Baptism for the remission of sins. And I look for the Resurrection of the dead, and life of the world to come. Amen.

A century ago, the general opinion was that the Apostles' Creed was the earlier of these and that the other two were merely amplifications of it, but it is now believed that the Nicene Creed is the oldest of the three. Some sort of creed seems to have been in use in the Church from the very beginning. In fact, in the days when the Christians were persecuted they used a very short form of the creed as a kind of password to secure admission to their meetings; a few words such as: "I believe in God the Father in whom are all things and in God the Son by whom are all things," but the form varied very much in different places and at different times.

The earliest mention we find of the Apostles' Creed is in the fourth century, by Rufinus,[27] who tells us that each of the Twelve Apostles wrote one of the twelve clauses of it. I may mention that Rufinus is not a reliable author and that this curious idea of his is certainly not held by any scholar at the present day. The earliest date at which we find the Apostles' Creed in anything like the form in which it now exists in the churches of Rome and England is in the eighth century, and it is supposed by the historians who have investigated the matter to be a mere conglomeration, a gathering together, of a number of separate and shorter creeds.

The Creed of Nicaea

As to the Nicene Creed, there is no doubt as to its origin. It was drawn up, though not exactly as we have it now, in the year 325 at the Council of Nicaea. That council was convened for the purpose of dealing with what is called the Arian heresy. There was a certain priest named Arius who maintained that the orthodox beliefs were in various ways inaccurate and, in consequence of his teaching, great controversies raged between his followers and the materialistic ecclesiastical party as to whether the Father had existed before the Son and whether the Father and the Son were of the *same* nature or of *like* nature. In English, we have two distinct words to express this difference of meaning, but the distinction in Greek is marked only by a very slight thing, the difference of a mere point. "Of the *same* nature" is *homos*; "of *like* nature" *homoios*. It is *oi* instead of *o*, and when the *i* comes in a word like that it is generally written as a small *i*, but when it comes as the second letter of a diphthong it is frequently written as a little dot. So the difference about which the whole Church fought for years was a question of a dot!

When we consider that the exact truth about the matter is a thing which no human being could possibly know, and, moreover, it could not possibly make the slightest difference to any of us which of the two theories is true, it is clear that the squabble was futile and unnecessary. It is noticeable in all those theological controversies that the smaller the difference of opinion, the greater was the amount of bitterness and hatred aroused in connection with it: probably there was never a worse squabble in the Church. It is not altogether surprising that Arius should have maintained that the Father must have existed before His Son; there is a certain claim of reasonableness about such an idea. However, the Council of Nicaea, largely directed by the emperor Constantine, decided that that was not so, but that they were coeternal and coequal. Undoubtedly they are from one point of view, for one must not be bound down by material conceptions of Father and Son when these words are employed symbolically. The Nicene Creed, as it was drawn up by that council, omitting the final clauses (it ends with a terrible curse on all who would not accept it) is as follows:

> We believe in one God, the Father Almighty, Maker of all things both visible and invisible; and in one Lord, Jesus Christ, the Son of God, begotten of the Father, only-begotten, that is to say, of the substance of the Father, God of God, Light of Light, very God of very God,[28] begotten, not made, being of one substance with the Father, by whom all things were made, both things in heaven and things in earth—who for us men and for our salvation came down and was made flesh, and was made man, suffered and rose again on the third day, went up into the heavens and is to come again to judge the quick and the dead, and in the Holy Ghost. (Translation by G.R.S. Mead)

Comparing it with the form in which it appears in the Prayer Book of the Church of England, we notice several differences. There is not a word about Christ being crucified. It does not mention the birth from the Holy Ghost or by the Holy Ghost from the Virgin Mary, which is found in the more modern form and is a wrong translation. We also observe that there is nothing in it about Pontius Pilate, and, furthermore, all the latter part is omitted. That, with the exception of the words "and the Son," was added to it at the Council of Constantinople in the year 381, so that really it is the Constantinopolitan rather than the Nicene Creed which the Church uses now. That other very important addition, the word *filioque*, which means "and the Son," was made by the Western

Church at the Council of Toledo in the year 587, and thereby hangs the whole of the difference between the Greek Church and the Western Church of Rome and England as to whether the Holy Ghost proceeds from the Father alone or from the Father and the Son.

Three Sources

This is the history of the creed as generally accepted. Clairvoyant investigation has modified these conclusions to some extent.[29] It has shown that there are three separate sources which we must take into account if we want to understand how the creeds grew to be what they are now. These are: (1) an ancient formula, explaining the descent into matter, given by Christ Himself to the Essenes;[30] (2) the rubric for the guidance of the hierophant in the Egyptian form of the first initiation;[31] and (3) the materializing tendency, which sought to bring the whole teaching down to the physical plane and to interpret it as relating to the biography of an individual.

Let us consider each of these sources in a little more detail. Every religion in the world has some theory, some statement, as to how the world came into existence. In Christianity we have, unfortunately, very largely accepted the Jewish statement, which contains two contradictory versions. In the Book of Genesis we find one very elaborate statement which runs through the first chapter and up to the third verse of the second, and then another account begins, which does not agree with the first one at all. Neither of these is a clear or comprehensive statement, and each needs a great deal of explanation to make it agree in any way with our scientific knowledge.[32] It can, with a certain amount of latitude, be translated into some kind of symbol of the order in which things came forth from the Deity. The idea of creation in six days is, of course, sheer nonsense, and all the higher critics agree that those days were vast aeons. Even so, the statement given in the creed is a clearer and better one, if people would only see it; but, instead of accepting it, Christians have preferred to accept the Jewish idea.

CHAPTER 10

The formula of cosmogenesis taught by Christ to His disciples was certainly the first source of our creed. I do not profess to be able to give the exact words used by the Christ, but merely a paraphrase of its meaning as enshrined in the hearts of those to whom it was taught. It runs as follows:

> We believe in God the Father, from whom comes the system—yea, our world and all things therein, whether seen or unseen;
>
> And in God the Son, most holy, alone-born from his Father before all the aeons, not made but emanated, being of the very substance of the Father, true God from the true God, true Light from the true Light, by whom all forms were made; who for us men came down from heaven and entered the dense sea, yet riseth thence again in ever greater glory to a Kingdom without end;
>
> And in God the Holy Ghost, the Life-Giver, emanating also from the Father, equal with him and with the Son in glory; who manifested through his Angels.
>
> We recognize one brotherhood of men as leading to the Greater Brotherhood above, one initiation for emancipation from the fetters of sin and for escape from the wheel of birth and death into eternal life.

That is a very rough approximation to the original formula as it was given by the Christ—not to the general public, but to the Essenes, the community among whom Jesus was brought up.

In considering the second source, we have to remember that in the Mysteries of ancient Egypt there was a very elaborate symbolical ritual in which the candidate for initiation was made to play the part of a mythical hero; he was put through a figurative death burial and resurrection, and was laid upon a wooden cross at one part of the ceremony. That is where the idea of the crucifixion of Christ took its rise. It is not historical, because the death of Jesus took place before the Romans occupied Judea, and crucifixion was a Roman, not a Jewish form, of punishment.[33] But the rubric for the guidance of the officiating hierophant in the Egyptian ritual became incorporated with our creed, though it had existed thousands and thousands of years before the time of the Christ. Jesus had visited Egypt and had been initiated there, so the Christ must have been entirely familiar with all these ideas, as were most of the Essenes whom He taught. It is very natural, therefore, that He should have used that rubric to illustrate the descent of the Logos in His Second Aspect into matter.

The Materializing Tendency

Let us now examine the third source, the materializing tendency. At a very early period in the history of Christianity we find three schools or sections in the Church arising from different phases of the Christ's life work. We read in the Gospels of His preaching to the people. We are in one passage given the impression that He did this for one year only, but in others we find the idea of three years. He did, as a matter of fact, teach for three years after He took possession of the body of the disciple Jesus at His Baptism by John the Baptist.[34] Two of these were devoted to teaching the higher philosophy to the community of the Essenes, these being already very highly spiritually trained people. This private teaching contained certain secret formulae which were never written down. Later on, when the original Essene community had been broken up, the different Gnostic sects alone represented something of the inner teaching given to the Essenes, though in many cases it was considerably influenced by Zoroastrian beliefs or by Assyrian and Babylonian teachings, so that we find various fragments of creeds very much mixed and often very confused and mutually contradictory.

After his sojourn with the Essenes, the Christ, for one year, did as is related in the Gospels—He wandered about the country preaching to the people. During this time He seems to have delivered two distinct kinds of addresses, the first being the *logia* or "sayings," a series of short sentences each containing an important truth or a rule of conduct, and the second, the *paraklēteria* or "words of comfort"—moved by the deep compassion he felt for the misery and degradation of the lower classes. The *logia* are mentioned in the Church Fathers. We find a number of them in the Gospels as they are now: "I am the light of the world" [John 8:12]; "judge not that ye be not judged" [Matt. 7:1]; "Whatever ye would that men should do unto you, do ye also unto them" [Matt. 7:12]; and so on. During the first two centuries after Christ's death, many of His disciples seem to have made and written down collections of the sayings which were ascribed to Him by oral tradition.

There was a great stir when Grenfell and Hunt, working in Egypt, found a portion of one of these collections.[35] Many of the sayings it contained were those which already exist in our Bible, but there were some new ones also of great power and beauty. An exceedingly graceful one runs: "Cleave the wood and there thou shalt find Me; Raise the stone and there am I." This is a very beautiful statement of the omnipresence of the Deity, of the immanence of God. There was a large body of Christians who took these logia as their guide in life. These were quiet and respectable people who did not embroil themselves with the authorities or get into trouble but quietly and steadfastly tried to follow these teachings. They represented what might be called the moderate party of the Church.

The third section consisted of a turbulent and troublesome set of "poor men" whose only religion was a vague hope of revolution. Our Lord was profoundly impressed with the terrible oppression of the lower classes, with the slavery which was then universal, and with the degradation and the despair by which all these unfortunate people were overwhelmed, and it was in the endeavor to comfort and to help them that He uttered the *paraklēteria* or "words of comfort." Again and again He told them that they must endure nobly unto the end, but He never advised rebellion. He said: "If you will but follow my teaching, out of your sufferings will certainly arise a better time both after death and in your future lives. Work hard, take courage; there will come a time when those who oppress you will suffer in their turn, and you who have been oppressed will rise into higher and happier condition." As there was a great deal of human nature in the first century as well as in the twentieth, there is no wonder that comparatively soon the people to whom these addresses were given forgot the qualifications: "If you bear this nobly and well, if you live according to my teaching," and they translated His words into a vague general idea of a good time coming. Most of them thought that the injustice under which they suffered was to be righted by savage retribution; they imagined a time when they would be the oppressors and those who now trampled them down would suffer at their hands.

This lower section of the early Christian Church become like David's cave of Adullam in which all who were in distress, or in debt, or discontented, gathered together [1 Sam. 22:1; 2 Sam. 23:13; 1 Chron. 11:15]; in fact, there was a good deal of what we might call riffraff in that early Christian Church, and they very soon eliminated from their doctrine the condition of good living and simply banded together as believers in a good time coming when they would enter into possession of wealth and enjoyment of luxury. As this tendency developed they became imbued with all sorts of political and revolutionary ideas, and it was this great body of ignorant followers of Christ that made all the trouble between the early Church and the Roman government. I suppose there never was a more tolerant government in the world than that of Rome with regard to religious beliefs. It even went out of its way to take into account all the religions of all the people subject to it. For instance, as soon as it penetrated to the Roman authorities that Christ was being worshipped as a deity they promptly set up a statue to Him in the Pantheon. Most of them believed little themselves and they cared not at all what other people believed, but they were deeply concerned about what people did, and when the curious revolutionary beliefs of some of these early Christians led them to get athwart the government, they were at once suppressed with a heavy hand not because of what they believed but because of what they did or did not do.

As time went on, these ignorant people became jealous of the Gnostics and their higher teachings. They utterly decried the idea that it was necessary that any one should know more than they did. They took the attitude that the Christian teaching was revealed unto babes and regarded ignorance as practically a qualification for salvation. As Christianity spread and the Church gained a certain amount of influence, the respectable people who followed the logia and the "poor men" drew together and gradually united to form what was called the orthodox party. Being united in its distrust of the higher teachings of the Gnostics, this body found itself compelled to develop some sort of doctrinal system to offer instead of theirs. The formula given to the Essenes by Christ had by this time become known among them in various more or less perfect forms and accepted without much understanding as a creed; and, of course, some interpretation of it had to be produced to set up against the one propounded by the Gnostics. Then it was that they translated the great Mystery drama—that beautiful allegorical illustration of the descent into matter of the Second Person of the Trinity contained in the symbolic ritual of the Egyptian initiation—into the life story of a human being whom they identified with Jesus the Nazarene. Thus, through this materializing, it was made to mean something that had never before been thought of in connection with it. If we try to contain it all in the life history of a man it plainly will not fit; as a physical-plane story there are great gaps. It does not cohere; it is contradictory to the history of the time. No idea could have been more unfitting or misleading, yet one can understand its welcome by ignorant people as being more nearly within the grasp of their limited mental caliber than the magnificent breadth of the true interpretation.

The slight additions necessary to engraft this theory upon the growing creed were easily made and, not very long after, fragmentary versions of it began to be made in writing. These early fragments are imperfect recollections of an oral tradition out of which eventually a very fair representation of the original was compiled and formally adopted by the Council of Nicaea. Thus we have seen that though the creed, as is generally believed, is a conglomeration gradually gathered together, the true genesis of the greater part of it is a very high one indeed, coming direct from Christ Himself. It is the materialistic quasi-historical corruption of the centuries which has obscured the magnificent truths it embodies. How these great truths are still mirrored even in what is left to us of the creeds I hope to show as we consider them clause by clause in the following chapters.

11

THE FATHER ALMIGHTY

T he Nicene Creed begins, "I believe in one God the Father Almighty, Maker of heaven and earth, and of all things visible and invisible."

Now when we think of God the Father, it seems to me that we have three ideas simultaneously in mind.

1. God in the abstract—the all-pervading, all-embracing;
2. God the Father as the First Person of the Blessed Trinity;
3. God as the protector and father of His people.

All our ideas connected with the Deity are exceedingly vague. In one sense, of course, they must be, because God is far above, out of our sight and our comprehension. And yet at the same time that they are vague and usually quite unphilosophical, they are often also altogether too anthropomorphic. There are many among us who still believe in a God who is a Providence, who is prepared to interfere with the action of his own laws at our request. That is no doubt a comforting theory for those who wish to feel they have the Deity on their side in personal difficulties, but it is scarcely a dignified or philosophical conception. All these limited and material ideas of the Deity are largely due to our inheritance of the Jewish traditions of the Old Testament. There is no doubt whatever that the Jewish Jehovah was a tribal deity—one among many, constantly asserting that he is superior to the other gods; constantly jealous and fearful lest any of his people should abandon him in order to attach themselves to some other. There are many statements in the Bible which clearly prove this. For example, there is a very striking statement in the first chapter of the Book of Judges in which it is said that the Lord was with Judah and he prospered mightily and he drove out all the inhabitants of the mountains, but he could not drive out the inhabitants of the valley because they had chariots of iron [Judges 1:19]—a text that very fairly shows that we are not dealing with a supreme and infinite God but with a tribal deity distinctly limited in power.

Later on, the power of the infinite and all-embracing Deity was grafted on to these earlier and cruder conceptions. Some of the prophets undoubtedly had glimpses of this grander creed, and when they were carried away to Babylon in captivity they met, probably for the first time, with a great philosophical and civilized religion.[36] I know that there are texts alleged to be of earlier date than the Captivity which can be interpreted in this way; but we have to remember that all the sacred books were written down from memory after their return from that captivity, so they may very well have been tinged with Chaldean thought. Many of our churches still adopt very primitive statements about God and thereby involve themselves in the most extraordinary inconsistencies.

The Logos of Our Solar System

Of the Absolute, the Infinite, we can postulate nothing but that He is. Within Him are millions of solar systems, probably other universes beyond those which we can see; and, even though in Him we live and move and have our being, our connection or relation with Him must be on so high a plane that it can mean but little to us. For all practical purposes, He is represented to us by one who is in very truth a part of Him—though even that word is a misconception and a materialization. He is represented by what is sometimes called the Logos of the solar system, or the Solar Deity. This solar system of ours is a partial expression of Him. All the physical matter contained in it is His physical body; its astral matter is His astral body and so on. We accept the pantheistic idea that all that is, is God, but we go far beyond it because we say that He is also transcendent, that He has a great and magnificent life above and beyond the manifestation in system. As an ancient Indian scripture expresses it: "Having created this universe with one fragment of myself, I remain."

We have seen that this Solar Deity is spoken of in all religions as triune; in the Christian religion, the First Person is called God the Father. It is He who is the Great Architect of the system, for His thought creates the intelligible world of the Greeks, that is to say, the thought-form into which the matter of the system is built. From Him, of Him, part of Him, are the Monads or the eternal Spirit in man. From Him all came forth, and into Him all that came forth must one day return.

Thirdly, there is the thought of God as the father and protector of His people. In spite of all the sorrow and suffering which we see, in spite of the terrible catastrophes which happen, all things really are working together for good; so that the idea of God as a loving father, which Christ puts before us, is one that we may reasonably accept. It cannot always be justified if we see and judge only upon the physical plane— the lowest part of His manifestation; but as soon as one develops the higher sight and is able to look down from above one finds that all the evidence points to a benevolent Deity; and one realizes that for the soul of man all is always going well.

"Maker of Heaven and Earth"

In the Apostles' Creed this evidently refers to the Logos of our solar system. The Nicaean symbol,[37] taking a wider range, is cast into a form equally applicable to the First Cause of all, and so it speaks of the One God, maker not only of heaven and earth, but of *all things visible and invisible*. The idea of "heaven and earth" seems to be a corruption of that more clearly expressed in the formula in which the Christ indicates that the Logos called into existence "the scheme or system" [our solar system] "yea, our world and all things therein, whether seen or unseen."

There is a common misconception associated with the word "heaven." It is derived from *heven,* meaning "that which is heaved or raised up." Great confusion has arisen in consequence of its use in two totally distinct senses—first, the physical sky, the clouds, the sun, and stars; secondly, the nonphysical, glorified state of bliss which is the portion of man after his astral life is over. The heads of the Essene community were already in possession of fragments of more or less accurate information with regard to the origin of all things. Their knowledge of Chaldean and Egyptian astronomy undoubtedly enabled them to identify the planets of our system and the fixed stars which are the suns of other systems, and they would therefore appreciate the exact meaning of the teaching of the Christ.

The ignorant section of the Church would naturally blunder here and place thousands of solar systems under the control of one Logos. Later still, the yet more uncomprehending theologian imported the concept of the post mortem home of bliss—a physical location in space from which the majority of men are to be excluded—and so all knowledge of the original meaning disappeared.

12

THE SON

There are three separate ideas involved in the words of the Apostles' Creed: "In Jesus Christ his only Son, our Lord." The average Christian, hearing the simple formula which ends almost every prayer—"through Jesus Christ, our Lord"—thinks of one Person who is both God and man. He regards Jesus as God in the same sense as the Father. To the student of occultism, however, that phrase conveys three separate ideas; first, Jesus the disciple, who was not a great adept, though a very holy and beautiful character; secondly, the Christ, the great World Teacher; and thirdly, Our Lord, that is to say, the Second Person of the ever-Blessed Trinity. We shall try to explain how these three ideas are connected, and how closely they are linked.

First, as regards Jesus, the great disciple. To make his position intelligible, we have to understand that Christ is the World Teacher, a great official of the Hierarchy of Adepts which rules the world on behalf of the Solar Deity. We know that God manifests at many levels, that while there is undoubtedly the one supreme, eternal, all-embracing Deity of whom we know nothing but that He *is*, the representative of that Deity, with whom we come into contact, is the Logos or Deity of our solar system, who within Himself is three Persons just as is the Ultimate, the Absolute, the Highest above all.

The Deity of the solar system is represented in each planet by the spiritual king of that world. That spiritual king has his ministers like an earthly king, and under him, in charge of different departments of the work, are great saints, adepts, and Masters. One of the most important of those departments is that of the World Teacher, who comes not to preach one particular faith, but to provide the world with religions. All religions are different presentations of one eternal truth. Truth is one, but it is many-sided; it has many facets, and it is not possible that one man or one set of men should possess the truth in its entirety. It is noteworthy that when we speak of the Ancient Wisdom (which is the truth behind all religions) to Christians, they say: "You are giving us something of Hinduism, something of Buddhism"; and if we preach that same great truth to the Buddhists they say: "But surely you are trying to Christianize us." That every great religion is part of the central truth that lies behind them all is shown by the fact that each person takes what is new to him as though it belonged to some other religion. He often thinks that we are trying to seduce him from his own religion, instead of trying to explain to him its inner meaning.

The World Teacher

The great World Teacher might be described as the minister for religion and education. His mission is not to preach one particular faith but to present the one eternal truth in different forms at different periods and to men at different stages of development, so that it may be assimilable by all of them. The mistake that many make with regard to religion is to seek for, and emphasize, the difference between their particular presentation and that which has been given to some other nation or set of people, instead of trying to find the common ground which lies beneath the points on which all religions agree and then endeavoring to harmonize the minor points on which they differ. It is true that they differ in name, in externals, in various superficial matters, but the important part of every religion is the teaching by which its people live. They may present different methods of attaining the highest, but they all agree as to the sort of life a man ought to live. If we, as good Christians, compare the teaching that is given to us, not with the outer forms of worship but with the ethics of Hinduism or Buddhism, we shall find that the good Hindu or the good Buddhist is living precisely as we live; that he also recognizes that love and kindliness and fraternity and honor and decency are qualities that the good man must possess, and that he agrees that the bad man is the one who is selfish, who rides roughshod over all, who is unkind, unloving, unfraternal, who steals, who murders, and ill-treats his fellowmen. All religions alike agree on those points because they all come from one great Teacher. He has already appeared under many different forms, because when the world needs Him He either comes himself and teaches it afresh or else He sends one of His disciples to preach new forms of the one eternal faith.

That, then, is the conception of the Christ held by the occult student. He is a mighty Teacher who looks after not one but all the religions of the world and makes a new statement of the truth whenever He thinks that the world needs one. All religions decline somewhat as time goes on. They are taught first by the great Teacher Himself, who knows that of which He speaks. Round Him He usually draws a set of disciples who know also that of which they speak at first hand, but soon these are followed by a generation that does not know, that has to rely on that which has been said or written. Then there begin to be various traditions and slightly different presentations of the truth until, by the time a religion has existed for a thousand years or so, it has gradually become overlaid by error and distortion. Thus in Christianity we have a great number of different sects all professing to give the genuine teaching of the Christ. No doubt they each contain one or two points, but only by taking them all together, not any one of them alone, are we likely to arrive at the real truth of what Christ wished His people to believe and to do.

This great World Teacher is known and spoken of, and His coming is expected, in other religions besides our own. The Buddhists believe in the coming Lord Maitreya Buddha; those who have lived in Buddhist countries know that this future Teacher is represented as quite different from the Lord Gautama Buddha, the Teacher of the past. The

Lord Gautama Buddha is represented as an oriental, sitting cross-legged and often with a dark skin. The Lord Maitreya, the coming Teacher, is always depicted as a white man, seated like a European. The great Kalki Avatara is also expected in India. In Mohammedan countries the people believe that the Imam Mahdi is to come and restate the truth for them, and they say that he will come soon. Those who are old enough can remember that a great deal of fighting took place some years ago in the Sudan in central Africa because there arose a man who claimed to be the great Teacher and gave himself the title Mahdi, and consequently thousands of tribesmen followed him.[38] He was a pretender, but the true Imam Mahdi will come some day, and he is identical with the Lord Christ whom Christians expect.

All religions deteriorate and become more or less corrupted as time goes on, until there comes a time when a religion is so far entangled with merely human ideas, when it is so far removed from the simplicity of the original doctrine, that it becomes of little use except to the few who can see behind the accretions and get back to its original purity. When a religion is at that stage, the World Teacher comes forth again and gives a new presentation adapted to the new conditions and to the new set of people. This will assuredly happen in the case of our religion also. We have made so great an advance in science and general knowledge that the presentation that was suitable for the Jews in Palestine two thousand years needs some restatement in order to be fit for us. A far wider view of the truth could be put before us now, one which would have been quite incomprehensible to them.

Jesus the Disciple

When the World Teacher comes to earth, He cannot afford to waste time. It is not only when He comes to earth and founds a religion that He is doing the work of His office. At all times He is directing the world's great religions and inspiring every man who lays himself open to His influence. He has hundreds, nay, thousands of servants working for Him—great angels, and great men both living and dead. He has His hands always more than full of work, and when He abandons for a time the higher level at which He usually works in order that He may descend to earth to make a restatement of religion, He does not want to spend more time in doing that than is absolutely necessary. Consequently, it is very rarely that He takes a body in the ordinary sense of the word. It takes too long a time to be born, to enter into the body of a little baby and live through the time during which that body is growing up and being trained; it would be no use to Him until it was old enough to go forth to preach and teach. Therefore the usual plan is that a great Teacher coming to earth takes the body of one of His disciples. The pupil is more than glad to lend it to the Teacher; he is full of reverence and delight at the honor that is done to him. In such a case the disciple may have to leave the body permanently, or he may stand by and take it again whenever the Christ is not using it; it matters little to him, for he feels it the greatest of honors that he can help in the mighty work.

Thus Christ took the body of the disciple Jesus, who is now one of the Masters of Wisdom. A very pure and holy man must that disciple have been. There are many hints of that in the Gospel story, which tells us that he was a Nazarene from his youth up; that he remained continent, that he developed his mind in all the wisdom of the Essenes when he went down into Egypt.[39] This great disciple Jesus yielded his body to the Christ at the Baptism by John in the river Jordan. At that time, when the voice from heaven said: "This is my beloved Son in whom I am well pleased" [Matt. 3:17], and the Holy Spirit hovered over him in the form of a dove, the Christ took possession of the body and began to work through it.

Jesus was a man of noble birth, a descendant of the royal line of King David. When he was about thirty years of age, he yielded up his body for the use of the Christ, who then held it for three years, of which He spent two in teaching work, chiefly in the community of the Essenes in eastern Palestine, and one in traveling all over the country preaching to the people.

The Christ is the Master of Masters; He is high indeed above all the great saints, but yet near and approachable. We do not think of Him as far away in some distant heaven, but as working constantly in this world, even though as yet He is visible only to those who have the inner and higher sight. He may even now be visited by them and from Him may be obtained information and teaching such as He gave many times in the past.

Abraham and Melchizedek

Although we are thus presenting a different idea of the Christ from the one usually accepted, there is nothing vague about it. We are speaking of that which we ourselves have seen and know. Our own scriptures tell us these things, if only people would understand. Did not the Christ say: "Before Abraham was, I am"? That is usually supposed to be a statement of His Godhead, but earlier He had told the Jews: "Your father Abraham rejoiced to see my day and he saw it and was glad" (John 8:56–58). Now when did Abraham see Jesus of Nazareth? Of course he did not see Him, but surely he saw the Christ, the great World Teacher, manifested in the august personality of the mysterious Melchizedek, of whom it was said that he was "without father, without mother, without descent, having neither beginning of days nor end of life; but made like unto the Son of God" (Heb. 7:1–3); who, bringing forth bread and wine (the sacramental symbol of the initiation into a higher mystery), instructed Abraham in the supreme fact of the manifestation of the Cosmic Christ. Hence that was to Abraham a day of Christ, a day in which indeed he rejoiced because it was a day of great spiritual enlightenment for him. People read these things in the Bible and they vaguely think that the language is beautiful and it uplifts them, but they seldom try to attach any meaning to such statements. There is always a meaning, if we will take the trouble to understand.

The Second Person of the Trinity

Very appropriately may we call him "Our Lord," as they do in the East, but when that term is used in the creed, it generally refers to the Cosmic Christ, the Second Person of the Blessed Trinity. Yet the great World Teacher is so mystically, so wonderfully near to the Second Person that it is not surprising that some confusion should arise. He is so entirely a manifestation of that Second Person that indeed it does seem as though They were one—one in a manner far beyond our comprehension, but manifestly, truly one; for the Godhead flames out through Him so that indeed we may say They are indistinguishable. There is indeed a difference, but to us looking as from below, it is difficult to distinguish in any way between them.

In the Nicene Creed we have the phrase, "the only begotten Son of God." That is a very unfortunate translation of the Greek word *monogenes*, for *genes* means "born," and *mono* (*monos*) means "one." It does not mean "only begotten," but "alone born": To discover its real meaning, we must study contemporary philosophy. We know that words change their meanings with the passage of time; we find many instances of that in English. But even at this distance of time the word *monogenes* could not legitimately be translated "only begotten." The correct rendering is "alone born," that is, born from one and not from a syzygy or pair.[40] Everything else throughout physical life is produced by the interaction of a pair, whether they are separate entities as they usually are, or merely two poles included within the same organism. Always there is the interaction between two in order to produce a third. Only once in nature has there been one born alone, for the manner in which the Second Person comes into existence is absolutely different from all later processes of generation. We see at once that this passage refers not to Jesus or to Christ the World Teacher, but to the Second Person of the Blessed Trinity, which leaps forth from the bosom of the Father, called into being by the mere action of His will.

Hence comes the expression "before all worlds." It is undoubtedly true that the Second Person of the Blessed Trinity came forth from the First "before all worlds," but that does not alter the fact that that is a flagrant mistranslation of the Greek words that can mean nothing but "before all the aeons."[41] To those who are acquainted with the philosophy of the Gnostics or of Philo Judaeus or with the Hermetic philosophy, the meaning of those words is well known. The Second Person of the Logos is the first in time of all the aeons or emanations of the Godhead, differing from all the others, and so is "the first-born of many brethren."

Next comes the emphatic and reiterated assertion that Christ is "of one substance with the Father," is identical in every respect with Him from whom He came, save only that He has descended into matter and has thus for the time being limited the full expression of Himself, so that He has a dual aspect. As the Athanasian Creed expresses it, He is "equal to the Father as touching his Godhead, and inferior to the Father as touching his Manhood." Still the eternal unity is triumphantly proclaimed for "altogether he be God and man; yet he is not two, but one Christ," now as ever, "God of God, Light of Light, very God of very God." It should be remembered that there is no genitive case here; the Greek word means "out of" and so this clause should read "God coming from God, Light coming from Light, very God coming forth from the true God."

The Second Person of the Logos, the Son, sacrificed Himself for us by His descent into matter; He laid aside His kingly crown, descended to earth and put on the robe of flesh, the veil of matter. He is both God outside of matter and man within matter, and yet just as much divine in matter, though not showing the whole of His divinity. This divine essence of Himself which brought us into being is through us rising again into Himself. The culmination, the highest point of that rising, is the Christ. He is the head and front of humanity, the highest living man, the spear point of humanity pouring back again to God. He only of the human race has taken back His humanity to that stage of approach to the Godhead, therefore He is an expression of the Second Person of the Blessed Trinity to a degree and in a way that is quite beyond our gasp. That is the meaning of the words in the Athanasian Creed, and assuredly there is no grander statement of the eternal truth, that He is "One; not by the conversion of the Godhead into flesh [by the descent into matter] but by taking of the Manhood into God"—by the power to bear back into the Highest all the fruit of that descent.

There is a high mystical union between Christ and His people, but we must remember that this is always to be taken in two senses. Christ is within every man because that is God's plan for the evolution of His world. But remember that the Christ is both God and man; He is always to be looked at from those two points of view. It is very difficult for us to separate them in our minds, and yet sometimes it is well that we should do so in order that we may try to understand what is taking place and what is the real meaning of those wondrous gifts of His to His Church.

Christ the Son of God is always the Second Person of the ever-Blessed Trinity, the Second Aspect of the Solar Logos, but Christ the World Teacher is a man like ourselves, but perfect where we are imperfect. He also is the Christ: He is so utterly an expression or manifestation of the Second Person of the Blessed Trinity that, for us at our stage, we can make no distinction between Them—one is, as it were, the very incarnation of the other.

Christ as God, Christ as the Second Aspect of the Logos of our solar system, is within every one of us, and the whole of our spiritual life is an effort to bring the Christ within into full activity that it may be one with the Christ without, that all our vehicles may be permeated with His. We find many strange sayings in the Christian scripture, some seemingly contradictory of others, but in many cases, if we bear in mind these two aspects of the Christ, we shall see that some of these references are to one aspect and some to the other. The Christ within us is always the Christ principle manifesting through that which in us is an expression of Himself—the *buddhi* or the intuitional wisdom in man. That rests in every one of us, but it has to be awakened. Even that statement is misleading; the Christ principle itself cannot be awakened, for already it is the Christ, it is God, but we have to learn to adapt ourselves to it so that our vehicles may be, each at its own level, perfect expressions of that hidden Deity within.

13

THE INCARNATION

Since but for the descent of the Second Person into matter we could never have existed, it is true, and that in a very beautiful way, that "for us men and for our salvation [He] came down from heaven." Truly we might say, "for us men and for our very existence He came down from heaven." It is true that the immortal spirit of man is of the nature of the Father Himself. But for the sacrifice of the Son, who poured forth His substance as monadic essence into the limitations of the causal body, heaven and earth could never have met together, nor "this mortal have put on immortality." So the Christ is indeed at once the Creator and the Savior of men, because without Him they could not have been; without Him the gap between spirit and matter could never have been bridged, and the individuality—the soul in man—could never have been.

"And Was Incarnate of the Holy Ghost and the Virgin Mary"

This clause needs special consideration because there is an error in it.[42] No knowledge of the Greek language is required to appreciate this particular point, which is concerned with the two prepositions *by* and *of*. In the original Greek, there is only one preposition. The phrase there means He was made flesh or incarnated "out of" or "from" the Holy Ghost, *kai*, "and" the Virgin Mary. There is no word between "Holy Ghost" and "the Virgin Mary" except the word *kai*, which means "and." So it is unjustifiable to translate it: "And was incarnate by the Holy Ghost of the Virgin Mary" and thus, by inserting another preposition, make the function of the Holy Ghost entirely different from that of the Virgin Mary. The actual meaning is that He was incarnate of, or took flesh of, the Holy Ghost and the Virgin Mary, and nothing else can be made of it. If a schoolboy with a rudimentary knowledge of Greek, translated *kai* as it has been done in the Prayer Book, he would get into trouble with his teacher!

This mistranslation is not modern; it was St. Jerome who translated the Greek creed into Latin who first made this mistake,[43] and its perpetuation is due to the tendency that blinded the eyes of translators to any but the most material interpretation of the whole sentence and introduced, instead, a totally different idea.

The sentence is not found in the original Nicene Creed. There the text ran: "Who for us men and for our salvation came down and was made flesh, and was made man." There is not a word about either the Virgin Mary or the Holy Ghost; all of which was inserted afterwards, probably with the laudable intention of making the meaning clearer. It was correctly stated in the Creed of Constantinople. It was not until at least a century later that the Latin translation caused such confusion. This same Latin translation has been used ever since and, apparently, no one has ever thought of looking at the original Greek. In the Apostles' Creed, which as far as we know was put together in the eighth century, the idea became still more grossly materialized, and we now have the phrase "conceived by the Holy Ghost, born of the Virgin Mary," thus bringing the matter right down to the level of a physical plane marriage.

The real meaning is that the Second Aspect of the Divine Life, the Son, having already poured forth of His substance as monadic essence, now materialized Himself still further by assuming visible, tangible matter; by taking form, not of virgin matter, but of the vivified matter into which the force sent out by the Third Person of the Blessed Trinity, God the Holy Ghost, had already descended. He does not come into the mere sea of primitive matter (the true Virgin Maria) but into the seas over which the Holy Spirit has brooded. That is an important point to notice because this root of matter, this primitive matter to which the name "virgin" has frequently been applied, when untouched by the action of the Holy Ghost, does not aggregate itself or enter into any combination of its own motion, but remains in the atomic condition in which it is inert and unfruitful.

The life of the Holy Ghost, which at the First Outpouring interpenetrates that matter and vivifies it, is not to be separated from it. Indeed, as far as we have seen from our investigation there is no such thing as dead matter. Into this living matter the Second Outpouring of the divine life descends, giving it further powers of combination and fashioning therefrom the manifold forms of nature. Thus the Second Person of the Trinity takes to Himself a vesture or garment, not of the virgin matter alone, but of matter which is already instinct and pulsating with the life of the Third Person, so that in very truth He is "incarnate of the Holy Ghost and the Virgin Mary."

Here we may draw attention to a striking instance of the introduction of a totally different idea by a very trifling alteration. In some of the old manuscripts we find that the name of the Blessed Virgin is not "Maria" but "Maia," which means mother, dame, or foster mother. It is curious that in the Greek mythology, Maia was a daughter of Atlas, who supported the world upon his shoulders; and she was the mother of Hermes, who was the messenger of the gods. For Christians, the Blessed Virgin is the mother of the Christ who is the Messenger of the High Powers of this system. When we remember that Maya was the name of the mother of the Lord Buddha, and that this Sanskrit word is also used for the illusory veil of matter which the Logos draws round Him in His descent, we begin to realize that all these things are symbols.

The Virgin Birth

As soon as the creed is translated from Greek into Latin, we have the possibility of a play on the word Maria (which in Latin means "seas"), and yet another suggestion of the true meaning of the descent into the seas of virgin matter—the Virgin Maria, which, although impregnated and permeated with the life of the Holy Ghost, nevertheless remains pure or virgin because when that life is withdrawn the matter is as it was before. This is the original idea behind the dogma of the Virgin Birth around which so much controversy has raged, the difficulties, of course, being caused solely by the materializing tendency mentioned earlier.

Behind this mystery there lie in reality three meanings; first, the birth or manifestation in matter of the Second Person of the Blessed Trinity; secondly, the birth of the human soul, the individuality; thirdly, the birth of the Christ principle within man at a later stage of his development. We have already dealt with the birth of the Logos into matter and with the birth of the individuality which is made in His image. In this latter case we may think of the causal body—the permanent body which goes on from life to life—as the mother, itself immaculately conceived by the action of the Second Person upon matter already prepared by the Holy Spirit. Later, after the man, the soul, has developed intellect, we have the third meaning of this symbolism, namely the birth of the Christ principle in the soul of man when the intuitional wisdom is awakened. Then very truly the soul becomes, as it were, a little child again, is born anew into the higher life of the initiate, which is the true kingdom of heaven. That is the meaning of what is called the "second birth." It will be remembered that Christ said to Nicodemus: "Marvel not that I said unto thee, ye must be born again" (John 3:7). And when Nicodemus failed to understand, he was asked: "Art thou a master of Israel, and knowest not these things?" meaning, "You ought to understand; it is part of the inner teaching of your sacred books."

It should be remembered that the doctrine of the Immaculate Conception, as understood by the Roman Church, has nothing to do with the birth of the Christ but refers to the birth of the Virgin Mary Herself. The Roman theologians hold that Her body was born in the usual way of Joachim and Anna, but that Her soul was free from the original sin which was supposed to be inherited from Adam.

"And Was Made Man"

This clause does not appear in the Apostles' Creed. Its insertion into the Nicene Creed is significant as showing that the arrival of the monadic essence at the level of humanity was a stage separate from, and later than, the descent into matter and that therefore the taking flesh of the Holy Ghost and the Virgin Mary previously mentioned could not and did not refer to a human birth. That is even more distinctly shown in the draft made by the Council of Nicaea, where the text runs: "And was made flesh, and was made man," the assumption of the flesh clearly referring to the previous passage of the monadic essence through the animal kingdom. Those who take all this to refer to the physical birth of a human being take the three stages to mean one and the same thing. But when we understand the symbolical significance of the clauses, it is evident that they are meant to describe three distinct stages in the descent and have nothing to do with one another except that they follow one another.

"Suffered under Pontius Pilate"

In this clause we have a remarkable instance of the narrowing influence of the materializing tendency, for by the insertion of the smallest letter of the Greek alphabet (the *iota*, often represented by a dot) into the manuscript the original idea was entirely lost and forgotten. The word *pontos*, meaning a sea, was thus altered to Pontius, a Roman proper name. Instead of Pontius Pilatus, the earliest Greek manuscripts which clairvoyant investigators have yet been able to find, all read *pontos piletos*. (It must be remembered that the interchange of "a" and "e" is by no means infrequent in various Greek dialects.) Pilatus is another proper name, but *piletos* means "thick," "solid,"[44] so that *pontos piletos* means really a compressed or dense sea, by no means a bad description of the astral plane which is often symbolized by water. This clause should be rendered "He endured the dense sea"—that is to say, He allowed himself to be limited by, and imprisoned in, astral matter.

One consequence of the alteration was that it fixed the death of the Christ on a wrong date because He was already dead many years before Pilate was born. These things may be known to certain scholars, but they are not generally known to the man in the street, for few people have the time or inclination to study theological works. This particular alteration may quite easily have been made by the copyist under the impression that he was merely correcting the unimportant mistake of an earlier scribe.

In those early times people had no idea of literary honesty. Nowadays we take pains to be accurate; we think it wrong to insert a passage from somewhere else and not acknowledge it as a quotation, but in those times they simply included whatever they thought was good, whoever had said it, and they probably considered that they were doing the original author a favor! In those earlier centuries there was no such thing as printing whereby thousands of copies of the same work can be turned out without any possibility of making an error. Until the fifteenth century, every book was written by hand, and therefore in every copy mistakes are found. There are something like two thousand of those manuscript books, hardly two of which are alike. Errors have crept into all of them, giving often quite contradictory readings. It is clear, too, that in some cases the difference is not due to a mistake on the part of the scribe but has arisen because the copy was made from the slightly different original.

Originally, most of these things were written down from memory. The disciples heard what the Christ said, but quite a long interval might have elapsed before they wrote it down. If the members of any congregation attempted to write down what they remembered of a sermon they had heard in church, it is not likely that the result would be alike in each case. The same general idea might be presented but there would be considerable variation and, most assuredly, no two people would use exactly the same words. The same thing is true in the case of the apostles. Their memories were by no means infallible. They made mistakes in reporting just as anyone else would do and, as each account was copied hundreds of times, it is a wonder that we have not even greater variations than actually exist.

Finally, I must draw attention to the order in which the clauses of this part of the creed occur. Neither of the creeds as they stand at present contains quite the whole of the original idea. In the Apostles' Creed, though the order is accurate, several stages are omitted. While the Nicene is fuller, there is a confusion in arrangement. However, it is perfectly clear that in both there is a definite attempt to symbolize the different stages of the descent into matter, and this is even more evident in the draft of the Council of Nicaea. First, "for us men and for our salvation" the Son "came down from heaven"; that is, He came down from a higher level. Then having done that, He "took flesh"; that is to say, He passed into association with living forms and finally entered the animal kingdom. After He had taken flesh, as quite a separate step, He was "made man"; the divine force or life, rising from the animal kingdom, entered the human on receiving that other downpouring from the First Person, which gives the divine spark to man and creates his permanent soul or Ego that persists through all his lives until he has passed beyond the necessity for rebirth. Then came the suffering under "Pontius Pilate," or descent into the astral sea; and only after that the crucifixion on the cross of physical matter in which He is graphically described as "dead and buried." To regard all these details as referring to the physical plane life story of a particular man does not explain them in the least, whereas if we take the symbolical meaning, we at once see that they all come in the right order, and we arrive at an interpretation which it is possible for reasonable beings to accept.

14

THE CRUCIFIXION

"Was Crucified, Dead, and Buried"

Here we have a misunderstanding of colossal proportions—an astonishing transformation of a perfectly reasonable allegory into an absurd human biography. This has had a very sad effect on the Christian Church and on the faith which it preaches, because it sets forth as fact something that is demonstrably untrue, a fallacy which must appear to any thinking man as devoid of all rational meaning unless, as is the case, there is a higher symbolical interpretation.

The body used by the Christ was not crucified but stoned, that being the Jewish method of execution. By putting back the birth of Christ to its true date, which is 105 years before the time generally fixed for it, we find that His death occurred *before* the Romans conquered Palestine, and therefore He was undoubtedly put to death by the Jews in the Jewish way and not by the method of crucifixion which the Romans are said to have introduced. Thus an enormous amount of devotional sympathy has been poured out all through the ages in connection with a wholly imaginary story of terrible physical suffering. It has been, perhaps, the most extraordinary and most lamentable waste of psychic energy in the whole history of the world. For neither the creed nor the Gospels were originally meant to relate the life story of the Christ but were intended as an allegory setting forth the story of the evolution of every man, not of one particular incarnation.

This is no new theory; Origen, the greatest and most learned of the Christian Fathers, thoroughly understood this. He speaks of "the popular irrational faith" (based only on the Gospel story) and he says of it: "What better method could be devised to assist the masses?" He points out that the ignorant multitude is best taught by means of stories, for thus they can be led to grasp something of the higher things. But the spiritual Christian no longer needs the crucified Christ because his faith is founded upon definite knowledge of the truths of which these things are only symbols.[45]

The Crucifixion and the Resurrection clearly belong to the Christ allegory; this is evident from the fact that the date of their commemoration by the Church is not a fixed one, as would be the anniversary of an actual event, for it is movable and determined by the movements of the heavenly bodies, showing clearly that it was associated with their worship in pre-Christian times. Easter is always celebrated on the Sunday following the first full moon after the vernal equinox. This would be a grotesque method for fixing the date of a historical anniversary such as, for instance, the battle of Waterloo. But a commemoration whose date is made to depend upon astronomical calculations is not a commemoration in the ordinary sense and can be understood only when we consider it in relation to the festivals connected with the worship of the sun god thousands of years before the birth of Jesus.

As a matter of fact, this part of the creed is taken direct from the ritual of the Egyptian initiation, which was intended to illustrate the later stages of the descent of the monadic essence into matter. Let us consider first how this descent came to be symbolized as a crucifixion and then how it was represented before the eyes of the neophytes in ancient Egypt.

The Symbolism of the Cross

To understand this clearly, we must first try to ascertain the meaning attached to the emblem of the cross in the sacred Mysteries of antiquity.

Each form of the cross has its particular meaning. The Greek cross is the symbol of God the Holy Ghost, the Third Person of the Blessed Trinity. The swastika and the Maltese cross, belonging to an elaborate set of symbols with which some students are familiar, are both symbols of the Holy Ghost in activity. First, God the Father is symbolized as a point within a circle. Then the point extends into a line and divides the circle into two parts, and that is a symbol of God the Son who is always represented as dual. In some cases that duality is expressed as male and female, like Osiris and Isis in Egypt; sometimes it is represented as God and man as in the Christian scheme, but always the Second Person is dual. Then the Third Person not yet in manifestation is represented by a second line crossing the first at right angles so that we get a cross within a circle.

When He prepares for a further descent, the symbol changes. Sometimes the circle falls away altogether, leaving the equal-armed Greek cross as the sign of the Third Logos, the Divine Activity, ready to manifest as Creator at the commencement of a great cycle. The next stage is the swastika, which implies motion—the creative power in activity; for the lines added at right angles to the arms of the cross represent flames streaming backwards as the cross whirls round and thus they doubly indicate the eternal activity of the universal life, first by ceaseless outpouring of the fire from the center through the arms, and secondly by the rotation of the cross itself. We find the same idea in the Maltese cross, in which the arms, diverging from the center, once more typify the divine energy spreading itself forth in every direction of space.

Along another line of symbolism, the cross, instead of dropping the circle altogether, extends in all directions outside it and we then have the equal-armed cross with a small circle at its intersection. Later, the small circle becomes a rose, giving us an emblem which is well known in one of the higher degrees in Freemasonry.[46] Again not only does the cross bear the mystic rose in its center, but itself becomes rosy in color as a symbol of the divine love which is the beginning and the end of all things.

The Latin Cross

The Latin cross, which has a long stem and a shorter horizontal arm above, is often represented—more especially in the Roman Church—in the form of a crucifix with the Christ hanging upon the cross. When our investigators began to trace its symbolism back through the ages, they expected to find that the figure would fall away leaving behind the simple cross which they supposed to be its earlier form. They were greatly surprised therefore to find that exactly the reverse took place and in the earlier representations of the crucifixion the cross fell away but the figure with the arms extended persisted.

The cross has for ages been a symbol of matter. The Divine Man is bound upon it, cramped and confined by His descent into matter which He takes upon Himself in order that we might exist. That is the real idea which lies behind this symbol and the others connected with it—the nails, the wounds, the blood.

For several centuries, the Christ was always depicted reigning from the cross with hands uplifted in blessing and with no mark of suffering. It was only in the thirteenth century, in the time of Cimabue and Giotto, that He ceased to be represented as living and triumphant on the cross. Those different stages may be seen in successive paintings in the Uffizi gallery at Florence.

There are certain passages in some of the apocryphal scriptures which are very significant. In *The Acts of Judas Thomas* there is a most beautiful description of the Christ standing in glory above the cross, and also of a splendid vision of a cross of light, by looking into and through which all the manifested worlds were to be seen. At the same time, the aura of the Christ included and interpenetrated them all. That surely is the true mystical and gnostic interpretation; it has nothing to do with the ordinary theories of crucifixion but is clearly meant to symbolize the descent of the Second Person of the Trinity into matter.

The cross, even though the body worn by the Christ was never physically nailed upon it, still remains a symbol of the ineffable self-sacrifice of the Deity when He descends into matter and of the enormous patience with which He holds Himself within that limitation, so that the manifold forms which He takes may expand gradually and not be broken by the too rapid movement and expansion of the life within. It is still for us the symbol of the mightiest sacrifice that the world has ever known. The limitation of the Deity must be to Him, if not exactly suffering, a veritable death by being linked with, and confined by, all these lower forms. That sacrifice He undertakes and patiently carries through "for us men and for our salvation" that we may come into being and eventually return to the level from which originally He came.

This symbol may also be used to remind us that man, as a part of the divine, is himself thus crucified if he did but know it. The soul, the living Christ within him, is still blindly identifying itself with the cross of matter upon which it is bound—with the physical, astral, and mental vehicles, which are not himself but his instruments to control and use. So whenever we find, as it were, two selves warring within us, we must remember that we are in truth the higher and not the lower—the Christ, not the cross. The symbol of the cross may then be to us a touchstone of self-sacrificing love, to distinguish the good from the evil in the difficulties of life.

The disciple is taught in certain inner Mysteries even now that only those actions through which shines the light of the cross are worthy of a disciple. He is taught to try himself, his actions, and his thoughts by that, and see whether they are the product of selfishness, however delicate and subtle, or whether they are really prompted by self-sacrificing love. Only in the latter case does the light of the cross shine through his life. It is said again in these inner Mysteries: "When the disciple enters upon the path he lays his heart upon the cross; when the heart and the cross have become one, then hath he reached the goal." This should remind us, too, that all true sacrifice must be like that of the Logos—a willing sacrifice; so long as it causes us pain and suffering we have not reached the goal. Only when self-sacrifice is natural to us; when, seeing the opportunity for it, we cannot do otherwise than take it; only when we are willing to give ourselves absolutely, fully and freely, can our sacrifice be one with His; then, and then only, have we truly signed ourselves with the sign of the cross of the eternal Christ.

The Ancient Egyptian Ritual

The great sacrifice of the descent of the Second Aspect of the Logos into matter in the form of monadic essence was somewhat elaborately set forth in symbol in the ritual of the Egyptian form of the first of the great initiations. It is not difficult to see that the idea of the crucifixion of the Christ originated in the rubric or direction given to the officiating hierophant which ran thus:

> Then shall the candidate be bound upon the wooden cross; he shall die, he shall be buried, and shall descend into the underworld. After the third day he shall be brought back from the dead, and shall be carried up into heaven to be on the right hand of Him from whom he came, having learnt to guide (or rule) the living and the dead.

The hall of initiation was generally underground in an Egyptian temple, probably both for the sake of secrecy and as part of the symbolism. At the culmination of a long ceremony the candidate voluntarily laid himself down upon a huge wooden cross, which was hollowed so as to receive and support the human figure. To this his arms were lightly bound, the end of the cord being carefully left loose in order to typify the entirely voluntary nature of the bondage. He then passed into a deep trance and, while in this condition, his body was borne away into a vault beneath the floor of the hall of initiation and laid in an immense sarcophagus—a process which, as far as the physical body is concerned, was not all inaptly symbolized as death and burial.

15

THE DESCENT INTO HELL

In the Apostles' and the Athanasian Creeds we find the clauses "He descended into hell" and "the third day he rose again." Concerning these passages there has been a great deal of misconception. I have already indicated that the words "hell" and "damnation" in the original Greek or Hebrew in no case mean what they have been commonly supposed to mean. I mentioned that our English word "hell" is derived from *helan*, to "hele" or conceal, so that "hell" means the "hidden place." As explained before, the ancients imagined this world as a vast plane floating in space, and they thought that the dead passed to a region situated underneath this plane, and hence it was called the "underworld" or Hades, which was the term commonly used by the Greeks. That hidden world is undoubtedly a fact in nature, but it is not on the underside of a great plane, because this earth happens to be a sphere.

When a man passes through the change which we call death, he sheds his physical body in just the same way as a man may take off an overcoat. When a man removes his overcoat he is still dressed. It is exactly the same with the man who puts off the physical body at death; he remains in what St. Paul called the "spiritual body" [1 Cor. 15:44], which is his astral or emotional body.

The Astral World

In the astral world there are a number of subdivisions roughly arranged according to the density of the matter of which they are composed. We find the same arrangement on the physical plane also. Broadly speaking, most of the physical matter is under our feet, although there is a certain amount floating in the atmosphere as smoke, and most of the water of the globe lies upon the surface of the solid matter, though some of it interpenetrates it, and there are underground rivers and lakes. The air lies on top of both the solid and the liquid, and above that again are various kinds of ether. These are lighter still and, although they interpenetrate all the other kinds of matter, they lie chiefly on top of the air, further away from the center of the earth than its atmospheric envelope. Generally speaking, although there is a good deal of intermixture, the various components of the astral plane lie in the same way—the densest matter at the bottom and the lighter above. Thus, the densest astral matter is down on the physical plane; next above that comes the next lighter variety of astral matter—what we call the sixth subdivision; above that, but also interpenetrating it, the fifth, fourth, third, and so on. All these interpenetrate one another, but they collect chiefly at their own levels.

In the astral body of each one of us there is matter of all these different kinds, just as in the composition of our physical bodies there is dense solid matter, a large proportion of liquid, and a considerable quantity of air and gas of various sorts. There is also etheric matter within and around our bodies.

When we come to live in the astral body, there is a great difference in the way in which we perceive things. In this physical body we have, by slow degrees in the course of our evolution, specialized for ourselves organs of perception—eyes to see, and ears to hear—but we still retain the sense of touch all over the physical body. In the astral body what corresponds to the sense of sight or hearing is spread all over it. There is no special astral organ of sight, but we can see with all parts of the astral body. While we are what is called "alive," all the different kinds of densities of astral matter are intermingled in the astral body. After death, these types of matter rearrange themselves, and the densest and hardest is drawn to the outside so as to minimize the disintegration of the matter by friction and thus prolong the astral life as long as possible. Since what might be called the sight of the astral body is spread over its whole surface, it is clear that having the densest and coarsest matter outside, the only vibrations the dead man can respond to are those coming from the lowest and coarsest level of the astral plane. That part of our hidden world is, on the whole, distinctly unpleasant because of the fact that all this coarse matter is the vehicle for the vibrations belonging to the more undesirable qualities.

When a man dies, he does not suddenly become a different kind of man, much worse or much better than he was before; he does not suddenly acquire new habits but remains exactly the same. If he has lived an ordinary decent life and has not been in the habit of yielding himself to coarse and low desires, he may have a certain amount of coarse matter arranged on the outside of his astral body and may, for the time being, be cut off by that pall from the higher and more beautiful vibrations of the astral plane. But because he has not been in the habit of using the coarser matter, he remains to all intents and purposes asleep during that early stage of his life after death. He is surrounded by all sorts of unpleasant influences, but his consciousness cannot be affected by them, so he floats about quite undisturbed in the midst of all the emotional turmoil and disorder. When, gradually, the coarser matter wears away and the finer type of matter which he has been in the habit of using comes, in its turn, to the surface, he becomes conscious of external impacts and is able to enjoy them.

Purgatory

The theory of our Roman brethren—stated very roughly—is that the hopelessly wicked drop into hell immediately while the saints go at once into heaven much in the same way that Our Lady is said to have been swept up there at Her Assumption. The ordinary good man between those two extremes has a great many faults and failings, which unquestionably unfit him to step immediately into the presence of God in the conventional heaven, and he would certainly be very uncomfortable and out of place there. Besides, these faults and failings would be offensive to those already there. Since he is not yet fit for heaven, he is thought to need a longer or shorter stay in an intermediate condition in which his faults will be eliminated by a painful process.

Within certain limitations that theory of the Church of Rome may be said to be true enough. Of course, there is no such thing as eternal hell. It is an outrage to common sense and most assuredly it gives an utterly wrong concept of God to any man who believes in it. As to heaven, according to the Roman theory, it is not quite like that; nevertheless there is a condition which we may call the heaven-world, with which I have dealt elsewhere. And it is true that the saint—the specially good man—does not linger in that intermediate world which we call the astral, but passes on almost immediately into that higher heaven life. But the large majority of people, who are neither great saints nor what we might call distinctly bad, pass through both these stages, first the stage that is depicted as purgatory and then the heaven-world. It is not a question of "going to heaven" or to "hell" but rather of passing through both these conditions—the lower first and then the higher—and all the difference is the relative length of time spent in the two conditions.

This "purgatory" is not at all inaptly so called because it is indeed a place where a great deal of refinement and improvement takes place. It is the lower part of what we commonly call the astral world into which man passes almost immediately after death. The Roman Catholic doctrine has a great deal of truth in it, but it is marred by the theory of indulgences, which holds out the possibility that a man can buy his way out of this inconvenient stage without going through the purification for which it exists.[47] There is no such possibility; no number of millions of pounds could make one pennyworth of difference to what happens to a man after death. No one can buy his way out of the action of the laws of nature.

Of course, it is clear that all these material ideas, such as burning by fire, are symbols; they could not be anything else. First, we must eliminate all ideas of purgatory as punishment. God does not act like an ill-tempered schoolmaster looking out for an opportunity to punish people. As a loving Father, He has, for the good of His creation and its evolution, established certain eternal laws. If there were no laws of nature (and the laws of nature mean the expression of the will of God), we should be living in chaos with nothing upon which we could depend.

The first and greatest of all these laws is that of evolution. Man and all the other creatures upon earth are slowly but steadily evolving— growing better than they were before. But they grow under a law of cause and effect which is always and inexorably just. The law works automatically, and we cannot in any way avoid its action. If we fall over a cliff, we are dashed to pieces or seriously hurt at the bottom because of the law of gravity; the reason for which we fell over the cliff makes no difference whatever. If we fall over, we fall, and we get the uncomfortable result of the fall; it would not occur to us to say that God had punished us. Nor must we say that God punishes us when, as the result of some action of our own, the effect of that action comes upon us.

And so, in the life after death, there may be suffering for the man who has broken the law, but it is not a punishment. It is simply the result of a cause which the man himself had set in motion. It is the only effective, and therefore the most merciful, process for the elimination of wrong or evil desire, for that is what the suffering which sometimes occurs after death really is. But in almost every case, the life after death is a far higher, pleasanter, happier life than the life on earth, even in the case of those whom we would call wicked. It is a better life for such people because instead of going on doing evil they are usually checked in their evil career by the suffering that comes to them. For most wrongdoing is caused by evil desire, and by suffering, the evil desire wears itself out so that in his next life the man is free from it.

A man who has been of the low, coarse type on earth would be conscious only of most of the vibrations which belong to the lower levels, though, as he had been in the habit of responding to such vibrations, they would not seem so terrible to him as to the more developed man. Still, he would certainly suffer keenly from the cravings which he would not be able to satisfy and this suffering would continue until the lower kind of matter was eliminated from his vehicle. Thus every man in that early stage of life after death finds himself in precisely the sort of surroundings that he deserves. He will be aware of only those impressions that he was in the habit of attending to during physical life.

The Origin of the Idea of Hell

What is the origin of the idea that hell is a punishment? First, let us take the case of a drunkard or a sensualist who has just died. These are not, in my opinion, the worst crimes; there are many meannesses which are greater evils, but I take them for the moment to illustrate what I wish to say. In the former case, the man has been under the domination of the most intense desire. The craving of the drunkard for drink is so powerful that he forgets honor and duty and even his love for wife and children in the mad desire to satisfy it. After death, he will have the same tremendous craving tearing at him. He will be fully conscious in the lower part of the astral world, and, having lost the physical body through which alone he can satisfy his craving, the condition in which he finds himself will seem to him a very real hell. Though, in terms of earthly time, it might not last very long—only the length of time which may be necessary to wear out the desire and get rid of it—yet it might seem to him long indeed because of the suffering connected with it.

The same thing would be true of the sensualist or of one who dies filled with jealousy, for example. I have seen a case where a man had a terrible time because of jealousy. He would spend his time watching the object of his jealous affection. He would be able to see enough to realize what she was doing but, having lost the power to interfere, he was compelled to remain a helpless witness, and so he suffered intensely until the coarser matter had worn away. Yet it was absolutely within his power to stop the whole trouble at once. Neither the drunkard nor the sensualist would have been able to cut off in a moment the desires that they have been diligently nourishing all their lives; it would have required some time to conquer these. But the jealous man had only to make the effort to overcome his evil feeling and there would have been no more suffering. At any moment he could have declared: "I decline to be jealous; I will think only of the happiness of the one whom I love; if she loves someone else, so be it." If he had had the strength of will to bring himself into that frame of mind, his suffering would have been over. Perhaps these examples may serve to show that there is no injustice and there is no punishment imposed from without; there is the result which follows on the man's own action, the absolutely natural and inevitable consequence of what he himself had done during life.

Some of the old Hindu writers were evidently observers of these things. In the *Garuda Purana*, for example, which deals with these low conditions of life from the popular and much overdrawn point of view, it is said that the miser goes along crying out: "Give up, give up, my wealth; from the world of Yama I see my wealth being enjoyed by you."[48] It is true that people who inhabit the lower astral world are very often far from happy and are sometimes intensely unhappy, and though the existence of this condition may have helped to inspire the popular concept of hell, there is no such hell except in people's disordered imagination.

The Descent into Hell

Let us now consider the meaning of the descent of the Christ into hell. We have seen that in the Egyptian ceremony of initiation there is a stage where the candidate is taken out of his physical body which is left lying in a condition of deep trance. During that time, the man himself is functioning in his astral body and is fully alive and conscious in that lower world. The Christ, as every other man in the course of his development must one day do, left His physical body and passed, not into the hell of the gross Christian conception, but into Hades, the world of the departed. We are told that during the three days before He rose again from the dead He went and preached to "the spirits in prison" (1 Peter 3:19) and, assuredly, those recently departed from this life may very truly be thought of as being in prison so long as they are yielding themselves to those coarser vibrations. As has been said before, the average decent man would be unconscious during this period and so would need no assistance except, perhaps, a little stimulus to help him rise out of his surroundings into higher conditions. But it was to those wretched creatures who had recently departed from this life and were still imprisoned and held down on the lower levels of the astral plane by unexhausted desires and unsubdued passions—it was to that vast army of unfortunates that the Christ went in order to help them by pointing out the true course of their evolution and the best method of hastening it.

There is a beautiful story in the *Gospel of Nicodemus*[49] about the entry of the Christ into Hades. It tells how Adam came forward to welcome Him and, as he prostrated himself before Christ, the Lord took him by the hand and led him, and the many pre-Christian saints and prophets that were with him, out of hell. Thus, according to this story, as Adam was the first to die, so also was he the first to be made free. That is only a legend, but it shows how they thought about these things in the early Church. They believed that the entry of the Christ into that hidden world would set free all those who, having had the misfortune to live in times long past, could attain salvation only by thus after death hearing and accepting the Christian faith.

It is as the prototype of all Christian men that the Christ descended into hell. Every Christ descending into hell will preach to the spirits in prison and try to help them. Even now, every time a candidate is received into the Great White Lodge, the Brotherhood of the Adepts, he also has to go through that experience. He is examined and is asked: "Here is such-and-such a case; how would you go to work to help it?" Then he is sent out to make his first experiment in preaching to the spirits in prison—to make his first attempt to help the unfortunate people in the astral world who have not yet reached the higher part where they could be happy—unless, perchance, he had previously been taught how to do so, in which case the ceremony of his initiation would be considerably shortened.

A Field for Work

But long before that great advancement comes to a man, it is possible for him to help in this work when he leaves his physical body and passes out into the astral world during sleep. He also can "preach to the spirits in prison" just insofar as he has the knowledge which enables him to tell them how to escape from their different limitations. Before he can do that effectually he must, of course, know something of that higher world, must prime himself with advice which he can give according to the cases which may come before him. Assuredly, if we resolve to give such help and to look for opportunities to help, we shall do so. Any resolution of that kind which we make in our waking consciousness will be put into practice in that higher world because, though most of us cannot bring through the recollection of the higher, the recollection of the lower passes automatically into the higher.

So when we go to sleep at night we shall remember our intentions perfectly but when we come back to our physical bodies the next morning, it is quite uncertain whether we shall have any memory of what we did in the astral world. All that the average person may hope to bring through is an occasional vivid dream of having done or said certain things.

There is a vast need for help and for more helpers. As time goes on, more and more people will raise themselves to the condition where they can be effective helpers during their physical lives and, afterwards, when they have cast off the physical body and are themselves living in the astral world, it will be one of their principal occupations to help other people, to go about giving them advice and assistance.

Thus the descent into hell is an opportunity for Christlike work in the relief of suffering. That hidden world—hidden from our physical eyes, but nevertheless perfectly clear and open to our astral vision—is a field where we can go and work; where nightly, during sleep and after death, we can bear the good news to those who are heavily burdened with sorrow or remorse and lift them out of their suffering, out of darkness into light.

16

THE RESURRECTION

"The Third Day He Rose Again from the Dead"

According to the Gospel story, Christ died on Friday afternoon or evening; the different accounts do not agree as to the exact time. Then it is said that He rose at midnight between Saturday and Sunday. It has been argued, a little disingenuously, that that fulfils the idea of rising again on the third day; that if the Friday (which, however, was nearly over before His death) is counted in with the Saturday and the Sunday (at the dawning of which He rose), it may be said that on "the third day He rose again from the dead." But this does not agree with that other statement attributed to the Christ that "so shall the Son of man be three days and three nights in the heart of the earth" (Matt. 12:40).

I have already drawn attention to the Egyptian rubric which the Christ Himself seems to have used to illustrate the teaching He gave to His followers about the progress of man through the different stages of initiation. There it is said that the candidate shall die and be buried and pass into the underworld and that, after the third day, he shall rise again. For three days and three nights the candidate was left in a state of trance; then on the morning of the fourth day he was lifted from his sarcophagus, carried into the outer air, and laid against the eastern side of the Great Pyramid so that the First Rays of the rising sun might fall upon his face and awaken him from his long sleep. But that was quite clearly and definitely *after* three days and three nights; therefore, insofar as this tradition is founded upon that rubric (and undoubtedly it is so to a great extent), three days and three nights would be the proper period.

That seems to have been universally accepted in the early days of the Mysteries, but, as is well known, the Mysteries deteriorated as time went on, and candidates were accepted because they were people of importance rather than because they were spiritually developed. In the early days of the Eleusinian Mysteries in Greece no one, not even the greatest king, would have been accepted unless he was in every way ready. In later and more degenerate days, the Mysteries became widely spread, and it is evident that it could not have been very difficult for people to join them, for one reads of a meeting of one of the degrees which was attended by no less than 30,000 initiates. It is certain that some of the later candidates could not fulfill all the requirements and were unable to remain in trance or even in sleep during the original period of seventy-seven hours. So "after the third day" became "on the third day." Of course this change could not have been made until the original intention had been forgotten or allowed to lapse.

There is a definite reason why this particular period of time was chosen; it refers to the other side of the symbolism—the descent of the Second Person of the ever-Blessed Trinity into matter. Students are aware that that descent is divided into great periods called "rounds," because of the fact that the divine life-wave passes seven times round a "chain" of seven worlds during the life-period of what is called a "planetary chain." The descent into matter takes three and a half such rounds. For three long journeys round our earth-chain and part of a fourth, the monadic essence sinks deeper and deeper into dense matter. We read in *The Secret Doctrine* that *fohat* (the Tibetan name for one of the manifestations of the Divine Life) has taken three turns and half a turn. It is only after the middle of the fourth round that certain mighty beings came down to our earth and gave a tremendous impetus to human evolution. Therefore in the symbolism of the ritual, the Christ is buried in the heart of the earth for three days and three nights, and only then is brought out again and rises, symbolizing the moment the monadic essence begins that mighty sweep of its upwards arc which, in the end, shall seat it "at the right hand of the Father."

Other Meanings

There are other meanings involved in this symbolism which I can only touch upon here. In the Epistle to the Romans, St. Paul writes: "We are buried with him by baptism into death; that like as Christ was raised up from the dead . . . even so we also should walk in newness of life" (Rom. 6:4). We have died with Christ; that is to say, just as the Second Person has descended into matter, so have we as souls descended into incarnation again and again. So we must also rise out of matter with Him into the higher and fuller life.

At the first initiation—a man's first birth into the higher life—we speak of him as rising from among the dead because, from the higher point of view, those who live in the world and for the world may be thought of as dead—dead as yet to the higher possibilities before them, dead to the spiritual side of their lives—and so the man who attains that level thereby becomes "safe" for ever and has definitely raised himself out of that death into life. All that many people think of as life— worldly ambition, power, and the indulgence of the self—is from the higher point of view merely a kind of living death, and the man who lives for such things has not yet risen from death in the mystical and inner sense.

The rising from the dead is also part of the symbolism of the fourth initiation. Connected with that is always much suffering, for the man must clear away all the karma that may yet remain to him. Up to the very end there will cling to him something of the results of his actions, whether they be good or bad, and in that initiation he finally winds up all connection with the affairs of earth. The man who has reached that level need not take birth again on earth unless he wishes, though almost invariably he decides to be born again in order to help mankind. For whatever advancement a man may gain, whether it be the first or the fourth initiation, he gains not for himself but on behalf of us all. The "great orphan humanity," through him, takes one more tiny step on the way to its collective escape from the chain of matter. When a great one rises from the dead, the whole world is brought a little nearer to its own rising, and there is great rejoicing among the angels of God whose great object (those of them whose work belongs to this side of things) is to help on evolution.

The whole world rejoices when the *arhat*[50] attains; "all nature thrills with joyous awe," as it is expressed in that wonderful little book, *The Voice of the Silence*. In *The Light of Asia* Sir Edwin Arnold describes most beautifully how, at the attainment of the Lord Buddha, the whole world was affected and felt a pulsing of sympathy; the prisoner leapt to lose his chains, people on sick beds felt themselves for the moment better and stronger without knowing why. Whether all that happens on the physical plane, I cannot say—most probably it does. But whether it does or not, I can testify from what I have seen myself that on all the higher planes it is so. Perhaps one may say it is after all but a small thing, because what is so stupendous an advancement for one man is, when divided among the hundreds of millions in the world, but a very little advance for each one, but it still means quite a definite uplift for everyone. So true is it that humanity is One.

We Shall Rise with Christ

Therefore those of us who understand a little of the truth are eager to run in advance, as it were, and are determined to work definitely for evolution instead of hanging back and just allowing ourselves to be carried on by the current. If we are anxious to make the swifter progress in order that we may help our fellow men and that we may take part in the great plan of evolution, if we are acting unselfishly and working in the spirit of God, then shall we rise as did the Christ. As the Christ had the Godhead behind Him, so have we within us the same power, although not yet unfolded as fully as His was. Nevertheless it is there; it is only a question of development, and that development is absolutely certain.

We shall indeed rise with Christ, and our rising must be continually repeated because there are always still higher levels to be reached. We must continue to cast behind us the burdens which hold us down and steadily, even though it may be slowly, rise towards the glory which lies before us in the future. "Christ being raised from the dead, dieth no more; death hath no more dominion over him. For in that he died, he died unto sin once; but in that he liveth, he liveth unto God" (Rom. 6:9–10) is true not of Christ alone, but of every man. We all have to die unto sin, and when we have once done that and risen above it, we live unto God for evermore. When we have raised ourselves above the temptations of the lower world, we live for the Christ and for His world and no longer for the personal self. That is indeed the true resurrection, and that is the goal which we must set before ourselves. When we have cast behind all that may hold us, it will indeed be true that "death hath no more dominion" over us, for we have risen with Christ and are partakers of the glory and of the higher life of God Himself.

17

THE ASCENSION

"He Ascended into Heaven"

The account of the Ascension given in the Bible states that Christ rose before the eyes of His apostles from the ground into the air and floated up until a cloud received Him out of their sight. This account need not be taken as historical. The whole Gospel story is a mystery drama setting forth the stages in the spiritual advancement of every Christian man.

The account given in the New Testament is not at all as definite as we should expect of so singular a phenomenon. There is simply a reference to it at the end of the Gospel of St. Mark,[51] and the story as we have it depends upon St. Luke. The Gospel attributed to him (we do not know anything about the author) and the Acts of the Apostles, which he is also supposed to have written, contain two contradictory accounts of this event. In the Gospel it appears that the ascension took place on the same day as the resurrection; that the Christ rose perhaps at midnight or very early in the morning while it was still dark, and in the evening of the same day He ascended [Luke 24:51]. In the Acts of the Apostles, forty days are made to intervene [Acts 1:3–9]. In the *Pistis Sophia* it is said that a period of ten years separated the two events.

These discrepancies become of little importance when we consider the symbolical meaning. To say of the archetypal man—in this case Christ—that "He ascended into heaven" means that He reached a certain higher level. In the old Egyptian ritual, it will be remembered, while

149

the candidate was in a deep trance, he had to enter not only the astral world of the emotions and learn to function and help there, but he also had to experience his first touch of consciousness on the *buddhic* or intuitional level. It was this transcendent experience, changing as it did his whole conception of life and of evolution, which was spoken of as the ascent into heaven.

Again, at a higher level, that of the fifth or *asekha* initiation, the ascension into heaven means the attainment of adeptship, the level at which the man has nothing more to learn as regards this particular chain of worlds. It means that the Christ which was born in him has once more become one with the Father. That is the highest meaning we can attach to the symbolism.

The Heaven-World

This symbolical interpretation is, of course, remote from the orthodox idea of heaven, which is that of a place somewhere far away to which the redeemed or the saved are conveyed and where they spend eternity playing harps and singing hymns. That view is, to say the least, inaccurate. Assuredly there is a heaven, but it is not eternal; neither is it a place but *a state of consciousness*, a condition into which a person passes when he has left his astral body behind.

When we begin to understand what death is, we realize that it is the true man, the soul, gradually withdrawing from his vehicles. When he has dropped his outermost vehicle—the physical body—he lives on in his astral body. Then, gradually, that body becomes more refined as the coarser particles are thrown to the surface and are worn away by friction. So the man may be said to pass through two stages of astral life—a coarser and then a more refined one. These stages correspond to the purgatory and the paradise of the average Christian. Eventually he drops his astral body at what is called the second death, and he finds himself living in his mental body in what would ordinarily be called his mind. Because life in that vehicle cannot be otherwise than blissful when compared with anything we know down here, it is called the heaven-life.

The highest level which any man can touch is heaven for him. The Red Indian of North America, who enjoys nothing so much as success in the chase, looks forward to passing to the "happy hunting grounds"— the highest state of bliss that he can realize and enjoy. If by any chance he should find himself in the Christian heaven, with harps and clouds and palm branches and crowns, he would be entirely out of his element and, as may easily be imagined, very uncomfortable. Each man gets that for which he is fitted, so he would stay on the lower levels of the astral world, where he was able to imagine himself as hunting, that being all the heaven that he is capable of appreciating. The orthodox heaven is found at a slightly higher level, but it still belongs to the astral world, as do all the material heavens of the average believers of other faiths. There are higher subdivisions still, where the more highly developed man can live a happy and useful life while his astral vehicle is gradually wearing away.

When this vehicle has finally been cast off, the man reaches the true heaven-world, where he lives in his mental body. That condition is always one of indescribable bliss, glory, and joy. There is nothing comparable to it here in physical life. There we have all that the heart can desire and are entirely free from all lower encumbrances. The average man has not developed that vehicle at all fully, and so he finds himself shut up in a body only part of which will respond to his will, but he does not know it. That is all of the mental body he has ever felt or known, so when he rises to that level he is perfectly satisfied with it. He has no idea that there are possibilities which he cannot touch. There is no feeling of doubt or limitation; he is perfectly happy in his heaven, whatever it may be. There is an Eastern proverb which says that "every man brings his own cup, and whatever may be the size of that cup, God fills it." It is always full; the man has the utmost that he can receive and can enjoy. It is a world full of all possible bliss, a world of divine thought, and each man draws from that divine thought what he is able to draw. There must always be that in the thought of God which is quite beyond our capacity of response, but from it every man draws what he wants, and all he wants, all he can possibly need, and so he makes his own heaven.

Our Friends and Loved Ones

Many of us need most of all the company and the affection of those we love. No heaven, however glorious, could be perfect for us without that. How is that to be managed when, of those whom we love, some are here on earth and others have passed away long ago? How can it be possible to have them all around us? In the most natural way in the world. Whenever we think of a person we make an image of him in mental matter. If we think often of a particular person, then we have floating round us a thought-image of that person. Here in the physical brain, our thought is a comparatively poor thing, but in the mental world where there is no longer a physical brain with heavy, dull particles to be set in motion, where there is no more interference of astral vibrations, where there are no feelings except the highest and most unselfish emotions of love and sympathy and devotion—where there is nothing to interfere with our thought—the making of a definite and powerful astral image of our friend constitutes a direct appeal to him, and he responds instantly.

The mistake generally made by people is that they think of the physical body as the real man, so that when he lays aside that body they think they have lost their friend. That is not so; the man is there still, but he has, as it were, taken off his overcoat and, because they have been used to seeing only the overcoat, they think they have lost him. He is there just the same; and he reacts to our love just as much as before and fills the image which we make of him in the heaven-world. If he should be living on earth, the physical brain may not know of that, but he, the soul, knows it perfectly, and pours himself into the image which we make, and through that he is very much nearer to us than he was through his physical body when we were both together in incarnation, because the physical body is a constant limitation.

The friend whom we love so much may have another side to him, which, if we saw it fully, we should perhaps not like so well. This "other side" may occasionally obtrude itself down here on the physical plane. It could not do so in the heaven-world because the manifestation of him there is exactly what we make it. He can show himself to us through the thought-form only as we think him to be. The fact that he has another manifestation going on in the physical world makes not the slightest difference. It does not prevent him thinking and feeling in that way any more than my taking hold of two separate objects with two hands prevents me feeling them both. I can tell the difference between these two things while at the same moment I am just as much conscious of one as of the other. Exactly in the same way our friend is as perfectly conscious through two manifestations of himself—or through two hundred—at the same time, or even through many thousands, as there may well be in the case of a much beloved and world-renowned personality.

The World of the Soul

Assuredly, the soul is filling all those thought-forms absolutely and perfectly though the physical brain down here may know nothing about them. The separate fingers do not know what the hand is feeling, but the brain, where all the lines meet, knows all; in the same way, the soul knows all the manifestations through which it is working. It is in the heaven-world that all the spiritual force which a man has set in motion during his earth life finds its full fruition. All our highest thoughts and aspirations belong to the realm of the untrammeled soul, and this lower world is incapable of providing a field for their fulfillment or realization. Nobody knows this better than the artist or the poet. A man who paints a picture or writes a poem hopes thereby to convey to others what he has seen in a vision of that higher world; none knows better than he how utterly the expression of the thought fails, how the most satisfactory reproduction he can make falls infinitely short of the reality. That being so, all these higher ideals and aspirations remain a vast force stored up, which can never be exhausted on the physical plane or during physical life. But there is this higher unseen world of transcendent beauty and unimaginable splendor, where it is possible for all these grander forces to work themselves out. All religions have tried to picture its glories, but they have all fallen miserably short of the truth.

It must be conceded that the orthodox heaven, with its harps and palm branches and crowns, might not be entirely satisfactory for everyone. Some people are not musical, and others are so musical that the harp might not fully satisfy their aspirations. Clearly the occupation of ceaseless singing to that instrument might not be equally enjoyable for everybody. One cannot think of any objective scheme where everybody would be satisfied to the uttermost. The only possible way in which that could happen is precisely what we find to be the truth, namely that each person makes his own surroundings and that everything in it is to him just what he wants it to be, and as he thinks of it.

Out of the fathomless sea of the divine consciousness each man draws that which he has made himself fit to draw, that which is suitable to him, that to which he is able to respond. If a man has a wealth of the grandest aspirations, he draws down a corresponding outpouring from above. If another has only a little grain or two of anything unselfish in his nature, even that little grain still brings forth its appropriate result. There is, moreover, no question of one entering and the other being shut out; it is not only for a faithful few, but for all who can reach it. All are not equally happy, nor are all happy in the same way, but every individual is happy to the fullest extent of his capacity. Each vessel is filled to the uttermost; though some vessels are small and some large, they are all filled to their respective capacities.

The Judgment

"He sitteth on the right hand of God, the Father Almighty; from thence he shall come to judge the quick and the dead." The creed has followed the Egyptian rubric closely through the phrases with which we have been dealing in the last few chapters and which are popularly supposed to refer to the history of the Christ. Here, for the first time, there is a definite divergence of meaning from it, though there is some evidence that it once followed the original formula more closely.

In the Egyptian rubric this clause is only an extension of the preceding one. In it the text runs: "He shall be carried up into heaven to be the right hand of Him from whom he came, having learnt to guide the living and the dead." That expresses very beautifully the object of the whole course of evolution. There is one trace left in exoteric writings to support the idea that this may have been the original reading. In the *Regula* of Apelles, who was a disciple of Marcion, this clause runs, "He sits on the right hand of the Father whence he *hath* come to rule the living and the dead."[52] This is a very slight divergence from the creed as we have it, but the meaning is quite different. It takes away at once any reference to the expected second advent of Christ, and so it becomes a very important statement which not only emphasizes the great fact that the life which is poured forth returns in fullest measure to Him from whom it came; it also declares that the whole vast process of evolution was undertaken precisely in order than mankind, so returning, should be the right hand of the Father in the work of guiding the living and the dead. Perhaps the great truth that all power gained is only held in trust and is given to us not for our own use or, rather, not for our own benefit, but to be used in the helping of others, has rarely been more clearly set forth than it is in those words.

Another point about which there is much misunderstanding is the meaning of the word "judge." The idea is ingrained in most of us by tradition that this refers to a second coming of Christ when He will judge between good and evil men and deal out eternal reward or punishment respectively. There is a certain truth in the idea of a day of judgment, but that is not what is referred to here. At the time when the Bible was translated into English, many words had a more general significance than we give them now, and this word "judge" is a case in point. We can see that this is so if we examine certain texts in the Bible. In the fourth chapter of the book of Judges, we find it stated that Deborah "judged Israel at that time." Evidently it means that Deborah was the ruler of Israel, because at that time there were no kings. In the tenth chapter of that same book, we read that "after him arose Jair, a Gileadite, and judged Israel twenty and two years." Here again, "judge" is simply a synonym for "rule." This brings us much nearer to the magnificent conception of guiding and helping which is given in the Egyptian formula. It may well be said, in the words of the Nicaean symbol, of a spiritual ruler who exists only to guide and help his people that "His kingdom shall have no end."

18

THE HOLY GHOST

"I Believe in the Holy Ghost"

The statement appears in this simple form in the Apostles' Creed also. It was very much amplified by the Council of Constantinople in 381, when the succeeding clauses were added: "The Lord and giver of life, Who proceedeth from the Father and the Son, Who with the Father and the Son together is worshipped and glorified, Who spake by the Prophets." We have seen that the clauses connected with the descent of the Christ into matter—His crucifixion, His resurrection, and His ascension—were molded on the rubric belonging to the Egyptian ritual for initiation. In the clause now under consideration we come back to the original formula as given by the Christ.

I have already explained that the Holy Ghost is the Third Person of the ever-Blessed Trinity, the aspect under which the Logos of the solar system manifests Himself to His world. It is, to a large extent, through and by this activity aspect of the Deity that the work is done down here. Nevertheless, although there are passages in the Bible which are liable to lead to that idea, we must not for a moment think of God the Holy Ghost as a mere instrument or messenger.

The Christ Himself said to His disciples when telling them He was soon to leave them: "I will pray the Father, and he shall give you another Comforter" (John 14:16, 26), and later on He explains that the Comforter is the Holy Ghost. That sounds as though the Spirit were a "something" which could be sent—an emanation rather than definitely a part of the Godhead who would act for Himself. It is much nearer the truth if we think of Him as the arm of the Lord stretched out in activity.

Of the Persons of the Holy Trinity, the Holy Ghost is, as it were, the nearest to us, and it is chiefly through Him that the divine force is outpoured down here. When a candidate comes up for confirmation we first make the "traditional call which has always been addressed to Him, which He stands ever ready to answer—the *Veni Creator:*[53] "Come, Holy Ghost, our souls inspire." This hymn has been used from the earliest days of the Church to invoke the descent of this mighty power.

Later the bishop places his hand on the head of the candidate and prays: "Receive the Holy Ghost for the sweet savor of a godly life." Let no one for a moment doubt that the Third Person of the Blessed Trinity does descend when thus invoked, that His power is directly poured into the candidate, and that that power remains ever to encourage, to strengthen, and to help. His influence opens up certain channels which were not opened before, and it widens those which were already open. It is through Him that all blessings, all sanctifying power descends, whether it is at the consecration of a church, the blessing of holy water or of the congregation by the priest or bishop. The blessing is always given in the name of the Father and of the Son and of the Holy Ghost, and thus three varieties or types of power are sent out in that benediction, but they all come through that lowest aspect which is yet so inconceivably high—God the Holy Ghost.

The Paraclete

The most prominent characteristic of the third aspect of the Blessed Trinity in relation to us is that of Encourager. That is the real meaning of the word *Paraclete,* which is so often employed in reference to Him and is frequently translated in the New Testament as the Comforter. That word is derived from a Greek word, the principal meaning of which is "to cheer on" or "to encourage."[54] True, we can also make it mean "to comfort," because if a man be in sorrow or difficulty, to cheer him up is certainly to comfort him. Without doubt, He is a comfort to His people when they are in sorrow or trouble, but He is very much more than that, because in whatever state they may be, at every point from the cradle to the grave, He is constantly encouraging and strengthening, heartening and urging us on to better and higher things.

God the Holy Ghost dwells ever within us; He is always near when we appeal to Him; His strength is poured out upon us whenever we turn to Him for help and for encouragement. He is God the Encourager, God the Strengthener, ever working within us towards righteousness.

It is the whole aim of man, having come forth from the divine, to rise again towards his origin; in the course of that steady evolution when he comes into touch with the divine, he naturally must come into touch with the lowest point first. We use the expression "lowest" with no sense of comparison or with any implication of greater or lesser. But it is true that the Holy Spirit presses further down into our world than the other Persons do, and therefore it is with Him that the man who is getting to be more than man, comes first into touch on the higher part of the mental plane. He becomes one with God in this, if we may call it so, outermost manifestation of Deity. That is imaged in the Christ drama when the Lord ascends into heaven.

When a man leaves the ranks of ordinary humanity, he rises to the stage beyond humanity and becomes one with God—he ascends into heaven and sits on the right hand of the Father. But immediately following the festival of the Ascension comes the festival of Pentecost, which celebrates the outpouring of the Holy Spirit. The adept, when he has passed beyond ordinary humanity, pours down upon his friends and disciples the power of the divine life and light—pours himself forth as the Fire of God, that being one of the titles often applied to the Holy Ghost. He is also sometimes called the Flame of God or the Fire of the Divine Love because He is especially a manifestation of that love which is the very life of God. His symbol is fire—a very apt illustration of the burning love far above all earthly passion or emotion, that wonderful spiritual love which, in truest alchemy, burns up all dross, burns away all that is not good, all that is not of the highest, all that is not able to stand in the flame of its consuming fire.

"The Lord and Giver of Life"

This phrase is generally taken to mean "the Lord of Life and the Giver of Life," which is an entirely unwarranted construction. In the original Greek there is a comma after the word Lord, and then the beautiful name—the Life-Giver—is given as a separate title. The proper translation is therefore "The Lord, the Life-Giver."[55]

God the Holy Ghost is the life-giver in no less than three separate senses. We have seen that life came forth from Him in the beginning when He brooded over the face of the waters of space and brought into existence matter as we know it today.

It is His life that pulsates through the ultimate physical atoms and gives them the power to combine in certain ways so as to form the chemical elements. Thus, the atoms with which modern chemistry deals are monuments of His work. His action brought them into existence in a certain definite order—an order which, as far as investigation into this subject has been carried out, appears to correspond to that of their atomic weight, so that substances having high atomic weight, such as lead, gold, or platinum, are of much later formation than elements of low atomic weight, such as hydrogen, helium, or lithium. His great outpouring of life is still going on, and we have reason to believe that chemical elements of a still more elaborate kind are in process of creation, as we shall discover as time goes on. Probably His "workshop" is down in the center of the earth.

Only a few years ago it was supposed that an atom of any of these elements could not possibly be broken up into anything smaller. Recently, however, it has been discovered that these so-called atoms are not true atoms at all. "Atom" means that which cannot be cut, which cannot be further subdivided, and so is the ultimate to which a thing can be reduced. It has been found that chemical atoms of all kinds are built up of very much tinier bodies called electrons.

Long ago, Sir William Crookes and Mr. Sinnett engaged in research along this line, and I had the honor of helping in a great many of their experiments.[56] We tried to discover what lay behind all these chemical elements, and Sir William Crookes came to the conclusion that there was a substance out of which all of them were built which he called *protyle*, meaning the first form of matter. Of course, the electron which has since been discovered goes further back than that. What he had found was the earlier physical form of matter—the earliest condition in which it can be regarded as really physical—which is built up of what occultists call ultimate physical atoms.

The Ultimate Physical Atoms

These are much smaller than the chemical atoms. For example, eighteen ultimate atoms go to make one chemical atom of hydrogen.

The ultimate atoms are all alike except that some are positive and some negative. A definite number of them arranged in a certain way make a chemical atom of hydrogen, and a great many more arranged in a different way make an atom of lead or silver or gold, and so on. All through, a distinct line of development is traceable in these chemical atoms.[57]

At first, they consist of a mere bundle of tubes, or sometimes of spikes through which force is poured out or drawn in according as to whether they are positive or negative. But presently, a central globe made of a few ultimate atoms is formed in the middle of this and, as we follow the line of evolution from the lighter to the heavier chemical atoms, this little sphere in the center becomes larger until, in radium, we find it is very distinctly the principal part of the whole, and the rest of the framework—the spikes and the funnels—exists simply for the sake of this central sphere. It becomes progressively more and more alive, developing more power of motion, unfolding, in all sorts of ways, unexpected qualities until, in radium, it is sufficiently alive to draw matter from without and shoot it forth again and so is able to go on, pouring out force for millions of years. The reason why it can do that has not yet been discovered by the scientists, but someday they will find out that it does so because it is like a living cell, a living spore.

These ultimate atoms are complex things. We call them ultimate physical atoms because, when we break them up further, they become astral matter. There is reason to believe that the electrons of science are what we call astral atoms, because it is said that in a chemical atom of hydrogen there are somewhere between seven hundred and a thousand of these electrons. Now it happens that in a chemical atom of hydrogen there are 882 astral atoms. This may, of course, be only a coincidence, but that seems improbable. If there is any real connection between these two facts it seems that in some of their experiments our scientific men must be actually disintegrating physical matter and throwing it back onto the astral plane.

The physical ultimate atoms are themselves built up of still smaller bodies which we call bubbles in *koilon*. If we look with clairvoyant vision at one of those atoms, it is seen to be composed of a number of spirals or tubes arranged in a certain order, each tube being made of seven still finer tubes spirally coiled, set successively at right angles one to the other. These tubes, which we call spirillae, are not all in activity as yet. We are now in what is called the fourth round—the fourth journey round the chain of planets on which we are evolving— and only four out of the seven sets of spirals are awakened and in full working order. The other three are not yet in activity, and judging by the past, in each future journey round the planets the atoms will develop another set of spirillae until all are fully vitalized and this particular part of the work of the Holy Ghost will be accomplished. Thus it is His life which is slowly unfolding the very atoms of which our matter is built. The fact that matter itself is evolving means that our work will become much easier as time goes on. What is called the resistance or inertia of matter is one of its qualities which at present often stands in our way and causes us trouble. Many difficulties will be removed for our remote descendants in later rounds, because matter then will be much more developed, much more alive than that in which we are working now.

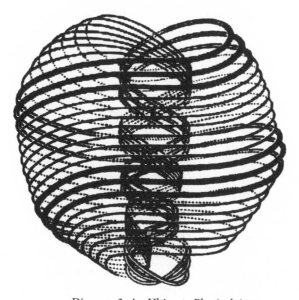

Diagram 3. An Ultimate Physical Atom.

The atom itself is nothing but the manifestation of a force; the Deity wills a certain shape which we call an ultimate physical atom, and by that effort of His will some fourteen thousand million "bubbles in *koilon*" are held in that particular form. The atom here represented is male or positive. It is a heart-shaped structure, composed, apparently, of ten sets of spirally-arranged "wires," of which three sets are thicker than the others. Under observation, an atom is seen to be extremely active, three movements being chiefly noticeable: first, it spins rapidly on its axis; second, it moves rapidly round a small orbit; third, it is expanding and contracting, pulsating like a beating heart. All the so-called chemical elements are made of geometrically arranged groups of these ultimate atoms.

The Serpent Fire

There is a third way in which God the Holy Ghost is the Giver of Life. It is through the force called the Serpent Fire or *kundalini*. I wrote in my book *The Chakras*:

> This force is the physical-plane manifestation of another of the manifold aspects of the power of the Logos, belonging to the First Outpouring, which comes from the Third Aspect. It exists on all planes of which we know anything. . . . It is not convertible into either the primary force already mentioned or the force of vitality which comes from the sun, and it does not seem to be affected in any way by any other forms of physical energy.
>
> We have known for many years that there is deep down in the earth what may be described as a laboratory of the Third Logos. On attempting to investigate the conditions at the center of the earth we find there a vast globe of such tremendous force that we cannot approach it. . . . The force of kundalini in our bodies comes from that laboratory of the Holy Ghost deep down in the earth. It belongs to that terrific glowing fire of the underworld. That fire is in striking contrast to the fire of vitality which comes from the sun.
>
> Kundalini is the power of that Outpouring (the First) on its path of return, and it works in the bodies of evolving creatures in intimate contact with the primary force already mentioned, the two acting together to bring the creature to the point where it can receive the outpouring of the First Logos, and become an Ego, a human being, and still carry on the vehicles even after that. We thus draw God's mighty power from the earth beneath as well as from heaven above; we are children of the earth as well as of the sun. These two meet in us and work together for our evolution. We cannot have one without the other, but if one is greatly in excess there are serious dangers. Hence the risk of any development of the deeper layers of the Serpent Fire before the life in man is pure and refined. . . . But kundalini plays a much larger part in daily life than most

of us have hitherto supposed; there is a far lower and gentler manifestation of it which is already awake within us all, which is not only innocuous but beneficent, which is doing its appointed work day and night while we are entirely unconscious of its presence and activity.[58]

We see then that God the Holy Ghost is a giver of life in three ways. First, He sends His life through the atoms; then He pours through them another stream of life which enables them to combine and make the chemical atoms; thirdly, He works in the bodies of all evolving creatures through that mysterious force we call the serpent-fire.

"Who Proceedeth from the Father and the Son"

There has been a great deal of ambiguity surrounding this clause. It has attained a notoriety, a prominence out of all proportion to its intrinsic importance, because it was nominally the cause of the greatest schism which has ever taken place in the Christian Church—the division between the Eastern and Western churches in the eleventh century. The whole question turned upon the insertion of one word. "Who proceedeth from the Father" was the original form of the phrase, and the word *filioque*—"and the Son"—was inserted by the Roman Church about the year 600. The Greek Church took no exception to it at the time, but some four hundred years afterwards it suddenly discovered that it could not possibly have fellowship with people who held so strange and outrageous a doctrine. The real reason for the change of front was political and financial rather than doctrinal.

Relations between the two parts of the Church had been strained for some time. The west of Europe owed its allegiance to the See of Rome, whose policy it was to centralize everything in Rome itself. There were several patriarchs in the Eastern Church who ranked equally, whereas there was only one head of the Western Church, the Pope. He tended to draw authority more and more into his own hands, and the straw which broke the camel's back and finally decided the Greek Church to secede was the transference of the allegiance of the Bulgarians from the patriarchs to the Pope. That meant the turning aside of a good deal of money from the one organization to the other, and so the Eastern Church broke away and gave as pretext the insertion of "*filioque*." The Western Church in no way corrupted the doctrine when it added that word, but only expressed in words what must have been obvious from the first to anyone who read behind the mere letter of the formula, and yet there was a very real meaning in the protest of the Eastern Church.

We have already seen that when the life of the Deity appears in the highest world of our solar system it manifests as a triplicity, as three Persons or Aspects. The first of those Persons—the Father—remains always at the level of the first and highest manifestation. The second descends one plane and clothes itself in the matter of that plane. The third of these equal manifestations descends through two levels. Thus we have three separate manifestations whom, with all reverence, we may describe as standing on three steps. If we picture the planes to ourselves as the shelves of a bookcase, there will be three manifestations side by side on the highest plane. The First remains always on that plane, while the Second descends a stage lower and manifests there through the matter of that plane. The Third descends a further stage still and there manifests Himself. But as the three exist coequally on the highest plane, the Second Person must always retain that manifestation on the highest plane though He descends one plane lower. Similarly, the Third Person descends two planes but retains a manifestation on each of those higher planes. So clearly it was not an alteration of the doctrine of the Church to say that the Third Person proceeded from the First and Second Persons. He obviously proceeds from the first through the level of the second down to His own plane on the third. What the Latin Church meant when it included the word *filioque* in its creed was simply that God the Holy Ghost does not drop to the third plane *over-leaping* the intermediate stage of the second plane, but *passes through* that stage which is specially devoted to the manifestation of God the Son. The Greek Church misunderstood this addition and supposed it to indicate a confusion of the functions and manifestation of the separate Persons or Aspects of the Trinity. Both sides were right. The Eastern Church was perfectly right when it said that there was a clear line of descent from the level of God the Father and that therefore the Holy Ghost did not come forth from the manifested Person of the Son. St. John Damascene came the nearest of any of the disputants to understanding the truth, for he rendered this phrase; "Who proceedeth from the Father through the Son."[59] He was, however, considered a heretic by his contemporaries.

If they had reversed their phrasing and said that the Son proceeded from the Father and that the Holy Ghost was begotten of the Son, they would have been nearer to the occult truth. The second Person of the Trinity leapt forth of His own volition from the bosom of the Father, and so was born of One and not of Two. As I have explained elsewhere,[60] the real meaning of the word *monogenēs* is "coming forth from one alone" and not from the interaction of a syzygy or pair, as in all other births in our system.

The procession or generation of the Holy Ghost was no exception to the general rule, for in all systems the Son is regarded as dual, though in the modern Christian system the two poles or aspects are expressed only as divinity and humanity. In many of the earlier trinities, and even in the Gnostic traditions, the duality was regarded as corresponding to that of male and female and the Second Person was sometimes called "the Father-Mother" and was spoken of as containing within Himself the best characteristics of both the sexes.

"Who with the Father and the Son Together Is Worshipped and Glorified"

This phrase emphasizes the equality of the Three Persons, though this was by no means universally accepted. The followers of the Arian heresy held—certainly with a show of reason—that if the Son came forth from the Father, He must be younger and therefore in certain ways of less importance than the Father. But the orthodox party maintained that in essence these Three Persons had always existed, and that they were coeternal and coequal, a truth stated in this clause of the Nicene Creed and more definitely asserted in the Athanasian Creed, where it is stated that "none is afore, or after other; none is greater, or less than another; But the whole three Persons are coeternal together; and coequal." The Three Aspects are indeed equally worthy of our reverence and our gratitude, all equally to be glorified by man, since his debt of gratitude for the labor and stupendous sacrifice involved in his evolution is due to all three alike.

"Who Spake by the Prophets"

This touches another side of the work of the Holy Ghost and is more a misunderstanding than a mistranslation, because the original Greek is certainly capable of that interpretation. Those who have studied the writings of the Christian Fathers, the Gnostics, and the philosophers of Alexandria, know that the real meaning of this clause is obviously something quite different from the rendering given here. We use the word "prophet" nowadays to designate a person who foretells the future. The Greek word *prophēmi* (*phēmi*, "to speak," and *pro*, "forth" or "before") means to speak out, to preach, to deliver a message. The meaning of the original passage which this clause represents may perhaps best be rendered into English as "Who manifests through His Messengers." Now the Greek word *angelos* means both "angel" and "messenger." The angels are the messengers of God, and the original meaning behind this was not a reference to the Jewish prophets but to the idea that God the Holy Ghost manifested Himself to the world through certain Messengers.

It must be remembered that most of the early Christians were Jews, and they were always anxious to link the new Christian teaching with the old Jewish belief and to make Christ appear as the recognized Messiah whom their prophets had foretold. The prophets wrote and spoke poetically in large and general terms, but many of their utterances were twisted from their obvious meaning in order to make them fit in with incidents which were supposed to have happened in the life of Christ. We find that very frequently Christ is spoken of as doing or saying certain things in order that "the scriptures might be fulfilled." They supposed that He did or said certain things in order to fit in with what the prophets had said hundreds of years before. It was very natural that they should try to fit these things together, and when we remember their strong conviction that they were God's chosen people, perhaps it is not very surprising that they should regard this passage as indicative of the inspiration of the Hebrew prophets.

The Seven Rays

In order to find the real meaning of this clause we must go back to the teachings of the Jews not as found in the books of the Bible but rather in their mystical writings. There we find a tradition of the seven Archangels or the Seven Spirits before the throne of God—the seven lesser Logoi, who are the first emanation of the Godhead. Of course, it was manifestly impossible that the reference to them in the passage under consideration should later be understood by those already obsessed with the idea that all that was said of the Second Person of the Trinity was to be taken as the life story of a human teacher. If the Second Person were but a man and the Third Person a vague influence proceeding from Him, then the messengers through whom that influence had previously manifested must obviously be men also. The grandeur of the true conception was far above them.

That this manifestation through His angels is a vivid reality, every student of occultism knows. On every plane he finds the seven great types, not only of matter but of life and energy. Whatsoever has come forth from God, of Light and Life and Strength, has come through one or other of those seven great Spirits. They are, in a way very difficult for us to understand, entirely separate entities; and yet they are centers of energy in the Logos Himself. All life which is poured forth is His life,

169

but it is poured out through one or other of these great channels and whosoever passes through them receives an ineffaceable mark, so that thereafter one can always tell through which of the seven any particular portion of strength, life, health, may have come. We find these seven lines of energy running through all the kingdoms.

We call them rays; we speak of individuals as belonging to the fourth or the seventh or the Fifth Ray and so on, according to the line along which they came forth from the Divine. Men have always recognized these divisions. A century or more ago they were called "temperaments," and men were classified as being of the lymphatic or the sanguine temperament, and so on. Later on, astrology came into vogue and people were defined as being under the influence of one or other of the planets.

The original meaning of all these classifications is simply that all of us are on one or other of these seven great lines, all of us came forth through one or other of these seven great angels or messengers, and the life which came through one of them always remains His life even though it is also the life of the Logos of which He is a part. Thus verily is the Divine Life ever manifesting not only without us, but within us, yet always that life comes through His angels or Messengers, through one or other of those wondrous living lights who are yet centers in that still greater Light which knows no setting, but shines for evermore.

19

THE CHURCH AND THE SAINTS

The Holy Catholic Church

This clause appears in the Nicene Creed as "one Catholic and Apostolic Church" and has always been understood to signify the body of faithful believers all over the world. The word "catholic" (Greek *katholikos*) simply means "universal." The Catholic Church is therefore the one universal Church; there is no title more sadly misunderstood than that. Why should one particular section, however powerful, however estimable, of Christ's holy Church be allowed to appropriate that name and exclude all the rest? Assuredly every Church in which Christ is truly worshipped is part of the great Catholic Church.

This clause is in effect a statement of the brotherhood of man, for it proclaims that the community of interest in spiritual things draws together men of every nation. That is the real meaning of the word "church." The Greek for "church" is *ekklēsia*, meaning the body of those who are "called out"[61] of the ordinary life of misdirected energy by their common knowledge of the great facts underlying nature. They are those who, no matter to what nation they may belong or by what name they may choose to call their faith in spiritual things, know something of the truth about God and His relation to men; who cannot live as though they had not this knowledge, and, because they understand the relative importance of each, have "set their affection on things above and not on things of the earth."

In this sense the Church is indeed a very true and great brotherhood with the closest possible links between its members, yet there are many sects among the followers of Christ who do not realize their brotherhood, who distrust and misunderstand one another. But assuredly, as the world evolves, people will begin to realize more and more how foolish it is to quarrel about unimportant matters of belief. Men equally good in every way belong to all the different religions, to all the different sects of Christianity, though externally they differ in forms and names and ceremonies. The question as to what dress they shall wear when they worship God, as to whether they shall be baptized when they are infants or when they are adults, whether they shall use this word or that, this ceremony or that ceremony—all these things matter very little.

The really important point for those who regard things spiritual rather than things temporal is that they all agree in standing together on the side of God, that they have definitely ranged themselves on the side of good instead of evil, of evolution instead of retardation. The sharing of the higher knowledge and a community of aim constitute a very real spiritual bond, stronger far than any of the external divisions that separate them—stronger because it is spiritual and belongs to a higher plane than this.

This true Church of the Christ is *catholic* because among its members are men of every race and of every creed under heaven "of all nations and kindreds and tongues"; it is *holy*, because in every branch of the Church of Christ, those who are really part of it are trying to make their own lives and those of others holier and better; it is *apostolic*, not, as is so often thought, because it descends from the Twelve Apostles, who are probably mythical,[62] but because all its members are in very truth apostles—"men sent forth" by the Great Power who is guiding all. Though many of them know it not, every true follower of the Christ is sent forth by Him into the world that he may be His expression upon earth, that he may be an emissary to help his more ignorant brethren, not only by precept but by example and by influence.

One, the Church is called, and fundamentally it is so in essence, whatever its outward divisions may be—"elect from every nation, yet one o'er all the earth"—though it may be centuries before all its members realize their unity.

For the truth is that in all the world there are only two kinds of people—those who know and those who do not know. Those who know have realized God's plan for man and know that it is evolution—that it means onward progress from good to better, and from better to best. They are comparatively few as yet, but still, in the aggregate, a vast number. Then there are the many who as yet do not know of the divine scheme; they live for themselves and are very largely the slaves of their passions. When they come to know the truth, they will experience what is called conversion (Latin *con*, "with," and *vertere*, "to turn") and will begin to move in harmony with the divine law of evolution because that is God's will for man. Those who know are for God and for evolution, and it does not matter one iota whether they are Buddhists or Hindus, Moslems or Christians, freethinkers or Jews. That is not the question at all; the question is whether they are definitely on God's side, and whether, in the religion into which they happened to have been born (not by chance but by the will of God and under His great Law), they are doing their best. If they are living as they ought to live, they are on God's side, and they are the salt of the earth; they are the lifters, the helpers of the rest of the world which has to be lifted and helped. These are the holy Church throughout all the world, which always acknowledges its Head, though it may call Him by many names and image Him under many forms.

The solidarity of the Church is very little understood. The Christ Himself said, and it has been taught over and over again, that "no man liveth to himself and no man dieth to himself," but most people do not understand this. Truly, we, being members of Christ's body, do nothing alone. There is a commonwealth in the Church—a commonwealth of worship and of good works and of sacramental grace—and we all worship and receive and act not for ourselves alone but as parts of the whole. Not vicariously, as substitutes one for another, because that would be subversive of perfect justice, but we are one with one another by communication of blessing and of peace because we are all one with God. At the topmost pinnacle of the pyramid of religious life there is always one single stone—the stone of the Divine Love. That is the brightest jewel of the whole universe, the touchstone by which we may try everything else; that is indeed the central point towards which all paths converge, and holy souls journey thither by many roads, for all are pilgrims traveling to one and the same shrine.

The Communion of Saints

This clause is found only in the Apostles' Creed and is interpreted in three different ways. The first makes it merely an extension of the clause before it, that is to say, "The holy Catholic Church [which is] the Communion of the Saints." The more ignorant take it in that way; they believe that it includes Christians only, and often only one sect of Christians. They have not yet grasped the glory and beauty of the plan; they are still in the condition of the little child who thinks (and it is quite right at his stage that he should think so) that his father is the finest and the strongest and the greatest man in all the world. As he grows older, he comes to recognize that there are other men who are just as good and just as great as his father. So when we grow up out of the child stage of our religion, we realize that all religions are much about the same, differing but not necessarily one greater than another.

A second interpretation of "the Communion of Saints" is that which takes it to mean the members of the Church who have passed away. The idea is that the Holy Catholic Church is the Church of the living, whereas the communion of the saints is the Church of those who have cast aside the physical body. That idea is expressed in one of the hymns:

> One family we dwell in Him,
> One Church above, beneath,
> Though now divided by the stream,
> The narrow stream of death.

The third method of interpretation gives a more mystical sense to the word *communion* and makes it mean the intimate association which exists between the saints.

The truth, as is so often the case, includes all these, but yet is far grander than any of them, for the true meaning of the expression of belief in the communion of the saints is the recognition of the existence and the functions of the great Brotherhood of Adepts. These are they who have passed through human evolution and are standing on the threshold of that which lies above humanity. They are "supermen," to use the modern phrase, who are in charge of the evolution of mankind. This Great White Brotherhood, which lasts from eternity into eternity, is the "kingdom of heaven" of which Christ speaks, and they who enter it are the elect, the chosen—chosen because of the work they have done, because of the stage they have reached in advance of us—yet they, too, are part of us, and the proof of that unity is that each man who reaches that level helps humanity forward towards its final consummation.

The members of that mighty brotherhood are one to a degree that it is impossible for us to understand. They become one mighty consciousness, "the Heavenly Man," as it is sometimes called, and yet in becoming that they lose not the slightest part of their individuality. They lose no feeling of continuity, but with them the sense of individuality has increased to extend over the whole world, to include all those who, with them, are drawn into that divine consciousness.

Thus this clause is truly an extension of the idea of the brotherhood of man implied in the belief in the Holy Catholic Church; yet it also involves the closest association and even communication with the noblest of those who have gone before us. When a man once realizes this great truth, however keen may be his sympathy with the manifold sufferings of humanity, however much he may fail to understand much of what he sees in the world around him, the element of hopelessness, which before made it so terrible, is gone forever. For though he feels that many mysteries are as yet but partially explained, though questions may sometimes arise to which, at present, no answer can be given, he knows with the absolute certainty born of experience that the power, the wisdom, and the love which guide evolution are more than strong enough to carry it through to its glorious end.

He knows that no human sympathy can ever be as great as that of those who stand behind humanity, for none love more than they who are sacrificing themselves for man. When once a man begins even dimly to understand these things, it brings a sense of absolute peace and security which can never be shaken or lost through any of the changes and chances of this mortal life.

20

THE REMISSION OF SINS

"I Acknowledge One Baptism for the Remission of Sins"

This phrase did not form part of the original draft of the Council of Nicaea but was added by the Council of Constantinople in the year 381. The Greek words translated "the remission of sins"[63] may be more correctly translated "the putting away of sin," so the whole clause as it now appears really means: "I acknowledge one baptism for the putting away of, or emancipation from, sins." In the Apostles' Creed it is rendered as "forgiveness" of sins, but there is no idea of forgiveness involved in the original Greek words. We can read that into them only if we approach the subject with that idea in mind. Sin can be put away by our becoming no longer enslaved by it, or it can be put away by the divine forgiveness, but there is no reason to import into the words an unexpected and unusual meaning when there is a plain straightforward one. This is simply a declaration that the candidate acknowledges the necessity of getting free from the dominion of all his sins before attempting to enter upon the path of spiritual progress. Its spirit would be far more accurately rendered by an expression of belief in the "demission" (the original meaning of the word) rather than the "remission" of sins. This clause was primarily intended to be a reminder of the principle which requires moral development as a prerequisite to any kind of inner advancement and as a warning against schools which teach occult knowledge of various sorts without exacting strict morality as a necessary qualification. The pupils of such schools run a very serious risk because certain powers are put into their hands, but there is no guarantee whatever that they will use them in the right way for the furtherance of evolution. Unless a man is sure to use his powers rightly, it is far better for him not to have them at all because he may easily do more harm than good.

If a person is morally developed, if he has been taught that love of God and love of his neighbor must come first, he is not likely to go seriously wrong whatever faculty he may develop. Therefore, in the Christian scheme, moral purification has always been recognized as the first step.

This clause of the creed had another and inner meaning referring to a higher stage in man's development, and this is more clearly brought out in the Nicaean symbol: "I acknowledge one baptism for the remission of sins." Substituting the idea of emancipation for that of forgiveness and remembering that baptism has always been the symbol of initiation, we have a conception which is far removed from the later development of dogma and is identical with the meaning attached to this clause in the original formula of the Christ: "I acknowledge one initiation for emancipation from the fetters of sin." By this statement, the candidate proclaims his recognition that before him lies that great step, that he will devote himself as far as be can to that line of endeavor, to set before himself as his goal that first initiation given by the One Initiator through the Great White Brotherhood. For there is but one Initiator, the spiritual king of the world, and all initiations are given by His order and in His name only. Through that initiation a man gains the power to cast off entirely the three fetters of doubt, superstition, and the delusion of self which must be got rid of before he can take a higher step.

The One Baptism

During the ceremony of his initiation the man receives the first touch of what is called buddhic consciousness—that is, he definitely realizes the higher unity for the first time—unless in some way he has previously contacted it, which does not often happen; there is given to him then a touch of the higher power, the Christ power within him. And in that touch he not only receives a vast increase of knowledge which alters the whole face of nature for him, but he also enters for the moment into relation with his Master far more intimate than anything he had ever before imagined. In that flash of contact he received a very real baptism, for there pours into his soul a rush of power and wisdom and love which greatly strengthens him for further effort. In a very true sense, then, is this first great initiation a "baptism for the emancipation from sins," and the baptism administered to a child soon after birth was but a symbol and a prophecy of this—a kind of dedication of the young life to the effort to enter upon the Path.

Original Sin

When the materializing tendency set in, the true meaning of all this was obscured, and the extraordinary doctrine of original sin was invented to provide a reason for the baptismal ceremony. In many branches of the Church it is taught that baptism purifies the child from original sin.

According to the story in Genesis, Adam and Eve had been forbidden by the Deity to eat a certain fruit but were overpersuaded by the serpent and, because of that comparatively trifling error, all mankind since has been born in sin! Every man is held responsible for something of which he knew nothing, which happened thousands of years before he was born. A certain symbology lies, of course, behind this extraordinary story.

It is only when we accept the fact of reincarnation that the idea of original sin presents to us something more tangible. To accept this illuminating fact means that we believe that this is not for any one of us our first appearance on this field of action, it is not our first birth in this world; that we have had many lives before and shall have many more lives after this one; that all these lives are continuous and progressive, and, to use the ordinary phraseology, that it is the same soul which manifests itself again and again in a number of bodies successively.

179

Now, being the same man, he naturally brings over with him from the past whatever development he may have gained in previous lives. He brings over at the beginning of each life both good and evil germs; which of them will get developed first depends very largely on his surroundings; that is why those who have children in their care have a very great responsibility.

Very early in life the germs begin to put out sprouts and to grow. If we then expose the child to envy, anger, irritability, and so on, those qualities become active in him. If, on the other hand, we are careful to surround the child with good and loving thoughts, the good will be stimulated first and will grow rapidly. This is of enormous importance, because whichever starts growing first will leave little room for the other. Thus, if all the good germs are developed in the child first, there is little room for the evil ones to grow; but on the other hand, as so often happens, if the evil ones are first developed because he is surrounded by bickering, anger, and various kinds of undesirable feelings, it is much harder afterwards to draw out the good.

The object of baptism is to repress the evil germs and to strengthen and nourish the good ones. This is done to a great extent by the tremendous force of the divine power which is poured into the child at that time. He may not be sufficiently developed to respond, but the evil is repressed and the good is encouraged and strengthened. The rational meaning of the doctrine of original sin is that each man brings over certain evil tendencies as the result of his own actions in other lives.

The Meaning of Sin

The bogey of sin has done a great deal of harm in the world. Sin is supposed to be something awful, something polluting, something desperately terrible. Sin is really that which is not in harmony with the Divine Plan; whatever we do or say or think which is against God's plan is a sin. It would be better to use the word "mistake" instead of "sin," for that better conveys the way in which God Himself regards the matter.

To Him, the sinner is a man who simply does not know better yet, and therefore he makes mistakes; when he has learnt more he will cease making them.

God has called this universe into being, and it is His will that keeps the whole of creation working. It will go through its regular stages of development and at last draw back into Him from whom it came, but that final consummation is very far off as yet. All the life in the universe is Divine Life. His purpose for it is evolution and, since that is His will, the universe is filled with a pressure in that direction. There is a steady upward pressure at every stage; every one of us, however little we may know it, is subject to that slow, definite upward push so that even the worst are gradually becoming a little better than they were. On all planes there exists this strong current in the direction of improvement.

Anyone who does or says or even thinks contrary to that current sets up an opposition, a swirl in the current immediately round himself. It can easily be seen how such a disturbance in the current of the Divine Life amounts to a wrenching aside of that current. Happily for ourselves, our power to do this is very limited; but we can produce a distortion in what would otherwise be an even flow, and that means, as far as the individual is concerned, that he has set up in his aura a number of vortices which are not vibrating in harmony with the evolutionary current.

The steady pressure of God's Will will put all that right for him, but it may take a long time, and meantime these little unpleasant centers in the man's aura are acting upon him and tending to make further and wider disturbances in his different vehicles and in his surroundings. That is where the absolution or forgiveness of sins is of use. That is a scheme which the Christ Himself devised whereby this disturbance or distortion can be straightened out much more quickly than would otherwise be the case. Until this is done we cannot draw into ourselves the divine blessing and power. The effect of the priest's absolution is to comb out all these disturbances and help us start afresh. Of course it is only when we withdraw our strength and life from them that the disentangling can be done. We must cooperate with God to that extent, or the priest cannot help us.

Just as the idea of original sin descending from Adam is absurd, so is the common notion of the forgiveness of sin. The idea that God has made us what we are, and—knowing exactly all about us—is going to turn upon us and feel anger against us because in our ignorance we do this or that which is not in accordance with His plan is surely an outrage on the idea of the fatherhood of God.

The Deity knows perfectly well that we are not yet fully developed and that therefore we are sure to make many mistakes. We would not be angry with a flower in our garden for not having grown as we hoped it would, and it would be absurd to talk of "forgiving" it. We know that it is a human weakness to feel offense. We have no right to charge God with such a weakness and suppose that He needs to be placated. He knows far better than we do how and why we do wrong. He is not angry about it—perhaps He is pleased when we do well, when we take advantage of the opportunities which are put before us, because that goes a little further towards carrying out His great Plan. To suppose that He could be disappointed, displeased and become angry because some infinitesimal part of the scheme seems temporarily to fail is altogether an unworthy idea. The Deity is so far above all our petty errors and mistakes and failings that He could not possibly be angry with them or need to "forgive" them. He does not expect the impossible from us, but He does expect us to try our best. He expects us to try to understand the scheme and, so far as we can, to work in harmony with it.

21

THE RESURRECTION OF THE DEAD

I t is commonly believed by orthodox Christians that man will "at the last day," as they put it, rise in his physical body—the same one that he has at present—and will then be judged and rewarded or punished according to his deserts. Of course, anyone who thinks at all knows that that is physically impossible. We are told that the whole body, every particle of it, changes every seven years or thereabouts. My own opinion is that the change is probably more rapid than that. But a constant change is certainly taking place; particle after particle is being thrown out every minute, and other particles are being drawn in all the time. The physical body is therefore not a permanent but a fluctuating object. No one has the same body now that he had even ten years ago; therefore that body could not be got together at some time in the far distant future. Moreover, the particles which we throw off every moment may be absorbed by some other creature. Are we then to fight over those particles at some time in the dim future when this resurrection takes place? It might be argued that we shall have the particles with which we die; but that does not solve the problem because a dead body disintegrates, decays, and it is not conceivable that its particles could be collected and put together again.

Many people claim that this extraordinary belief is part of the Christian faith. It is no such thing. Its teaching certainly involves resurrection in a body, but not in the same body. It is simply the doctrine of rebirth or reincarnation. From earliest times that was a universal belief, but in later Egypt and in classical Greece and Rome it has already dropped out of popular knowledge, though it was always taught in the Mysteries and was mentioned quite clearly in the original formula given by the Christ to His disciples. There was a reference in that to the wheel of birth and death, which really is a term originating further east than Palestine, for it was used by the Lord Buddha Himself and is also found in the Zoroastrian teaching which very largely influenced early Christianity.

When we want to understand an ancient religion, we must go back to the circumstances under which it arose and see what were the influences which were playing upon it. In the case of Christianity there were many external influences besides the Zoroastrian religion, among them the inner teachings of Judaism and also such knowledge of the Babylonian religion as the Jews had brought back with them from captivity. It was only crass ignorance that perverted the simple statement that man returns to earth in a new body into the absurd dogma that everyone collects a certain number of physical particles and rebuilds a corpse. That which rises is the incorruptible soul; and since it rises in a body, it must be in a new body, that is to say, in the body of an infant. This belief was held by many people at the time of Christ. In the Kabbalah, the inner teaching of the Jews, metempsychosis—the movement of the soul from one vehicle to another—was a prominent feature. Josephus, the Jewish historian, testifies that the Pharisees held this doctrine in a curious form. They believed that the righteous returned to earth and lived again so as to draw nearer to perfection, but that the unrighteous did not.

There is a certain amount of truth in that connected with the dropping out of the backward souls in the fifth round, which, as we have seen, is the real fact behind the theory of the Day of Judgment. Jerome speaks of the belief in the passing of the soul from one body to another as existing in early Christianity. Origen, the greatest of all the Church Fathers, held it strongly and clearly, and it is significant that he maintained that he did not borrow it from Plato but that it was taught to him by St. Clement of Alexandria, who in turn learned it from Pantaenus, a disciple of apostolic men. Thus we have a clear statement that the doctrine of reincarnation came down from the apostles themselves.[64] It was one of the Mysteries of the early Church, taught only to those who were worthy, who had come into the inner circle of its organization and had proved themselves good and reliable members, fit to be trusted with the inner teachings.

Reincarnation in the Gospels

There are only a few references to reincarnation in the Gospels as we have them now, but these are quite definite. In the story of the man who was born blind, the question of the disciples is plain: "Master, who did sin, this man, or his parents, that he was born blind?" (John 9:2).

They clearly recognized that such a terrible affliction must be the result of some sin or mistake in the past, and so they asked: "Whose was the fault? Were the parents so wicked that they deserved to have the sorrow of a blind son, or did the blind man himself commit such crimes as necessitated his being born in this way?" Since he was born blind, whatever sin he may have been guilty of must have been committed before he was born, that is to say, in another birth. The question of the disciples clearly implies the two doctrines on which we lay so much stress—that man takes birth after birth, and that the justice of God could allow such a thing to happen only as the result of some sin or some mistake.

The answer of the Christ is noteworthy. It should be remembered that He was never backward in reproving errors or misstatements. He spoke very plainly and decidedly not only to His own disciples and to the Pharisees and Sadducees but also to the general public. When He had to tell them of any error or mistake, His language was decidedly forcible; it was sometimes, perhaps, less than we should consider quite polite or allowable in these more polished days. On this occasion there was an opportunity for the Christ to have said to His disciples: "What is this you are saying? It is a foolish thing to ask whether this is the result of what the man did before he was born!" Instead, He says that neither of their suggestions is correct; that it was not because the man or his parents sinned that he was born blind, but for an entirely different reason. Then there is a definite statement in the Gospel of St. Matthew which should settle the question once and for all for anyone who believes in the inspiration or the truth of the New Testament. Here Christ clearly says to His disciples concerning John the Baptist: "If ye will receive it [i.e., if you are able to believe it] this is Elias, which was for to come" (Matt. 11:14). Orthodox commentators explain that Christ did not literally mean what He said on this occasion; that He merely meant to say that John the Baptist was a type of Elias, was the same kind of man as the earlier prophet.

It must be remembered that Christ was familiar with the popular opinion. He knew quite well that the people were speculating about Himself; that some said He was Elijah, others that He was Jeremiah or another of the ancient prophets reincarnated. He was well aware also that the return of Elijah had been prophesied and that the people were expecting it, and so He must have known how His hearers would take what He said. He made a clear and unequivocal statement. If He did not mean it, it amounted to willfully deceiving the people, and we know He could not do that. Either Christ said it or He did not. If He did not say it, what becomes of the inspiration of the Gospels? And if He did say it, then reincarnation is a fact, because there is His statement that John the Baptist was Elijah in a new body.

There is a third and much higher meaning sometimes attached in the New Testament to the word resurrection. We have already seen that when St. Paul wrote that he himself was striving "if by any means [he] might attain unto the resurrection of the dead" (Phil. 3:11), it is clear that he meant that he was striving to attain to that great initiation of which the resurrection is a symbol, that initiation which liberates man from life and death alike, and which raises him above the necessity of further incarnation upon earth.

To rise from the dead, then, is sometimes merely to reincarnate, sometimes to take the first great Initiation according to the Egyptian rite, and sometimes to take that higher one for which St. Paul was striving, which permits the man to escape altogether from the wheel of birth and death.

"And the Life Everlasting"

The semipoetical form into which the translators have put this clause has led the orthodox to see in it a reference to eternal life in heaven, but that is not the true meaning. It is merely a straightforward statement of the immortality of the human soul. In the Celtic creed the form was simpler still: "I believe in life after death," while the Nicaean symbol expresses it as "the life of the world to come" or, to translate it more accurately, "the life of the coming age."

PART THREE

Various Subjects

22

OUR LADY

In all our thoughts about Our Lady and about Her festivals we must never forget that there is a triple meaning in everything that is taught. First, the story gathers round the historical mother of Jesus, who was a noble woman of the royal house of Judah, and who, after attaining adeptship, entered the angelic kingdom; and then there are two great lines of symbolism to which all the events of Her life are adapted. Much of what is written about Her can hardly be fitted into the historical story, but we know that it is added with a view to perfecting the symbolism, as in the case of the Gospel story of the Christ Himself. Much of what is written, sung, and spoken about Her refers to the feminine aspect of the Deity, and much more of it refers also to the conception of the great duality—the great deep, as it is called—the Divine Wisdom, the Father-Motherhood, the myth of Spirit and matter and the interaction of the one upon the other. All this has to be borne in mind in striving to interpret these beautiful allegories.

Star of the Sea

Our Lady Mary, the Star of the Sea, is represented always in robes of the blue of the sea and of the sky because She typifies the great sea or the waters of space over the surface of which the Holy Spirit brooded and upon which He acted. The very derivation of Her name Mary is *maria*, which in Latin is the plural of *mare*, "sea," referring to the seas of virgin matter from which the universe was created.[65] Why of virgin matter?

191

All space is filled with the ether of space, that strange substance, if we may call it so, more readily affected than the finest of all fine substances of which we know anything, and yet many hundreds of times denser than the densest steel. Into that ether of space comes the breath of the Logos. That breathing penetrates the ether in somewhat the same way as air is pumped into water in order to mineralize it and, of the bubbles so made by the divine breath, matter is built—built indeed very truly of nothingness; for that is the real meaning of the strange Eastern theory that all matter is but an illusion. In one sense it is quite true, because out of those bubbles (if one may call them bubbles), the world is constructed, for the chemical elements are built up out of arrangements of them. But when it pleases the Supreme to draw in His breath once more, the universe will cease to be, because these bubbles, which are the very bricks of which it is built, disappear. And when the breath is withdrawn, the matter remains virgin, immaculate, exactly as it was before evolution began.

That is the inner meaning of the story of the Immaculate Conception. It is not a question of physical contact or physical sense at all, but it refers symbolically to the scientific fact that the ether of space is the basis of all manifestation and that when the manifestation is withdrawn it becomes precisely as it was before, showing no sign whatever of all that had happened.

So Our Lady is spoken of as the mother of all, and yet the Virgin Immaculate. But besides that, She is indeed a bright light of purity for our example, and so She is called the Star and is described as crowned with stars and clothed with the sun.

We must remember when we praise Our Lady for Her purity and thank God for the example which She gives us, we do not mean only what the word "purity" generally connotes. It has come to mean purity from one particular kind of physical grossness, but that is not in the least the only side of its original meaning. There is purity of intention as well as purity of thought, purity of feeling as well as purity of action. Purity also means one-pointedness, and so the unmixed motive is pure;

utter devotion is purity also, and it is in these ways as well as in the purely physical meaning that She is an example to us all.

Truly for us, for humanity, She performed that great service of giving a body for the Lord Jesus—a body which afterwards was taken and used by the Christ Himself; and because of the greatness which made Her worthy to be chosen for that, it was possible for Her later to become the Queen of the Angels, high among the offspring of this our small cycle of evolution. It is true that there have been others as great as She; but for this our cycle She does stand very high. And so we are thankful to God, not only for the help that the Divine Mother gives to so many people, but that in Her humanity has done well, has gained so great a victory, has made such a great advance.

Mother of the World

Just as there is an office of the Bodhisattva or the World Teacher, so is there an office of the World Mother. These offices are held by great adepts who have reached the utmost point of development within humanity first and then have taken a step beyond humanity and have become superhuman.

This office of World Mother is held by Our Lady Mary. Our Roman brethren speak of Her as the Mother of God, the Mother of Christ. Our Church differs slightly from that. We would say that the Holy Lady Mary was the mother of the body of the disciple Jesus—the body which was taken by the Christ and used by Him on His last appearance on earth as World Teacher, and that, because of the noble work which She did in that life, because of the wonderful purity and the great wisdom and devotion which She showed, because of the splendid patience and courage with which She bore the terrible sufferings that came to Her when She saw Her Son misunderstood and murdered, because of all that She made great advancement on the Path and became, indeed, an adept.

Adeptship can be reached in a woman's body just as in a man's, although after that position is gained he who takes that step may use the vehicle which is best suited to his work, either a man's or a woman's. Indeed, he need not take a physical body at all; he may remain on higher planes if he so chooses, and from there shed his blessing if he sees that to be more useful.

After passing beyond humanity, and because of all that She had done, Our Lady Mary was chosen for the great office of World Mother. All over the world, that part of the Christian Church which maintains the apostolic succession—our Roman brethren, our brethren of the Greek Church, our brethren of the Church of England—and holds the sacraments in their fullness reverences Our Lady. They give Her many beautiful titles, some greatly symbolical, as when they call Her the Star of the Sea, referring to the symbol of womanhood in the very Deity Himself and to the development of the worlds when Spirit and matter worked one upon the other.

Queen of the Angels

As Queen of the Angels, She is the leader of many thousands of angels, who are her representatives whom She sends down into the world. For She is present through Her representatives at every birth that takes place in the world. Never a child is born anywhere but the World Mother's representative stands by to give such help, such strength, and such comfort, as karma may permit.

This great department of motherhood is one of the most important in the carrying on of the work and the life of the world. So it is indeed well that while we think with love and reverence of our own mother, we should not forget the existence of the great World Mother who is the mother of us all, and that we should pour out our love and devotion at Her feet.

We do not ask Her, as our Roman brothers do, to intercede for us with Her Son. We do not think that the Christ, who sacrificed Himself that the world might be, needs any reminding of the fact. We do not think that it is necessary to ask Him to do His best for us. We know that He is doing for us everything that can possibly be done considering the karma and the circumstances of the case. Therefore we do not ask even Our Lady to pray for us, but we think of Her with the greatest love and devotion, and if we pray to Her it is not that She should intercede for us but we ask Her to use us in Her work, to pour through us the strength which She is spreading abroad on the world and principally on the women of the world.

We ask that She should make us channels for Her power and Her grace, Her wisdom and Her love, that She should use us to fulfill Her desire that every birth should be surrounded by the most perfect conditions, physical, mental, and emotional. She would wish that the highest honor should be paid to motherhood and that the greatest care and love should surround every birth and the education of every child.

The Work of Our Lady

It is not very easy to put the work of Our Lady into words, because it involves planes and dimensions very different from anything that we know. Our Lady is concerned with the evolution of womanhood throughout the world, in practically every detail, both physical and spiritual. It is an enormous department of nature, that of universal motherhood, and one of which remarkably little has been said. We have hitherto been preoccupied rather with the masculine side of this. But Our Lady draws the worship of thousands upon thousands of women throughout the world, and She is deeply reverenced and loved by thousands of men as well.

Let us begin with an example from the masculine side of life—the meaning of the perpetual crucifixion of the Christ. In one of its aspects this refers to His descent into matter, for He is "the Lamb slain from the foundation of the world" [Rev. 13:8]; but besides that, in quite another mystical sense, He partakes of all the sorrows and sufferings of men. Whatever humanity feels, of joy or of sorrow, the Christ in humanity also feels within Himself. The meaning of the Atonement is that He who holds the office of World Teacher shares the world's suffering and thereby lightens it for us, saving us from further and greater misery and sorrow. The Christ within each man is part of the greater Christ, and thus in Him there is the utmost sympathy for the sorrows of human life. The man who understands this great truth can lessen his own sufferings because he knows that it is thus shared with Him.

Our Lord the Christ bears in His own Person the sorrows of mankind, but in addition to that, and quite independently of that, our Blessed Lady Mary takes upon Herself the special burden of womanhood.

There is a vast field of labor here of which few know anything, and the few who know do not fully understand. He who enters the great Brotherhood learns to bear his share of the burden which the Christ is always bearing; and similarly there are those who learn to share the work of Our Lady, not symbolically but in reality. The sorrows of the world are great because of the blindness and the foolishness of men, and a part of that heavy burden is borne by the Great Ones who know and see. Everyone who comes into the Brotherhood joyously gives of himself in that way to help on evolution, to uplift his fellow men.

From the occult standpoint the greatest glory of woman is to provide vehicles for the souls that are to come into incarnation. That is not something to be half-ashamed of—to hide and put away—but it is the great glory of the feminine incarnation, the great opportunity which women have and men have not. Men have other opportunities, but the wonderful privilege of motherhood is not theirs.

Then there are the healing powers of Our Lady; they also are a fact in nature. The Healing Ray is a department of the Seventh Ray, but it is not confined to that. Our Lady and Her orders of angels contribute to it, each cooperating as may seem fitting to them. We may say that Our Lady is in charge of anything on the Healing Ray which has to do with the birth of children; that would come much more under Her charge than under that of the archangel Raphael. Our Lady plays a vast part in human life, and those who devote themselves to Her thereby make certain sections or parts of life more easily to be developed and awakened.

Her Influence

As the World Mother, She is the head of a mighty spiritual organization, more spiritual than physical, and yet Her influence reaches down into daily life. It is supposed that those who have attained perfection possess the highest and noblest feminine characteristics as well as the masculine.

Our Lady's influence gives great compassion and great patience, for women are wonderfully patient. We may realize this if we think of the drab and monotonous lives which hundreds and thousands of women live and bear so patiently year after year. And mother-love is one of the most beautiful manifestations that humanity can show. That mother-love is an expression of Our Lady—part of Our Lady's love; for She loves through the mother, just as Her Son, the Christ, loves through His devotee. All mothers are reflections of Her, manifestations of Her, insofar as they are true mothers. Motherhood is always a wonderful thing, for it has a transforming effect upon the whole nature, even though that effect may sometimes be only temporary.

We speak in Christian symbolism of Our Lady as being emblematical of the soul of man. The more we study the higher part of man, the more amazingly complex he seems to be. We think of an Ego as a single person; and yet within it there are so many different influences focused. It was once explained that all the rays are represented in each man, although he must belong especially to the one through which he has come up. At the same time, he contains within himself something of all the others—something within him vibrates to each ray. That alone is bewilderingly complex; but as soon as we have adjusted ourselves to that idea, we find that there are further cross-divisions. It is not only a matter of rays, but of the positive and negative in man.

We divide these aspects upon our altars, putting some upon the Epistle side and some upon the Gospel;[66] but they partake very largely of one another's qualities. Our terminology is greatly at fault, for nothing is ever absolutely negative or absolutely positive. We need a word which will express a being or a condition which is a little negative but principally positive, and another for one which is a little positive but much more negative.

There is within each one of us that which responds (or should respond) to the influence of Our Lady. In every man and every woman there is that which answers to the Christ, and there is also something in every man and woman which answers to Our Lady. And there are further and still greater complications. The further we advance, the more tremendously complex evolution becomes. All kinds of influences are playing upon us, and because they are undeveloped in us we pay no attention to them. But it would seem to be a possibility to take up one of those, intensify it, and make it more prominent in our lives. We find greater and greater complexity, and yet we are slowly beginning to realize that there is also a great simplicity in it all. Even while we are so far away from the greater heights, we can already see that there is a point of view ahead of us from which all is simple, in which some day we shall see that present, past, and future are all one.

The real difficulty is the undeveloped nature of our own consciousness. It is clear that God sees the whole sweep of this vast evolution and that by one action He can produce it all. For us it may appear to continue through many periods of time, but for Him it passes as swiftly as the twinkling of an eye. His consciousness must be of a nature which permits Him to see the whole at once and to understand it all at once. We have not yet developed such a consciousness, and consequently we cannot grasp the idea. All that we can grasp is this sense of bewildering complexity; but there is also the realization that although as we advance we see more and more details, yet we are drawing nearer to seeing it all as One.

23

THE HOSTS OF HEAVEN

I f we wish to understand the nature and work of the holy angels, we must begin by accepting the fact that they exist. We must realize that we are dealing with facts in nature, and that facts in nature remain always the same. It is true that we do not know much about the angelic kingdom, but we must try to learn what we can.

In order that we may study the angelic hierarchy and try to grasp something of the wonderful and mighty lives that the angels lead, we must approach the subject as definitely and as clearly as though we were going to study natural history or ethnology. We may be sure that the hosts of heaven are just as varied at their exalted level as are the tribes and nations of men on earth. And, furthermore, just as here on earth there are kingdoms leading up to the human, that is to say, there are the mineral, vegetable, and animal kingdoms—a steady line of evolution culminating in man—so there are other kingdoms leading up to and culminating in the kingdom of the angels. There are many different levels among those creatures which we call nature spirits, or fairies, and they hold somewhat the same position with regard to the angelic kingdom that the animal kingdom holds towards ours. There is much classification yet to be done before we can have even an outline of this great angelic evolution; but nevertheless it can be, and is, a matter of study, of research, and of respectful investigation.

To some this may sound strange, for these great beings are certainly not commonly seen because they do not descend so low into matter as we do. We come down to the lower part of the physical plane and are

veiled in dense bodies; we see and hear and feel through the sense organs of these dense bodies, and unless a being descends to our level we
cannot appreciate him until we learn to use our own higher vehicles. If
we master the etheric senses, then we can see and feel, touch and hear
etheric matter. If we use the senses of our emotional bodies or vehicles,
then we can sense astral matter. If we use those of the mental plane, we
can then perceive mental matter and the creatures living in mental bodies; and so on. But because in our waking hours we live in this physical
vestment we are apt to regard what we can see and sense through it as
the only reality and to forget all these higher things which are hidden
from us by our own limitations. They are facts, just as much as anything
with which we have to deal down here is a fact; but the limitation of our
senses prevents us from experiencing them. Because the angelic host
does not descend to the dense physical level, most of us know nothing
about it. We are apt to forget it, to ignore it; but we are quite wrong in
doing so. Sometimes these angelic entities have manifested themselves
so that men can see them for a few brief moments, and in any case they
are always to be seen by anyone who happens to possess the higher
sight. So we must rid ourselves, to begin with, of the idea that there is
any uncertainty as to the existence of angels and must realize the angelic kingdom, the hosts of heaven, as a glorious, a splendid reality, a
fact existing in nature.

In the past, man has unfortunately been far too self-centered in his
ideas about the world around him. For a very long time he has considered that all lower creatures exist only for his own pleasure or benefit,
not realizing that they also are manifestations of the divine life at different stages of evolution from his own.

If he believed in angels—and until about two centuries ago men generally did believe in such beings—he thought that they existed only to
wait upon humanity, since all creation was centered around the affairs
of men, and man was, so to speak, the hub of the whole universe. The
more we examine into things scientifically, the more we discover our
own extreme insignificance. We are by no means the highest evolution

connected even with this world in which we live, for the great angelic kingdom stands far higher than we do. Thus it behooves us to be humble in our study of these matters and try to understand the universe as its Creator sees it, as He meant it to be understood.

All a Manifestation of God

Everything that exists exists primarily as a manifestation of the divine. That is what we are; that is what these great and glorious angels are, and that is what all nature surrounding us is—a manifestation of God. Our first and greatest duty, therefore, is to become the manifestation of God that He intends us to be. Instead of holding this in mind, we so often think only of ourselves and of trying to please ourselves, to live as we should like to live, not in the least trying to understand and to live up to what He wishes us to be—which, after all, is the only thing that matters. These great angels live first of all to be a manifestation of the Divine Life at their own magnificent level, and if, incidentally, they sometimes help us, we should receive that help with humility and gratitude. That is but a minute part of their great and glorious lives; for they have an existence of their own which is incomprehensible to us—a life in which the glory of God is the first and most prominent thought.

Although angels do not exist in order to help us, they are nevertheless helpful to us in many ways, and we, I think, on our side, can afford them certain opportunities. But we must entirely destroy the idea that they exist for our service. Our pet dog or pet cat may very likely think that we exist entirely to minister to his wants. It is exceedingly probable that that is exactly what he does think. We have all kinds of other activities, and he sees many of those activities; he sees us reading and writing, for instance, but he can have no idea what we are doing. Our higher ideas—ideas of business, helping humanity—are a sealed book to the pet animal who, although he is so near us, knows nothing at all of our real life. We are in very much the same position with regard to the angels. We look up to them, we admire their power, but we do not understand. We may grasp little fragments of their work where their lives touch ours; but we cannot but see that that must be the very smallest part of the angels' existence.

Their Appearance

What do they look like? Those who have already developed something of the higher senses will know how man looks when seen with the open eyes of clairvoyance. They know that man appears as a globe of flashing, brilliant color, of coruscating light, of constantly changing hues—some of them very lovely, but some of them the reverse because as yet we are very imperfect. Now the great angelic evolution is far nearer to perfection than ours is and, consequently, their appearance, when looked at with this higher sight, is resplendent beyond conception. They are glowing, gleaming glories of color—no words that we can use can express their beauty. There are angels whose language is color, and there are other tribes, races, orders among them whose language is sound or music. I do not mean speech as we use the word speech, but music—ordered, harmonious sound. These last are called in India the *gandharvas*; we have no traditional name for them in Christianity, and so we call them the music angels. But it is that wonderful, scintillating, coruscating light that we should see most prominently if any one of those shining angelic forms could for the moment become visible to us. These great and glorious Spirits are generally human in appearance so far as the figure goes, usually of human size, though sometimes colossal, and they have calm, wonderful faces, with starry eyes full of the peace which passes understanding.

Almost always in Christian tradition we see them pictured as having wings; and yet no angel in reality carries such an adornment. Wings are emblematical of the powers which they possess.

They are, then, like human beings when seen with the higher sight. There is the same ovoid of living fire and a glorified form within it; but in the case of the angel it is very much more fiery, more coruscating, more glowing and radiant, and larger in size. The impression that an angel gives, if we can bear to look at him closely, is of a form of living fire, vivid in his life beyond the life of earth, flashing and fiery. One could not feel in their presence anything like terror connected with that tremendous manifestation of power; one would feel instinctively certain from the very first that the power was beneficent.

The Angelic Orders

There are nine orders of angels, of which seven are planetary and belong to our solar system, and two are cosmic and therefore beyond the limits of our system. The word *angel* is used to cover a number of Great Ones engaged in different activities. It is used first of all for the seven Planetary Spirits typified in Revelation as the Seven Lamps before the throne of God [Rev. 4:5]. In ecclesiastical nomenclature those Seven Spirits are often called the Angels of the Presence, but we must not confuse them with the Angel of the Presence in the Holy Eucharist. That angel is, in truth, a thought-form of the Christ Himself which He projects when the prayer of consecration is said. It is called the Angel of the Presence because it is the form in which the presence of the Christ is with us; whereas these others are spoken of as the Angels of the Presence because they are always in the presence of God. That is true of us also, since there is nowhere that God is not, and all that is is part of Him. But what is meant here is that, in a very special sense, these Seven Great Ones are part of the Solar Logos; they are manifestations of Him; they may be thought of almost as qualities or facets of Him; they are centers in Him through which His power flows out.

Some of the angels are known by the names given to them in the Bible and in ancient tradition. There is Michael, the prince, whose name means "The Strength of God."[67] All the names of the angels end in *el*, which in Hebrew is the name for God. "In the beginning God [the *Elohim*] created the heavens and the earth" [Gen. 1:1]. And we find that word *el* also in Bethel, the house of God.

Michael is the strength of God or the one who is like the Lord in strength, and consequently we find that he is connected with the planet Mars. Gabriel, the archangel who appeared to Our Lady at the Annunciation to tell Her of the honor in store for Her, is often called God's hero. The word means the omniscience of God. Raphael, the healing power of God, is often connected with the sun which brings the health-giving power to the earth. Others are perhaps less well known—Uriel, the light or fire of God, and Zadkiel, the benevolence of God, connected with the planet Jupiter. There are also Chamuel and Jophiel.

These archangels are qualities of God, and it is difficult to distinguish, so far above our comprehension are they, what they do and what is done through them. St. Dionysius, for example, speaks of them as the builders and cooperators of God.[68] St. Augustine says that they have possession of the Divine Thought or the Prototype. We find the same idea expressed in a certain system of Greek philosophy which held that the universe existed first in the mind of God, and that from that height—the intelligible world, the world of the Thought of the Logos—it was brought down into activity and worked out in detail in these lower planes.

St. Thomas Aquinas spoke of God as the Primary and of the angels as the Secondary, and he said that all visible effects were produced by God through the mediation of these planetary Spirits. In the same way, Basilides, a Gnostic writer, speaks of the lowest order of the angels as the builders of our material world. And we find in Kabbalah, the secret teaching of the Jews, that the cosmos is divided into seven worlds or planes one above the other, the highest of which are called the original, the intelligible, and the celestial. It is in the second of these planes—the intelligible world—that there first appear these seven Angels of the Presence, which are called the *sephiroth*.[69] We learn that there are ten sephiroth, the first three being, in fact, one, and also the sum total of all manifestation. They represent the three aspects of the Solar Logos, although, according to occult teaching, there are not only seven planetary systems working in our solar system, but three others which are on higher planes and so invisible to us. We may interpret the three sephiroth as the three aspects of the Logos.

The Seven Planets

They appear in the second of the planes, and it is only in the third, or the celestial world, that the seven planets are built by them and become their visible bodies.

Pythagoras taught that the earth moved round the sun,[70] and this fact was also known in ancient Egypt and India. Although it was forgotten during the Dark Ages, it was nevertheless preserved in what we call the Mysteries.

Astronomy tells us that our planets are aggregations of matter and, broadly speaking, there is a great deal of truth in Laplace's nebula hypothesis. It is a fact that this system was a vast mass of glowing gas and that it gradually condensed into the planets we see now. It was a perfectly natural process; but the fact that it was so does not contradict the other fact that it was directed and guided. For the aggregations occurred only in certain points because there, is a living intelligence which chose the points where they would balance one another. Certainly everything happens under natural laws, but these are the expression of the will of the Logos of the system and are directed by those whom He appoints. These Seven Spirits before the throne of God, which are really centers in Him, aspects of Him, are yet also separate intelligences; they are one with Him and yet they act separately.

The angels with which man comes into touch are not these seven great archangels but rather subordinate representatives of them. Each of those angels stands at the head of a ray or type, and it is for this reason that astrologers speak of a man as coming under the influence of a certain planet. He has come forth from God through one or another of these seven great ones, and through all his evolution he will bear the stamp of that line, of that great Spirit through whom he has come.

Each of the archangels is at the head of a great hierarchy that comes down in descending levels to about our own stage of evolution.

The Angelic Evolution

Angels are evolving just as we are, but not on our line. Investigation shows that there are several lines of evolution and that we come, not from the whole of the animal kingdom, but only from one part of it. The evolution of man is held by occultists to be from the mammals, whereas the Divine Life in all the other creatures—the birds, reptiles, fish, and insects—will never pass through humanity but through another parallel line, through those lower levels of the angelic kingdom sometimes called nature spirits or fairies.

The angelic life differs from ours in many ways. They appear to reincarnate in the sense that they descend from a higher level to a lower, draw round them matter of that lower level, and then, after a life period very much longer than our own, yield up that vehicle and retire again to a higher plane, only in due course to come forth once more. It would seem that to this extent a law similar to that of reincarnation holds true for them, but since the very word "reincarnation" implies the taking again of a body of flesh, we are hardly justified in applying it to the angelic evolution because they certainly do not take fleshly bodies.

The angels, then, have a splendid life of their own, which is full of varied activity. They are part, as indeed we also are part, of a stupendous evolution which as yet we do not understand. Certainly it involves a steady progress nearer and nearer to the divine center, for all of us, for angels and men alike. Of the work of the angels we know but very little as yet. We can only see them from below, can study such activities as are within our purblind vision. The higher vision extends far beyond ordinary physical sight and yet, in reality, it is strictly limited; for however great the powers of man may appear to be, they are not as yet fully unfolded in any but the great adepts themselves.

Man himself may become an angel, if he chooses, at a certain stage of his evolution. When he has reached adeptship—when he has passed through ordinary humanity and has become a superman—one of the possibilities before him is to enter into that mighty angelic evolution, as Our Lady has done. It is also possible for the lower stages of the angelic kingdom to pass into humanity, and anyone who is interested may find fuller information in a book which I wrote many years ago called *The Hidden Side of Things*.

Holy Places

One department of angelic work which is to some extent within our grasp is the maintenance of centers of influence in different countries. Among primitive peoples we sometimes hear of holy places, the origins of which no definite records can be found, or no reason for their alleged holiness; and yet, in very many cases, if we are in the least sensitive, we shall feel that there is some unusual influence in that place. In such spots it is often an angel who is responsible for that feeling, to whom the holiness of that place is due; for these great beings are sometimes directed to make centers of influence to be used for events which may take place far in the future. Such centers are to be found in many countries. In Ireland, for instance, I came upon two such holy places, each under the care of a great angel. What exactly they will do, I do not know; but the centers are being guarded for something which is to come in the future. Perhaps it may be that that land will become once more an isle of saints, as it was in ancient times; if that is so, assuredly those two great centers of magnetism will be holy places for those who approach them. Another similar center of angelic influence is Adam's Peak in Ceylon, and yet another exists in Sicily where a certain talisman lies buried, which is guarded likewise by a great angel who radiates out his influence over the surrounding country. There are such places all over the world, but it is only occasionally that people are wise enough to be able to recognize them.

Angels play a great part in the evolution of this world of ours, although we rarely recognize their influence. Certain of them watch over and practically ensoul the evolution upon certain sections of the earth's surface; and everything in that section is raised and strengthened at its level—whatever that level may be—by the influence of that great and holy Spirit, just in the same way as the atoms which are drawn into a man's body are distinctly vivified, improved, and strengthened before they pass out again. Many millions of physical atoms pass into the bodies of every one of us in the course of this life, and pass out again; but they are not the same when they leave as when they come to us. By being part of our higher organisms, which are more developed than the animal and the vegetable, they have been carried further in their evolution than the atoms which formed part of organisms in the lower kingdoms. In just the same way, though at a higher level, all entities, whether they be vegetable or animal, which come into the section guarded by an angel, are strengthened and helped at their own level by their contact with him.

National Angels

There are also angels of nations and angels in charge of districts. If we read the book of the prophet Zechariah, we find that he was constantly in communication with an angel [Zech. 1:9–19; 4:1–5; 5:5, 10; 6:4, 5]. That is a phenomenon familiar to students of the inner life. It often happens that people feel a sudden conviction arising within them or they hear an interior voice, and this happened also to the prophet Zechariah. In the book of Daniel we find a description of a great being called the Prince of Persia [Dan. 10:20], who appeared to Daniel in a vision and who spoke of his interests as being in opposition to Daniel, who represented the Jewish race. Commentators have suggested that it was the angel of the kingdom of Persia, who came to him and advised certain courses of action.

You will remember also how St. Paul dreamt of the man of Macedonia who asked the apostle to come and help him [Acts 16:9]. The Fathers of the Church believed that it was the angel of the country who thus asked for help. There is a passage in the book of Deuteronomy which says that when the Most High divided the nations He established their bounds according to the number of the children of Israel. But the Septuagint translation of that passage says that He divided them and established their bounds according to the number of the angels of God.[71] That is to say, the Deity arranged His tribes and nations according to the number of the angels who happened to be available to look after them.

Religious Ceremonies

One of the ways in which angels come most into contact with humanity is in religious ceremonies such as we celebrate in the Christian Church. Very many angels always come to help on such occasions. They, too, receive the outpouring of that tremendous power from the Host; they specialize it, bring it down to the level where we can best assimilate it, and then pour it forth upon the world.

They act as intermediaries, as invisible priests, in our services, and there is always a congregation far larger than can be seen with physical eyes, for the angels draw round the altar when these holy ceremonies are performed, since in them they are afforded a great opportunity of service. Whenever the Holy Eucharist is celebrated in any church, or in any house by the priest privately, always some members of the hosts of heaven will draw round and lend their aid. They attend because there is an opportunity for them to do the work for which they exist and by means of which they evolve.

At the beginning of the Holy Eucharist we ask God to send His holy angel. That is a definite invocation, and it brings an immediate result. An angel comes at once and takes charge of our work; he gathers the devotion and the love that we outpour, the worship that we give, and weaves it, as Tennyson poetically puts it, into the golden chain that binds our earth about the feet of God. Wherever there is earnest devotion outpouring, there comes at once a messenger to take this devotion, to elevate it and strengthen it, to call out as much from us as we can give, and then to send it up again to the feet of the Father. In our healing service, we begin by appealing to the archangel Raphael, who is the healing power of God. And in answer to that call there comes a majestic form by whom the work is done.

In speaking of angelic cooperation, I am claiming no monopoly for Christian ceremonies in that respect, still less for our own ceremonies in the Liberal Catholic Church. In this Church we have made some study of the way in which angels assist in our services, and, having made that study, we arrange our ceremonies so as to allow for that cooperation—and of course we receive it. But in every church and wherever men are pouring themselves out in love and devotion before God—whatever their form of creed or of ritual may be—we may be sure that the angels are present, adding their strength and their help. And this assistance of theirs is by no means restricted to Christians alone; for the angels help the Hindu and the Buddhist, the Mohammedan and the Parsee just as they help the Christian. They give assistance to every man in his devotional effort just as much as they do to ourselves; but the fact that we know them and expect them and allow for their help makes it easier for them to give it to us, rather than to those who know nothing about the matter, are not expecting it, and have not put themselves into a frame of mind to profit by it.

Difficulties of Classification

I am sometimes asked which of the nine great orders of angels correspond to the Seven Rays.

It is very difficult to assign angels to the different rays with certainty, partly because they are a great deal higher in evolution than any of us. They may belong to different rays—they must do so; they even claim to be angels of certain rays, but in so many ways they seem to have qualities borrowed from all the rays in turn. I am not sure that we have quite the right cross-divisions yet. But we have definitely established that those great angels to whom St. Paul gives the name of Thrones [Col. 1:16] are angels of the First Ray, and their head is he who is commonly called St. Michael. I believe St. Gabriel to be the archangel who stands at the head of the Second Ray. But I am not quite certain about the assignment of the various divisions.

It may well have been that St. Paul, or probably someone much earlier than he, encountering these great beings, would try to distinguish between the different types. He would see glorified entities so far above himself that they would seem to him to possess all possible good qualities; and he would no doubt come to think of some one quality as most dominant and would try to express that. Thus he would notice the tremendous power which flows through certain angels, and he might imagine them as holding up the very throne of God Himself. Furthermore, that power might suggest that God operates directly through them, that His almighty power rests upon them and pours itself out through them during certain of its acts of creation. Then he might notice those that appear to be taking a leading part in the work, and he might name them Dominations.[72] And so on with the other classes mentioned. I rather suspect that the Virtues belong to the Third Ray and represent the tact, the tolerance, and the adaptability of that line. St. Raphael might be connected with that, and yet he has about him a touch of the Seventh Ray. He is the Healing Angel, but he does not seem to fit in particularly with any one of the types named in the classification which we use in church.

The higher angels are of tremendous power. Those with whom we come into contact are mostly much more evolved than we are, and consequently the force which they pour into us is a tremendous and uplifting force, strengthening and helping our whole nature for good.

But we must not suppose that all nonhuman evolutions are necessarily greater than ours. There are lower stages leading up to the angel, and those lower stages are in no way greater than our humanity. There are the kingdoms of the nature spirits and the fairies, the gnomes and the sylphs—kingdoms leading up towards the angelic just as the animal kingdom leads up towards our own evolution.

Nature Spirits

We cannot all see nature spirits. If we could, we would have an exceedingly enthralling source of interest. Just as naturalists watch animals and ornithologists watch birds and learn their various characteristics, so one can watch these creatures. When we go out for a walk, we may be surrounded by them if they learn to like us.

But they generally profoundly distrust man because he destroys the things they like most. They are very fond of wild animals and birds, especially of the young, and man comes along and shoots their friends, or at any rate drives them away. They rejoice in the beautiful country air, in the scent of the woods and of growing things. But when man comes along he often pollutes this beautiful atmosphere with filthy tobacco smoke, or the smell of alcohol, or he is reeking of meat. The trees are their dear friends whom they love; men come along and cut them down and build hideous houses in their place. There are many men who go among them with all sorts of unpleasant thoughts and feelings, sometimes full of maliciousness, hatred, jealousy; all these things are loathsome to them. They do not like mankind at all, and yet they know that somehow he represents, or ought to represent, a higher stage of evolution.

So when they find men and women and young people whom they can approach and can like, whom they can come near without being disgusted by all these undesirable feelings and unpleasant smells, then— though they are very distrustful and shy at first—they are very pleased and delighted that there should be human beings who are what they would call the right kind. And so when these humans go for walks, they are generally surrounded quickly by these creatures. Some of these little creatures sometimes single out one person whom they especially admire and go after him everywhere. It is very interesting to watch their affectionate little ways, to see how utterly they differ from us, how they cannot understand some of the things we do. I have known a cluster of them surround a boy who was eating an apple. The interest of these creatures was immense. "What is he doing? What is he doing it for?" They themselves don't eat, and how is one to explain the action to them?

How Angels Communicate

Angels communicate with each other in various ways. Some of them have a definite language. Others have not any that we can *hear*, but indeed I am not sure that we really hear any of it, even of those who do speak. It is not physical-plane sound. It is that which corresponds to sound in the astral world, except in the case of creatures who wear etheric bodies. Then we have something nearer to what we mean by a sound. It is rather difficult to explain, because one has to qualify nearly anything that one may say in comparing these higher senses with our physical senses.

But angels communicate among themselves by impressing their thoughts one on the other. There are various ways in which that is done. I believe that those who in Sanskrit are called *arupadevas*—angels who wear bodies built of the matter of the causal plane—exchange ideas with the quickness of thought—in fact more quickly than we can think. The *rupadevas*—angels of the lower mental world—exchange ideas in much the same way as we might telepathically exchange thought. Then the *kamadevas*—angels of the astral world, the lowest kind of angels definitely individualized and above the nature spirits—would have to impress their ideas in some much more definite form and would take longer in doing it; not so long as we should take in speaking, but something between speaking and thought transference. But even then we should have to say, if we wished to be accurate, that we rather felt their thought than actually heard it—but it formulates itself as though in words.

The Mystical Four

The word "angel" is often applied also to the four that stand round about the throne of God, called sometimes the Four Beasts. There is a curious description of them in the Bible which speaks of them as full of eyes within [Ezek. 1:18]. That cannot be taken literally, but it has a deeply symbolical and poetical meaning behind it. In the Indian system, these four are called the four *devarajas*, and in the popular religion of India they are spoken of as the rulers of the four points of the compass—the angels of the north, the east, the south, and the west—and as ruling over the four elements of earth, air, water, fire. These are also the Four Living Creatures of the book of Revelation [Rev. 4:6], who adjust the destinies of men; they are not angels in the ordinary sense of the word, although they govern great hosts of angels. They are called the *lipika*, or the Lords of Karma, and they are sometimes spoken of as the Scribes or the Recorders because it is they who manage the whole tremendous machinery of divine justice. It is they who see that to every man comes the result of his own work. "Be not deceived; God is not mocked: whatsoever a man soweth, that shall he also reap" (Gal. 6:7). That is the great natural law which is called in the East the law of karma. All these laws of nature are in reality expressions of the will of the Divine Power, and they are laws which cannot be broken and which none can evade. We may act against them, but that can only be done by applying an equal force in the opposite direction.

Angels and Humans

Angels regard human beings as curious creatures. They say that we are so illogical, that we know certain things and yet do not act accordingly, and that to an angel is what we should call foolish. He does not understand such an attitude. For example, we know that it is a bad thing to worry, and yet we do it and go on doing it. The angel looks on aghast. "What can I do for this person?" he might think. "It is no use telling him, because he knows it already." They say: "We do not understand. You appear to know, you profess to know, in fact you *do* know; and yet your knowledge makes no difference to you." Such an attitude is incomprehensible to an angel.

There are certain times and seasons when the angelic host is in closer contact with humanity than at others; the Festival of St. Michael and All Angels on 29 September is one of them. Because this festival is kept by the majority of Christians all over the world, there is a vast current of thought going out towards the angels at that season, and that draws them more closely into touch with us.

The time is coming when the angelic kingdom will draw closer to our own. Mankind is supposed to have reached a stage in its evolution when it is better able to understand the angelic evolution and to enter into some relation with it and to gain from it great help and upliftment. The tremendous, rather blind devotion of the Middle Ages is passing away and the Seventh Ray, the ray of the relationship with the angels and of ceremonial, is now coming to influence the earth. It is our business to prepare ourselves for this, so that we may understand the angels, that we may live so as to cooperate intelligently with their efforts, and make ourselves channels for their work. We should adopt an attitude of receptiveness; we should try to make our lives such that the angels can cooperate with us and can work through us for the greater glory of God, who is ruler alike over angels and men.

24

THE COMMUNION OF SAINTS

There are many thousands of saints, and of course they do not all belong to the Christian religion. There have been, and there always will be, holy men and women in all faiths, for all religions are only different ways of approaching the one great truth, emphasizing in some of them one facet or one side of it and in others another facet or another side. The truth that lies behind them all is the same.

When we think of Christian saints, we usually think of those who have been canonized by the Church. Canonization amounts only to a recognition of a person's sainthood and a rather tardy recognition in most cases. It seems to have no effect whatever on any plane but the physical; it appears not to affect the Ego or soul in any way at all. But there are other effects.

A certain number of people begin to pray to the new saint, and their prayers, if there are any large number of them, will certainly make a difference. They amount to a call upon the Ego, and the Ego promptly responds. To explain how this takes effect, we have to link these ideas with other and more familiar facts. Practically the same thing happens to almost everyone of us when he is in the heaven-world. There are only a limited number of ecclesiastical saints, but most children are saints to their mothers, and there is hardly anyone who is not loved and respected by someone else.

When we withdraw to the heaven-world we make images of those whom we love and admire; immediately the Ego of the person responds and ensouls the image so that our friends are truly with us, although their personalities on earth may be quite unconscious of the fact. As far as I can see, there is no limit to the number of images which the Ego can ensoul at the same time, and it is simultaneously and fully conscious in all the different images. It is impossible to make this fully comprehensible down here; but the soul is conscious of them all in much the same way, to employ a physical analogy, as we are conscious of the different parts of our bodies when seated in a chair.

The one thing needed for the making of the image, and the consequent appeal to the Ego to ensoul it, is that we shall have thought so much of the person that his or her presence is necessary for our perfect happiness. In the heaven-world we possess all that we need to make ourselves completely happy, and the fact that a person is necessary to us in that way is sufficient to make the link. Thus, without being saints, we can all of us, as Egos, respond to the love and admiration of others, and if we could raise our consciousness into that of the Ego we should all find that we are centers of interest to many people. There will be departed friends and relatives who will have thought strongly enough of us to have our images in their heaven life. That image is truly ourselves; it is a very beautiful reality, for if any but we ensouled the image the people would be deceiving themselves. As it is, they are not deluded, for we are there—more there in truth than here—for we are without the limitation of the physical body.

This is exactly what is done by the saint as soon as people begin to make images of him; and that is how he may be said to answer the prayers of his people. They ask him for help; if there is anything that he can do, he will do it. They ask him for comfort in trouble; he will put before them such ideas as are of a comforting nature. They ask him for strength in difficulty; he will pour down what he can, and will give the impression of being exclusively occupied with one worshipper although he may in reality be simultaneously helping a number of others. The prayers help the saints as well as the suppliant; it is very good for the Ego to be appreciated, to have high thoughts centered upon it, and these certainly affect that portion which may for the moment be locked up in a personality. The analogy between the action of the saints and the action of the ordinary Ego in the heaven-world is very close.

The Festival of All Saints

All Saints' Day is intended to be a day of thankfulness to God for all His saints, from the greatest down to the least, including many not recognized as saints on earth. We should think of all who have shown forth the glory and the beauty and the loving-kindness of Our Lord, and thank Him for all those multiplex manifestations of Him. The festival falls, as a matter of fact, upon the date of an old pre-Christian festival in which the dead drew near to the living; so that at this time of the year it has become an established custom on the other side for people to try to communicate. At All Saints' and All Souls' the veil is thinner than at other seasons of the year; the worlds are nearer together and more open to each other, so communication between them is easier.

We do not know how it began. It was probably instituted because the living knew that this was a time when they could more easily reach out into the astral world, and the people of the astral world would very soon become aware of the reaching out and would respond to it. These great anniversaries are always known on both sides. Much the same thing happens with the angels on St. Michael's Day—for all religious people are thinking of the angels then—and that brings from any or all angels within reach a corresponding wave of thought. Because members of the two kingdoms are thinking strongly of one another, it is easier for communication to pass between them.

The influence of a saint is better than that of a sinner, so at least the influence outpoured is helpful and uplifting. There is a general flood of high and holy influence poured down. But the influence poured out at Christmas or Easter is distinctive, and all the saints, including Our Lady (for She is also a saint and the Queen of the Saints), join in. This influence is outpoured, and our devotion and love go up to meet it. There is a fine interchange and intercommunion—a sort of vortex of sainthood poured down upon earth, very beautiful and coruscating to look at. It is helpful and uplifting also because it brings the example of the saints before us.

Thus at certain seasons there is a very close relationship between the worlds visible and invisible, and we can take advantage of that condition. On All Saints' Day our adoration and love rise towards the saints with the distinct thought of receiving their help. Then on All Souls' Day we think of those not so highly developed whom we can help. It is the strength that has come down to us on All Saints' Day which we send out again on All Souls'. One who had not celebrated the festival of All Saints' would be very much less useful for the celebration on All Souls' Day.

"No Man Liveth to Himself"

We find the doctrine of the Communion of Saints mentioned in the Apostles' Creed. "I believe in . . . the Holy Catholic Church; the Communion of Saints." This has generally been interpreted in three ways, one of them being that the Communion of Saints is the Church. There is a deeper aspect to this idea.

The unity of the Church is generally little understood. It has been taught so often that "no man liveth to himself and no man dieth to himself." Most people really do not understand this; they insist on clinging to their separateness. It has taken thousands and even millions of years to accomplish our individualization, but now that we have that individuality we must learn to widen it. At one stage in our evolution it was necessary that we should feel selfish and think a great deal of ourselves in order that we should become strong centers of consciousness. But we have built it for the purpose that we may help in the divine scheme, that we may become even as He who is the greatest Self, the Christ who contains us all.

We must learn that we exist not for ourselves but for others and that our individuality must expand until it can take in all those others. There are special lines in this great oneness, and each man is best helped along his own line.

Some work along the line of Our Lady, some along that of the angels; some along the line of humility and love of St. Francis; some along the line taught by Pythagoras or by Hypatia, and others along the mystical teachings of Hermes. Some work along the line of courage and fire exemplified by St. Alban or St. Michael; others along the line of compassion and sympathy. Men may approach along many lines but the goal is the same for all. All those great ones continue to reinforce and sustain the stream of influence which they gave forth when they appeared on earth, and as members of Christ's Body they do nothing alone.

For there is a commonwealth in the Church—a communion of worship and good works. We worship and receive and act not for ourselves alone but as part of the whole, because we are all one with God. At the topmost pinnacle of the pyramid of religious life there is the single stone of the Divine Love. That is the brightest jewel in the whole universe and the touchstone by which everything may be tried. It is, indeed, the central point of the universe to which all paths converge. Souls journey thither by many roads, but all are pilgrims to one and the same shrine.

Once we realize that unity, there can be no more dejection or pessimism. There may still be sorrow and trouble, because all of us have gone astray one way or another and evil will bring its results just as good does; but there will be no more of that feeling of hopelessness and despair that often lies behind sorrow and suffering, when once we have grasped the meaning of the Communion of the Saints, which is another word for the brotherhood of man and also implies the fatherhood of God. It is true that there are deep mysteries around us as yet but partially understood. In the great drama of the world's history, questions arise to which man at present can give no answer. Yet we know with the absolute certainty born of experience that the power, the wisdom, and the love which guide evolution are more than strong enough to carry it to its glorious end.

The Brotherhood of the Saints

The Communion of the Saints also represents the mystical and intimate association which exists between them. It means the Great Brotherhood of Light—the Great Brotherhood of Adepts.

It should not be difficult to realize that there are such Great Ones because there are people at all possible levels of evolution. Since there are various stages of evolution below us, we should not think that we represent the highest that God has yet been able to evolve in His world. We know that there have been great men and women who stood out in their particular sphere as a lighthouse stands out above the waves far above us all—great saints, scientists, writers, artists, musicians. We cannot compare ourselves with them. Just as in music Beethoven, Bach, and all the great composers stand above us, so in spirituality the saints stand far above us. It is they who make up the great brotherhood which, under the Christ as representing the Logos, the Word of God, rules and directs the world.

They are those who are "saved" or safe; they are the true elect who are sure to go on with this particular wave of evolution. But we must not imagine that those who fall back will be lost. Under this divine scheme of evolution nothing ever was or can be lost, but there are those who may drop out of this year's "class" and come on with next year's class. That is what is meant by the Judgment Day—a day not of condemnation but a day when those who will be chosen can go on and the others will be kept back for further teaching.

Those who make up the Great Brotherhood are all one to a degree that it is almost impossible to understand. They are one; they form one mighty consciousness.

The Initiate

Everyone who passes into that great brotherhood begins at once to take his part in the work of the management of the world. True, the neophyte can take but a small share, for he is but a tiny cog in the great machine, a junior clerk in the great office of the spiritual world government, but still he has his particular work to do from the moment that he becomes a member of the brotherhood. At the first great initiation which admits him to its ranks, he takes a solemn pledge to devote himself to the welfare of the world; to have that always at the back of his mind as his principal duty, taking precedence of all else. The men and women who enter that mighty brotherhood have to live their lives in the ordinary sense; they generally have to earn their living just as before. They are not taken out of the world, yet they are in a very real sense not of the world because they no longer set before themselves mere personal ambitions. They no longer regard as their chief aim in life the winning of riches or fame, but rather to be as useful as possible in the helping and uplifting of mankind.

The initiate will never cause suffering to others, man or beast, if he can possibly avoid it. The pledge at the time of his initiation is that he will try to make his life all love, even as God is all love. He is not a man who is led away by mere outside appearances, for he deals with realities. Most people are like little children playing about outside the real world, and their lives, however happy and pleasant they may be from the lower point of view, are only a pitiful travesty of what life might be. They never know the real world at all; they are only very gradually growing towards the time when they may be able to enter that real life and work in it. At initiation, the real world opens out before the man and he sees clearly what is worthwhile and what not. It is like the passing out from a prison house into the glorious world outside. The world in general is pursuing shadows; most people are, as it were, sitting all their lives with their backs to the light watching the play of futile shadows on the wall before them, knowing nothing of the glorious reality; but at initiation (and before that in preparation for it) the man bursts out of the gloomy cave into the glorious sunlight—into the wider, fuller life—and he sees the glory of that real world before whose light all human lamps grow dim. He sees now the real object of life. So many people in the world spend their whole lives working at lower things, so much occupied with getting a name and making money, some of them perhaps with a good purpose in view, with the idea that they would use fame and money well, others not troubling about that so long as they make the money and the good name, all of them thinking themselves so busy and so wise. Long before the man approaches the portals of initiation he sees the relative unimportance of all these things and realizes that those who are pursuing worldly interests are living exactly like the man with the muck rake in *Pilgrim's Progress* who is raking away in the dust while all the time there stands above him a glorious angel offering him a golden crown.[73]

The relative importance of things is so little understood; it is so difficult for us to grasp, because we are surrounded by the turmoil of the world, by millions of people who are thinking as the world thinks; the pressure of public opinion on us is a thing we do not at all realize. We do not know what a tremendous power it has. All the time the thoughts of others are pressing on our mental bodies even though we may know nothing about it. The pressure of public opinion not only shows itself in the newspapers and common conversion but this heavy sea of intangible thought is all about us and, even though the thought may be foolish, even though it really means nothing because the people who generate it know nothing of the true facts, the weight of it is ever pressing upon us and, however strong we may be, it is an effort to stand against it.

The Four Qualifications

The four qualifications necessary for the attainment of the first initiation are discrimination, desirelessness, good conduct, and love, but we must not suppose that the necessity for the further development of these qualities has ended with the attainment of that great step. Assuredly those who have won this advancement must try to go on further in order that they may be more and more useful in life. They must, for instance, go on developing discrimination and learning what things are really worthwhile; must distinguish carefully between the really important things and those which only seem important. Knowledge is always a prerequisite of usefulness, for however well intentioned a man may be, if he has not the necessary knowledge he is liable to do more harm than good. The man who wants to help must know something, or else his helpfulness is far less valuable than it could be.

The consciousness of the initiate has, by the fact of the ceremony of his admission, become one with the consciousness of the Brotherhood, but how much of that tremendous consciousness he can bring through into his physical brain and his daily life depends entirely upon himself and upon the development which he afterwards chooses to make. To use the language commonly found in books on this subject, when this stage is reached the subliminal consciousness becomes one with that of the supraliminal consciousness. The subliminal consciousness is the consciousness below, and the supraliminal is that above the threshold of the consciousness which we use in ordinary life. The object of the initiate is to bring that wider consciousness up above the threshold so that it will be at his command for every purpose in daily life, so that he may learn to judge correctly and learn to choose rightly. That means that he must work unceasingly to become consciously one with that Brotherhood down here, as he is already one with it on the higher planes.

There is another way of imaging the idea of the two consciousnesses, which is perhaps clearer to some minds than to others. The common theory is that man has an immense consciousness but that most of it is below the threshold of his waking consciousness; that sometimes there is an irruption of this wider consciousness that results in all sorts of remarkable developments. The explanation given in some oriental teaching is just a little different from that. They say that the Ego of the man—what we should call the soul—puts down a hand and touches with the tips of its fingers the physical brain and that small part of the consciousness working through the brain: the touch of those fingers is the lower man, the personality, the temporary manifestation on the physical plane of the soul or individuality. The Ego is the consciousness that includes both the subliminal and the supraliminal. The subliminal consciousness is the consciousness which is in the arm and the hand, but not yet in the tips of the fingers. It is the nearest part to the great body of consciousness which lies behind, and sometimes, during a flash of intuition, the force floods down through the arm into the physical brain. Now that wider consciousness—the consciousness of the man himself—has become one with the great Brotherhood, but the tips of the fingers working in the brain down here do not know it yet, and the whole of that consciousness has to be brought down into them until it can all function through the brain insofar as is possible at that level.

The Birth of Christ within the Heart

The Christ is born within the heart at the First Initiation if He has not been so born before, as well may be with many people, but He has also to grow up in the heart so that the man may come to the "measure of the stature of the fullness of Christ" [Eph. 4:13]. How can this growth be stimulated? Our hearts must be ready, and our power to feel and think gradually expanded until the whole man becomes a fuller expression of the Christ. It is not, then, the Christ that grows, but we who grow in our power of response, in our power to accept the Christ within us. He is always there, and as we make ourselves more and more fit, He will shine out through us. Those who have not taken this step, who are still looking up to it from afar, would do well to remember that the very same process which encourages the growth when the step has been taken is also a fitting preparation for that step. So both alike must listen for His voice, must watch to catch the intuition from within so that they may profit by His wisdom. The initiate must qualify himself to receive that wisdom, to understand it, to distinguish it from other impressions, and then to have the strength to act upon it. In the words of that beautiful little verse quoted in *At the Feet of the Master* he must ever be

Waiting the Word of the Master,
Watching the Hidden Light;
Listening to catch His orders
In the very midst of the fight;
Seeing His slightest signal
Across the heads of the throng;
Hearing His faintest whisper
Above earth's loudest song.[74]

The attitude of the disciple both before and after initiation could hardly be more beautifully expressed than that, for the wisdom of the mighty Brotherhood lies behind the initiate just as the wisdom of his Master lies behind the disciple who is preparing himself for initiation. In each case we must make ourselves ready from below. We are the cup, and the purity, the love, and the wisdom of the Christ are the wine which shall be poured into it and fill it as soon as it is ready to receive it.

Just as soon as and just to the extent that we are ready to be filled, will the life of the Christ, and the power and wisdom of the Christ, pour down into us.

In very truth, this Christ life which lies hidden behind the ordinary life, is the real life, and it is the only life worth living. The Lord Buddha was right when He said that during his physical life sorrow fills man's "piteous time." There is indeed more sorrow than enjoyment in life; there is uncertainty, difficulty, and loss. Only when we are free from desire and enter into the higher life do we, for the first time, realize what life is meant to be. No life is worth living for the lower self, but all life is gloriously worth living when we are filled with the Christ spirit, the spirit of uttermost self-sacrifice for the good of the whole.

The Mystics and the Path of Holiness

The Path is always the path of spiritual development and holiness. The steps on it are the various initiations. It is difficult to say whether the states through which the Christian mystic passes bear any direct relation to the steps on the Path, for he is often vague as to his experience.

The dark night of the soul as described by Ruysbroeck and Suso could be identical with the great trial which comes at the fourth initiation. The unitive way reached by the greatest of the mystics may be identical with the state of union reached by the one who has taken the *asekha* initiation.[75]

The experiences described in *The Dark Night of the Soul* include the sense of being left utterly alone and cut off from the power of the Logos Himself. It is said that Jesus experienced this when He cried: "Eloi, Eloi, lama sabachthani," which is translated "My God, My God, why has Thou forsaken me?" [Mark 15:34].

The unitive way must be the way of union with all mankind and then with the Divine. The way of the mystic is always that of union with God. He tries to attain that union even at this lower level. There are said to be two main methods of spiritual development—the path of the mystic and the path of the occultist. They come to the same thing in the end. The mystic seeks to attain subjective union with his God here and now. "A single inward step, and all thy journey ends."[76]

Man is God, but he has to realize it, and this realization comes to most of us slowly and by degrees. Step by step we draw nearer to that possibility, and it is useful to know the steps on the way so that we may more or less measure our progress. One can see from the writings of the great mystics that they are seeking the same goal as the occultist, either along their own personal line or by an admixture of lines.

25

THE SACRAMENTS

All religions are paths intended to lead men to God. They differ because men differ both in temperament and in the stage of evolution which they have reached. They all teach man to cultivate the same virtues and to avoid the same vices. Each has its own plan of aiding its devotees on their upward path by offering to them such helps as seem suitable to them; in the Christian religion these helps are called sacraments. Some people are so constituted as to be able to assimilate the divine power poured out through the sacrament, and they are greatly assisted and uplifted by them; others disdain such help and consider them valueless, or perhaps as stimulants or crutches for the weak. Each man is fully entitled to hold his own opinions, but not to abuse, slander, and persecute those who differ from him.

The sacraments, then, are not necessities but valuable boons offered by the Christ to those who are ready to avail themselves of them. Christ's priests are those who have undertaken, and been duly prepared for, the work of the distribution of these helps to His people. In no case whatever must they exact any fee for such dispensation of His grace; it is His free gift to His children, and blessed indeed are they through whom it is given.

It will be seen that this theory of the sacraments removes all fear that a priest can ever exercise any sort of compulsion over his congregation.

And when we know that all will finally attain, that sacraments are not "necessary to salvation," though they are unquestionably great helps to progress, and that, in any case, they are free to all who are willing reverently to receive them, all possibility of ecclesiastical tyranny disappears.

In my book *The Science of the Sacraments*, I have tried to suggest a new point of view with regard to the sacraments of the Christian Church, a point of view which is new to us in the present day only because it is so old that it has been entirely forgotten.

The Definition of a Sacrament

A sacrament is defined in the *Catechism of the Church of England* as "an outward and visible sign of an inward and spiritual grace given unto us, ordained by Christ himself, as a means whereby we receive the same, and a pledge to assure us thereof." This is admirable as describing baptism or confirmation, but leaves much to be added when we come to speak of the Holy Eucharist.

That greatest of all sacraments is undoubtedly a means of grace as well as the highest act of worship and a wondrous and most beautiful symbol; but it is also very much more than that. It is an admirable and splendidly successful plan for hastening the evolution of the world by the frequent outpouring of floods of spiritual force; and it offers us an unequalled opportunity of becoming, as St. Paul puts it, laborers together with God [1 Cor. 3:9], of doing Him true and laudable service by acting as channels of His wondrous power.

This, then, is the postulate that I put before my readers—that the celebration of the Holy Eucharist is the culmination of all Christian service, because in it we not only worship God but actually, at our infinitely lower level, cooperate with Him and use such powers as we have to help in that development of the human race which is His plan for mankind.

Perhaps I had better explain how I know this. I was ordained priest in the Church of England in the seventies of the nineteenth century, but although I was always profoundly impressed by the Eucharistic service, I did not know then what I know now. A few years later, there came my way a unique opportunity of taking a course of lessons in psychic development, and I at once seized it. There are dormant within every man spiritual faculties by the unfolding of which he can learn to see beyond the range of physical vision. I happen to be one of those who, after many years of harder work than most people would care to undertake, succeeded in acquiring those higher senses; and it is by means of them that I have been enabled to conduct the series of investigations and experiments, the result of some of which is embodied in this volume and in *The Science of the Sacraments*.

I am, of course, aware that many people are incredulous as to the existence of such faculties. I must refer them to the publications of the Society for Psychical Research and other equally well-known works. I am not here concerned to argue about this subject; I am simply noting, for the benefit of those interested in the services of the Church, certain facts in connection with them which have become known to me through repeated personal observation.

An Outpouring of Divine Power

Each celebration of the Holy Eucharist is the occasion for a truly tremendous outpouring of divine power. At the risk of being considered materialistic and irreverent, I must insist on the absolute reality of this spiritual force which men call the grace of God. Many who believe in it because they have experienced it are nevertheless shocked to hear that its action can be seen and measured much like electricity, although it works in a finer grade of matter. Its distribution takes place under precisely the same laws as does radiation on our lower level, allowing for certain differences caused by the more rapid vibrations of matter in a higher state.

When a man awakens within himself the senses of the soul, every aspect of life at once becomes for him far fuller and more interesting, for he sees the whole of it instead of only a small and comparatively unimportant part. In the case of the services of the Church, he can see the result of the action in higher matter of the thoughts and feelings of devotion and love poured forth by the congregation, and of the stupendous inflow of divine power which comes as a response to it. A thought or feeling is a definite and real thing and, in the finer matter of the subtler worlds, it shows itself in color and form. The seer is thus able to observe in detail how the services work and in what way we can make them effective; for it is obvious that the way in which we do our part must be a point of some importance. There are various liturgies, and there are different methods of rendering each of them; the inner vision will show us which of them is most suitable for the end in view.

Repeated observation shows us that the ritual of the Holy Eucharist, as it comes down to us from past ages, is a complicated and elaborate ceremony, admirably adapted to the ends which it is intended to achieve, but requiring the nicely adjusted simultaneous action of several factors. Its purpose can be, and is, attained by those with no knowledge of this inner working, but only clumsily and with much waste; whereas men who understand what they are doing can gain a far greater result by the expenditure of the same amount of force.

Angelic Help

That force comes from altogether higher worlds and, in order that it may be effective in this lower life of ours, it must be condensed, compressed, transmuted. To do that work a vessel is necessary, and that vessel is constructed for us during the service by the angel whose help we invoke. The Angel of the Eucharist erects for us a thought-form of subtle matter, inside which the divine force can be stored and can accumulate until needed just as steam accumulates in the condenser of a distilling apparatus and is transformed into water.

That he may build this form, the angel must have a field purified from worldly thought, and this the priest makes for him by the prayer of the Asperges and by the effort of his will.[77] The angel must have material for his structure, and we provide that by our outpouring of love and devotion during the service. So the great Eucharistic thought-edifice is gradually built by the angel, and inside it the priest makes a kind of insulated chamber or casket round the sacred elements. Beginning from within that innermost casket, a tube is formed which holds the actual channel for the force, and inside that tube takes place the wonderful change at the moment of consecration.

The Christ Himself pours out the power. In order that He may do that easily and (if we may say so with all reverence) with the least exertion so as to leave the greatest possible amount of force for its real purpose, the Angel of the Presence, by the act of transubstantiation, makes the line of fire along which the Christ can pour it. The priest, by pushing up his tube and so preparing a channel, has made this action possible. There are many electrical experiments which must be performed in a vacuum, and when that is so, it is, of course, necessary to make the vacuum first. So, in this case, the tube must be made before that special line of communication can be inserted in it. But the priest could not make that tube by his thought and aspiration unless he had first constructed a properly isolated casket from which to push the tube upwards; and so he had to isolate and magnetize the elements. The people assist the priest and supply the material for the thought-edifice through which the force is later distributed. Thus all take their due part in the somewhat complicated process by which is produced so magnificent a result.[78]

Every celebration of the Holy Eucharist, then, not only strengthens and helps those who take part in it, but also floods the entire neighborhood with spiritual power and blessing. To what extent this blessing is assimilated by the souls upon whom it falls depends upon their attitude and their degree of development; but assuredly it must produce some effect even upon the most careless.

The rituals of the various liturgies have grown up gradually, and it need not be supposed that all their writers and compilers understood the science of the sacrament. But the living Christ stands ever in the background keeping watch over His Church, not interfering with its freedom of action, not driving it along this line or that, but always ready to guide those of its members who earnestly seek such guidance, using a gentle but persistent influence in the right direction. And it may well be due to that influence that the essential parts of this greatest of Christian rituals have been preserved intact through all the manifold changes which the passing centuries have brought.

Christ Experiments

Immersion in water as a symbol of the washing away of evil and the beginning of a new life was a tradition in nearly all the ancient religions. But the link with Himself in baptism which the Christ chose to make is, as far as I know, an innovation of His own. It is hard for many of us to get away from the idea that Christ came to earth only once. We must reconcile ourselves to the fact that the World Teacher has been founding religions in the past and that He will continue to found them whenever He thinks it necessary. Christianity is one of those religions. Though the World Teacher stands infinitely far above us, though He is so great in comparison to us that He seems godlike in His attributes, we must remember that He makes experiments, so to speak. He tries one scheme in one civilization but, when He founds another religion for another race, He does not reproduce everything that He did before.

All religions, as far as we know, have made it part of their work to spread spiritual force abroad, and they have done so in different ways. In ancient Egypt, for example, they did very much the same as we do every Sunday morning. Through their ceremonies they brought the divine force down from higher levels and spread it abroad upon the people.

The scheme adopted by Christ was a somewhat different one. Instead of only four high priests and their immediate entourage, as was the case in Egypt, He arranged to have priests in many places so that, although they carried out the ceremonies on a smaller scale, there were so many more of them that He hoped the general effect would be better. He established the orders of bishops and priests so that there should be someone in every parish to perform the ceremony of drawing down spiritual power and pouring it out over the people.

The idea of the average minister (whether he be Roman Catholic or Anglican or belonging to one of the other denominations) about the Holy Eucharist is that it is a wonderful and beautiful means of grace for the one who receives it. As a rule, he does not think of it as a means whereby he can cooperate with God by spreading the divine power over the surrounding district. But that is part of the original idea.

The congregation's main purpose in attending the service should not be the reception of communion, wonderful as that is, but to give something of themselves in order to help in the great work.

The scheme as it existed in Egypt was for the very few. Christianity made it democratic and arranged for larger numbers of people to take part in the distribution of the force. It has given us a very fine religion, if only people would take the trouble to understand it. We, in the Liberal Catholic Church, are, I hope, studying it and trying to apply its principles as far as we can, and if we can spread the information and help others to see something of what we have discovered, so much more good will be done all round.

26

THE HOLY EUCHARIST

The Eucharist, as we know it, is not altogether new. It was celebrated in some older religions but has now reached a more perfect form. It was found in Mithraism. Bread and wine and salt were used, but the form of their rite is somewhat vague. There was a secret ceremony in the Egyptian Mysteries in which consecrated bread—a sort of cake—was given, but never to the general public; only to a very small and specially prepared group something like a Masonic lodge. As soon as a man partook of this sacrament, the others bowed to him saying, "Thou art Osiris."

Our present scheme calls for a church in every village so that many points of radiation are found spread over the country. It is a beautiful thing to realize that people are taking part in this great work, although they may not fully understand what they are doing.

Where that first struck me rather specially was in Sicily when I was staying at Taormina. I used to go for long walks into the back country when I was just at the beginning of the scientific study of these things, and I especially noticed the wave of peace that came from the church in a distant village. It was some little time before I connected it with the celebration of the Mass.

When I was miles away, I would feel this powerful influence strike me like a wave of the sea and at first I did not know what it was. But I encountered it a good many times, and it was that which led me to attend the church and to make those observations upon which my book *The Hidden Side of Things* was based. When I had been in the

English countryside many years before, I had not the power of recognizing these things although I suppose I must have felt the effect many times.

There was nothing corresponding to the Eucharist in the Greek religion. They knew that every beautiful thing radiated an atmosphere of happiness, and for that reason they surrounded themselves with things of beauty. They knew that the gods manifested themselves through beauty, and so they were gathering around them tiny streams of divine force, but they had nothing so definite as this outpouring.

The Egyptian scheme was probably the nearest to our own. The rites were conducted by priests of the Mysteries and high initiates who radiated the influence over the country intentionally and with knowledge.

Furthermore, the priests represented certain qualities which it was their business to personify, and during their meetings each endeavored to develop his own quality to its highest and then to pour it out upon the world. Having faced inwards at a certain point in the proceedings and having gone through a certain ceremony, they then faced outwards and sent the influence out on the world.

The sacred cakes of Osiris were blessed by the priest and distributed to those present. It was believed that it was the very body of Osiris that was being given—Osiris who had descended into matter and had been torn to pieces by Set and had then risen again from the dead.

Four Main Functions

We in the Liberal Catholic Church hold that the Holy Eucharist has four main intentions or uses:

1. First of all, the Holy Eucharist is a symbol. It is a symbol meant to remind us both of the descent of the Second Person of the Blessed Trinity into matter and of the sacrifice of the World Teacher in descending into incarnation in order to help us forward on our way. The Second Person of the Blessed Trinity pours Himself down, as it were, into

matter, descending from the high plane on which the Solar Deity lives to our own level in order that we and all others may come into existence. But for His descent into matter, but for His sacrifice—the sacrifice of "the Lamb slain from the foundation of the world"—the world could never have come into being.

As described earlier, the first action in the foundation of the world is that the Holy Spirit broods over the face of the waters of space, calling life into being in the mineral kingdom, and so creates for us our chemical elements. But although that process has been going on for ages and is still going on (for God the Holy Ghost is still making newer and more complicated elements), we do not know the extent of His working. His workshop, so far as this world is concerned, is the interior of the earth, and we know all these things in science only as they come to the surface. Uranium is the last element that we have discovered and the heaviest, but heavier and more complex elements will come into being. So the work of the Holy Ghost is still going on.

But life could progress no further if it were not for the entry upon this great life drama of the Second Person of the Blessed Trinity. He sacrifices the higher life, or some part of it at any rate, in order to pour Himself down into matter; and then He descends into this matter which is already vivified and takes His robe of flesh from the vivified matter, for He is born, not of the virgin sea of matter alone, not of the Virgin Mary only, but of the Holy Ghost and the Virgin Mary.

Then He gives it the power of combination. These elements, which before were separate, now join together and, instead of simple elements, there are combinations; instead of just atoms, there are molecules; and so the Christ life pours down into the world and evolves steadily through the elemental kingdoms and through the mineral, the vegetable, and the animal until it reaches this human kingdom. Thus it is "for us men and for our salvation," yes, for our very existence, that the Second Person of the Blessed Trinity sacrifices Himself. It is to remind us of this that the Church celebrates the Eucharist in which, once more, the Christ descends into matter.

The Eucharist also reminds us of the sacrifice of the World Teacher who, having evolved far beyond men, comes now and again to the world which He loves, in order to teach and help. Again, truly, for us did the Lord Christ come as Sri Krishna in India and in Palestine as Jesus the Christ. He will appear again among men to give them the same teaching in some new and beautiful form suited to the times, just as the older teaching was suited to those earlier ages when it was given.

2. Then, secondly, it is a ready and beautiful means of showing the thanks and the worship and devotion which we feel towards our Lord Christ. The word "Eucharist" (which is perhaps the most beautiful title given to this service) means simply "thanksgiving."

There is a certain traditional chant which forms part of this service, where the priest, turning to the people at the beginning of the Canon, exhorts them to lift up their hearts, and the people answer, "We lift them up unto the Lord." And then he exclaims, "Let us give thanks unto our Lord God." The Greek word is *eucharistésomen*, so the meaning of the sentence is, "Let us offer the Eucharist," or "Let us offer the Eucharist to our Lord God."

From the time that the Church was founded it has used the same chant to those words—a chant that is familiar to the angelic hosts. For the words that follow are the call to the different orders of angels to come and help us in the work that we are doing.

3. It is undoubtedly a very great help and stimulus for those of us who take part in it, and especially if we communicate. Just as it is a spiritual sun shining forth from the altar and pouring its rays upon us, so may we be spiritual suns for the rest of the day to those among whom we go. We bear the Christ along with us when we have thus received Him into ourselves; we radiate His special influence, and so we are doing His work among our fellow creatures.

4. It is the greatest of all works that we can do for our fellow men. Here we join together to pour forth our love and devotion to Christ, and in return comes the response. If we send up our prayer, there comes

down the flood of grace from on high, and so, by joining in this act, we are calling down from heaven a special outpouring of spiritual force and blessing. That which is returned to us is far greater than that which we give, and yet it is in proportion to it. If there be here but a few of us and we pour forth our devotion and our love and our gratitude, that is indeed well, and we receive a hundredfold in spiritual grace and blessing. But if instead of two or three gathered together in His Name there should be twenty or thirty—if there should be two or three hundred—then surely the volume of devotion will be far greater and the volume of response greater still. For to everyone there comes a tenfold, a thirtyfold, a hundredfold return; according to the strength of devotion which he himself puts into it is the amount (if we may venture to measure in such a way) of the response which comes to him. So a greater congregation is a greater help to the world than a smaller. But, most assuredly, few or many, the help is always poured out not only upon us but upon the whole neighborhood and the city in which we live.

This is the chief reason why we should join in this most holy ceremony, in order that there may be more of this great spiritual outpouring to flow over our surroundings, to help and to strengthen every person in them who is capable of responding. There may be many so wrapped up in personal thought and feelings that but little of the higher spiritual force can touch them. But everyone whose soul is open to this dew from heaven will assuredly receive something of the downpouring which we call forth by our devotion and our love.

The Proper Elements

If a priest were to use other than pure grape juice or wine, or pure wheaten bread in the Holy Eucharist, no consecration would take place, for the force is withheld if the appointed elements are not provided. The Roman Catholic Church has gone very thoroughly into this question. There have been cases of celebrations on a battlefield where a zealous priest, unable to obtain the proper elements and wishing to give spiritual help to his people, used oatcake and whisky, and the question arose whether the consecration had taken place. The verdict seems to have been that under such very special circumstances a miracle may have been performed, but it was clearly implied that such a consecration would not have been valid under ordinary conditions. A priest, in an emergency, was once said to have used red currant wine; that consecration would most certainly not have been valid. In the Liberal Catholic Church we use pure, unfermented grape juice; if this should turn sour and become fermented, the presence of alcohol does not make any difference, for the fermented wine used in older branches of the Church is certainly consecrated. If the wine turns so sour that it becomes vinegar, no consecration takes place, but it could still happen in an intermediate stage where there was some wine left.

In cases of special emergency it would be possible to consecrate the Host without the chalice. Such a case might arise if someone needed the Viaticum and it was impossible to obtain either the reserved Host or wine.

Though grape juice and wheat must be used, an admixture of other elements would not necessarily impair the validity of the Eucharist. The Roman directions on the matter are quite explicit: "If the bread be not wheaten, or if wheat be mixed with other grain in such quantity that it no longer remains wheaten bread . . . the Sacrament is not consecrated." It is clear that they allow a mixture of wheat and barley, but the wheat must predominate.

After Communion, the disintegration of the molecules liberates the force; that is why the Roman Catholic Church directs that any particles of the Host which have in any way become corrupt or liable to decay should be consumed by fire. The Host continues to radiate tremendous force for several hours until it is broken up. The link does not remain permanently, because the matter with which it was made has ceased to exist as such. Although the actual wafer may only last for an hour or so after it has been received, the effects last much longer.

Taking Communion

The question is sometimes asked whether it would be wrong if one came to church in a troubled state of mind and partook of the Holy Sacrament.

It would certainly not be wrong to come to church when you are in a troubled state of mind, for that is precisely one way by which you may be helped to throw off the trouble. And it would not be wrong to partake of the Holy Sacrament. The whole service is intended to help us. The Asperges—the sprinkling with which the service begins—is intended to help drive away such thoughts, but if they persist, the act of Communion may very well give us precisely the strength we need to put them aside. Do not think of such Communion as a desecration. The Christ pours out His power for the use of all; and, indeed, the worse we are the more we need His help. He refuses the Holy Sacrament to no man who approaches it reverently. We do not ask a man if he has committed sins, because we know that he has. We all have; it is only a question of degree. The worse we are, the more we need the help of the Christ. But it will not really be of use unless we earnestly desire that help.

If I hold out a gift to someone, he, on his part, must put out his hand and take it. So if we are to receive this great gift from Christ and obtain what He means to give, we must come in the right spirit, and if we have been doing wrong we should set our faces earnestly against that wrong with the strong resolve not to do it again. That is true repentance; not sorrow and weeping and regret, but the firm resolve that that thing shall not be done again. If we come in that frame of mind, we shall unquestionably be helped to throw off our worries and troubles.

The Real Presence

The Liberal Catholic Church holds fully the belief of the presence of Christ in the Blessed Sacrament. There are other churches which hold that the Host ceases to be bread and becomes the actual physical flesh which the Christ wore two thousand years ago, that the appearance of the bread after the Consecration is a major illusion of our senses and that it is really flesh.

That is not as we see it clairvoyantly. The Host does not change physically. The physical wafer remains a physical wafer composed of flour and water even after the Consecration. But it is just as truly a vehicle of the Christ, just as truly ensouled by Him and filled by His mighty power as the body which He wore in Palestine. It has not changed its physical character; it is still the same on the physical plane, but what lies behind it or "stands behind" it on the higher planes has been changed.

The Christ Himself now "stands behind" it instead of the type of higher matter which normally does. The original substance has gone but the accidents remain the same. We hold the doctrine of the Real Presence to the fullest possible extent, but in a way that can be readily understood and does not offend our common sense. We believe that God intends us to exercise our intelligence and that He does not require us to believe anything which flies in the face of reason.

I do not say that the fact is simple; it is one of the great mysteries of God, but yet it is simpler than some of the theories advanced to explain the mystery.

Those who object to the idea of transubstantiation do not know what the word means. They are in the habit of speaking of physical things as substance; they might say, for example, that wood is the substance of which a table is made. But if you examine the meaning of the original Latin word you will find that the "substance" is not the outside form at all, but the reality within. That which stands underneath or behind the physical appearance is the real substance.[79]

And when the Church uses the word "transubstantiation" it does not mean that bread and wine are literally changed into physical flesh and blood perceptible to the senses. They are not, and it would be useless to pretend otherwise, and, furthermore, it would be a strange and horrible idea if that were so. The bread that you can see and the wine that you can see are, in ecclesiastical language, the *accidents*; they are the temporary form behind which is the reality called the substance. So when we speak of the substance being changed, we do not mean that the physical wafer is changed, but that the spirit and life behind it is changed.

Behind every physical object is what is called its counterpart: there is astral matter and mental matter; there is matter of higher planes running right up to the Logos Himself. All this lies behind the wafer, the piece of unleavened bread.

What is done at the moment of consecration is not to change the physical bread but to substitute for the life behind it a ray of the life of Christ Himself.

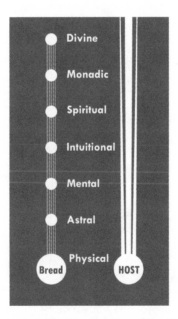

Diagram 4. The Consecration of the Host.

This diagram is an attempt to show the change which takes place at the Consecration, when the bread becomes the Host. The bundle of "wires" connecting the atoms in the bread with the corresponding atoms in the higher worlds (as shown on the left) is switched aside to be replaced by a line of fire which resembles a flash of lighting standing still (as shown on the right).

And so the Christ is truly there upon His altar manifesting Himself in an earthly form, not of flesh but of bread. So also with the chalice. There also His life is manifesting itself, but the outer form of wine is unchanged even though the substance within has been put aside in order that He may pour Himself down to the physical plane for the helping and the strengthening of His children.

27

HOLY ORDERS

It Is Christ Who Ordains

Christ works in His Church through those whom He has specially ordained and set apart for the work. When the bishop ordains, he lays his hands upon the head of the candidate and makes him a priest, but we must never forget that it is the Christ Himself who ordains, working through those who have been chosen to act for Him. It is always the Christ who administers every sacrament. The bishop or the priest may be a man of doubtful character and questionable morals, yet still the power of the Christ will flow through him. The unworthiness of the priest does not interfere with the validity of the sacrament, otherwise the congregation would never know whether they were receiving a true sacrament or not. There would always be uncertainty if validity depended upon the character of the celebrant. A valid ordination alone is necessary for the validity of the sacrament.

If a priest takes the full advantage of the mighty privileges which are conferred upon him at ordination, if he opens himself up to the full power and uses it always for the highest purposes, then indeed he has the most wonderful opportunities and is most blessed in his work. But even if the priest be careless, the sacrament is still valid. Even where the church building has been allowed to fall into decay; when services are irregularly conducted and are arranged for the convenience of the priest and not for the work in the parish; where the vestments, the altar, and its vessels are of the poorest description and badly maintained, the sacraments of Christ are given to His people.

They might have been better administered, they might have been surrounded with the reverence and the beauty with which those who understand ever surround them, but at least the Life is there. That Life lies ever behind His Church; even when men fail, the power of Christ never fails.

The Ordination to the Priesthood

When the *Veni Creator* is intoned at the ordination service, a great red glow slowly gathers in the church and increases in intensity as the hymn continues. Then it begins to gather together and eventually makes a vortex over the head of the candidate. The shade of red is what is called amaranth red, something like the color of the rose called "Kitchener of Khartoum." It is the fine red which, in the aura, denotes courage and high determination. It is not the red of anger, which has a touch of vermilion and orange.

There are two parts to this particular ceremony—the silent imposition of hands and the second imposition with the words of power, and their effects are entirely dissimilar. The silent imposition makes the man a priest, even if the other is omitted. The second imposition and the prayer which accompanies it brings the power of the Holy Ghost. The silent imposition seems to me to be the most impressive part of the whole ceremony, followed as it is by the beautiful prayer which begins: "O Lord Christ, whose strength is in the silence . . ."

After the silent imposition of hands, any priests who are present also lay their hands on the head of the ordinand. This conveys the particular spiritual qualities which they may happen to possess. The bishop, on the other hand, conveys power. The object of the silent imposition is to make the candidate a representative of Christ; it forms a direct link with Him. The second imposition opens up the reservoir of the church and bestows the power of absolution; the first gives the power of benediction—the Christ power. Not many of the priests who lay their hands on the head of the candidate fully realize their tremendous responsibility or that they are doing something of such far-reaching effect.

The power outpoured opens certain channels and, for the time, enormously increases the aura of the candidate, making it enlarge temporarily as it will not do permanently for a great many years or even lives to come. When it is in that distended and sensitive condition, the priests follow, and each gives whatever he has to give, the candidate then being not only capable of receiving, but in such a condition that he can hardly help receiving it.

During our evolution, we have spent many thousands of years in building up a strong center in which the Ego, or the soul, may grow; that Ego has shelled itself in fairly effectually. This has been done so that the center may become strong and self-reliant. When we undertake occult development of any kind, we must, without in the least lessening that strength and self-reliance, do away with the shell or scaffolding and throw ourselves open to the sense of unity. Until you try to do it, you do not know how difficult it is. When you attempt it in meditation you throw open a sort of diaphanous outer fringe, but the granite shell remains the same. It is very hard to get rid of, because for many lives you have identified that shell with the feeling of individuality.

Now, for one moment, at ordination, the work is done for the man from without and the shell is really melted for the time, so that the candidate may become one with the influence of the Christ and not offer resistance to it. And although, almost as soon as the ceremony is finished, the greatly magnified aura will slowly begin to contract, before it has time to do so each priest gives something of his own special quality. In some cases, the contribution will be much more suitable than in others, and it may well be that what some one priest has to give is not so suitable for the candidate, in which case he will be able to assimilate only a comparatively small part of it.

It is the Ego of the priest which is acting, but behind it is the power of the Christ pouring through the priest. It is not necessary for him to be conscious of all that he is giving, but he should be thinking intently about what he is doing.

Women and the Priesthood

The particular arrangement that we call the Holy Eucharist was ordained by the Christ to work through the male body. It is not arranged to flow through the female organism. It has been suggested that when the Christ comes again, that may be one of the modifications that He will introduce, but we cannot go beyond His previous instructions until He Himself alters them.

In *The Hidden Life in Freemasonry*, I referred to certain channels in the etheric part of the human body called *ida* and *pingala*.[80] The positions of these channels are reversed in the opposite sexes. That in itself would be sufficient to prevent a force which was designed for the one from running through the body of the other.

Women took a great part in the government of the ancient Church. They were made deaconesses and after they had attained the level of widow—a word used to represent a particular stage in membership in the Church—they sat in council with the bishop. In that respect, they ranked higher than priests, but they were never ordained priests and so never celebrated the Eucharist. The necessary force is not calculated to work through the female body.

The Episcopate

The ideal set for a bishop is rather stupendous. When he realizes what he is supposed to be, he cannot help feeling that he falls short of the ideal. The presence of such a one is itself a benediction because there are always flowing out from him forces very much higher than can be reached in ordinary life. Assuredly, a burden of responsibility rests upon bishops.

All his life long, the bishop is supposed to be a constant radiant center, a kind of sun. It would be quite improper for him ever to allow himself to feel depression or anything in the nature of interior weariness or slackness. He may get tired on the physical plane—one cannot avoid that—but there should be an inner joyousness that radiates out unconsciously all the time.

The bishop, too, must feel a tremendous sense of responsibility in the conferring of so great a power and must realize vividly that it is the Christ Himself who acts through him. There is probably no occasion on which he feels more strongly the reality of that tremendous Presence than in the ocean of power which is poured through on such an occasion.

Unquestionably, the consecration of a bishop and the result thereof is a help to the world. Many bishops are not aware of this fact and would only half believe it even if they were told. That is the trouble about not only Christianity but about some other religions; they are never precise about spiritual things. Generally they are so vague that they become unreal to people, and as they are, in fact, the most real, the nearest to reality of all the things that we contact, it is a great pity that they should be so misunderstood.

The consecration to the episcopate opens up so many great and glorious possibilities that the bishop may at first feel that it is impossible for him to raise himself sufficiently to take advantage of them fully. During the consecration certain higher centers are opened, vivified, and linked with the corresponding centers in the Christ. Afterwards, the use made of this relationship lies in the bishop's own hands.

The Angels of the Episcopate

I am sometimes asked whether special angels are attached to the bishops and priests of the Church to assist them in the carrying out of their duties. The priest does not always get the same entities, but he is in much closer touch with the angelic orders than a layman is, and on certain occasions angels come bearing the influence of the Christ. When he celebrates or baptizes, the force descends and is brought through angels, living entities. As I have said, all through life the bishop is expected to radiate an influence upon those with whom he comes into contact, to be ready at any moment to give a blessing. That is why angels are nearly always in attendance.

The Angel of the Episcopate, if we may use such a term, is in many ways different from the angels connected with church ceremonial. He resembles far more closely the Angels of the Presence. His power is always at the command of the bishop wherever he may be and whatever he may be doing; that aspect of the Lord is inseparable from him. The bishop has become by his consecration part of the very nature of the Lord—part of Himself. It is not so much that there is a special angel present as that the bishop himself is the representative of the Lord Christ—a vehicle of manifestation for Him—and he cannot divest himself of that Office or of its power. To fail to make use of such a gift would be a very grave dereliction of duty.

If we were to think of an Angel of the Episcopate in the same way as we think of the angels connected with certain degrees in the Mysteries, we may take it that that angel is a putting forth of the consciousness of the Lord Himself. He hovers over his bishop in the same way as those two mighty ones hover over the initiates of a high degree in the Mysteries. The Angel of the Presence is the materialized thought-form of the Christ, and the Angel of the Bishop is similar. Of course, I am putting the whole thing from one side only, because when we come to deal with the higher levels there is a unity of such a remarkable and inexpressible nature that distinctions seem to fall away and become somehow superfluous. One may be part of some Great One and represent Him to the uttermost, as much as anyone at these lower levels can represent Him, and yet one may also simultaneously be part of and represent another Great One. The union between them is so absolute that there is nothing in the nature of disharmony for, at a sufficiently high level, all are facets of the One. This cannot, of course, be expressed adequately in words.

28

HEALING

The system of curing disease by the laying on of hands is very ancient. According to the New Testament, the Christ told His Apostles that they should exercise that power in this way, and they frequently did so with great success, although, on at least one occasion, they met with a case for which their power was not sufficient, and they had to bring the patient to Christ Himself [Matt. 17:14–21; Mark 9:14–29]. Some might be surprised to hear that precisely the same power is manifested through the votaries of other religions. I myself have seen marvelous cures effected in the name of the Lord Buddha. The divine power is obviously much less restricted in the choice of its channels than many religionists think.

There can be no doubt whatever that such cures take place. Whenever someone has this gift of healing, there are always a large number of people who are greatly helped by his efforts. There are usually some sensational cures—wonderful cases of people who have been lame from birth or paralyzed for many years and are instantaneously and completely cured. But there are always a large number of cases which are not cured, or perhaps only slightly and temporarily affected. Why this should be so is at present uncertain, but it must be remembered that we know very little as yet of these matters and that there are probably very many factors in the case which are quite beyond our ken. It is often thought that the person who is not cured fails either in the strength of his belief or in the efficiency of his preparation. There is a great deal in that idea and in many cases it might be sufficient reason. In the Gospel we are told that when Christ was in Capernaum, "He could there do no mighty work" because of the unbelief of the people.[81] Certainly, a really hardened skeptic can put himself into such a condition of mind that it is all but impossible for him to be influenced. That is true with regard to mesmerism or hypnotism and of the influence of an outburst of religious fervor at a revival meeting; therefore it would be likely to be true of the effect of this outpouring of divine power.

In just the same way we find hardened skeptics among the investigators of spiritualistic phenomena. Such a man will often boast that nothing happens at a séance when he is there—the inference, of course, being that he is so much cleverer than everyone else, that he is always able to detect the fraud. The real reason is that he brings with him such a mental atmosphere that it is very difficult for the nonphysical operators to produce any results.

Many Methods

As to the rationale of the cures, there are several ways, even within our very limited knowledge, in which they may be performed. A strong thought in the mind of one person can be impressed upon another if that other be receptive enough. One method of mind cure is somewhat similar; it aims at the transference of good, strong, definite thought from the operator to the patient. The power of thought is a marvelous thing, and we know nothing as yet of its limits. Anyone of us can help a sick person by persistently surrounding him with thoughts of health. This is contrary to the ordinary practice in such cases; most people think, when a friend of theirs is ill, "Poor Mrs. So-and-so, how she is suffering; poor thing, I am very sorry for her." Of course you are sorry, and in thinking so you are trying to show your sympathy with the sufferer; and yet your method of doing so is entirely wrong. If you wish to help the sick person you should, for the moment, put out of your mind all thought of suffering and think strongly and brightly: "I hope my friend will soon get well. I myself am well and strong; I want to send her something of my own strength and of my own feeling of happiness and comfort." You must abstain from the kind of sympathy in which you try to make yourself miserable because another person is suffering. It is inevitable that when you see a man in pain you should feel sympathy with him, but you must show it not by weeping over his pain but by trying to bring him an atmosphere of calmness and health and even joyousness. Wonderful cures have occurred under the Christian Science system, though I must say that that is the method which least appeals to me because it begins by denying the existence of matter, which seems to be a little ridiculous. We know perfectly well that matter is, in one sense, an illusion, in that it is built not of solid particles but of bubbles which appear to be absolutely empty. Nevertheless, matter really does exist on the physical plane, although by rising to another and higher plane we can instantly become unconscious of it. But, even then, it is we who have changed and not the matter, which is, after all, one of the manifestations of the Logos of our system.

In Christian Science, if you think that your body is ill, you are considered to be in error because you have no body, and a body which does not exist can hardly have a headache or a toothache. If you can really persuade yourself of that, the headache or toothache will probably cease. It seems strange, however, that when a cure has been effected by this statement, the operator points to the body which does not exist and quotes it as evidence that the theory works. But, odd and irrational as it seems on the surface, there is no doubt that the scheme has worked, just as almost any scheme will work if you believe in it strongly enough.

Another system, which also works in some cases, is based on the theory that whatever is wrong with any person, whether it be in the physical body or in the astral or mental body, is the result of some lack of harmony with the Divine. The method of cure is to get the patient back into harmony. Usually the operator fills himself with the thought of love and harmony and then floods the patient with that thought, striving to make his own harmonious vibrations so much more powerful than those of the patient that they will, as it were, beat down the disharmony and bring his vibrations back to their normal rate. When the patient is thus harmonized, all his vehicles will also be brought into order. There is certainly a great truth at the back of this idea, yet, like all the rest, sometimes it will work and sometimes it will not.

Another method is simply to pour vitality into the suffering person. The operator in this case is usually a man of exuberant vitality who has learnt how to throw this force into his patient—to drench him with life, as it were. Quite a number of illnesses can be cured in this way. A man who is worn out with overwork or is suffering from weakness as the result of illness, can be very much helped by this flood of life. There is a certain danger that the flood may be too severe a remedy and that the pouring in of so much of it may overpower the person and do him more harm than good. Still, this is a method which meets with a good deal of success.

Another and somewhat more scientific plan requires a knowledge of anatomy. The operator should know the appearance of the different organs when they are in healthy condition. He makes a strong image of the organ which is affected, thinking of it as it ought to be and then planting that strong image upon the man. Nature is already trying to bring the organ back to its normal condition, so a strong thought-form which can be thrown into etheric matter may give great help to the vital forces of the body in rebuilding the organ.

An Interesting Case

Sometimes sudden and wonderful cures are effected by methods which we are unable to understand. I myself witnessed such a cure many years ago. One of the members of a well-known church with which I was connected was a lady whom I had seen many times, though I did not know her intimately. She had been partially paralyzed for years and could not walk without assistance; she had to be helped—almost carried—from her carriage into the church. One day she had a kind of vision in which she was told by a Shining One, whom she supposed to be an angel, that if she went on a certain festival to an early morning Eucharist and communicated, she would be cured.

She thought the thing impossible, and yet it impressed itself upon her so strongly that at last she went to the vicar, told him her dream or vision and asked what she ought to do. The vicar very sensibly said: "I do not know anything about this sort of thing; but we are told in the Bible that God used to reveal things to people in dreams, and I have heard of similar cases quite recently. I think you should try this experiment. It has been strongly borne in upon you; it can do no harm, and it may be God's will that something may happen." Accordingly, the lady was brought to church and helped to kneel at the altar rails, and when the sacred bread and wine had been administered to her she remained for a while kneeling, and then she rose without any help, made her genuflection and returned to her seat. There she remained kneeling in prayer for a long time and at the close of the service she walked out to her carriage without assistance. I knew her afterwards for eight years, and there was no return of the disease during that time.

Now thousands of people who have weaknesses and sicknesses partake of the Holy Eucharist Sunday after Sunday and do not receive such a cure as that. Therefore it is clear that this was a special case, but what made it so, we know not. The vicar spoke of it (and from his point of view he could do no other) as a special mercy of God extended towards this woman.

The water of the well at Lourdes is supposed to have been blessed for curative purposes by an apparition of Our Lady. It is perhaps more probable that it was an angel who appeared to the peasant girl, Bernadette, but at any rate the word went forth that those who came to this well could be cured of disease, and people flocked there. The Church at first banned the whole thing, but it was forced to reverse its opinion in face of the evidence that people actually were cured. Not all who went there were cured, but a certain number were. And the cures are still taking place. It is said that even Lourdes water carried away in a bottle has performed wonderful cures.

There are other similar cases, by no means confined to Christianity. It is not a religious question in the ordinary sense of the word. These things happen occasionally. All that we can safely say is that we do not yet know the circumstances which, in rare individual cases, make it possible.

This subject of nonphysical cures is much in the air at the present time, and we who belong to the Liberal Catholic Church ought to have clear ideas in our minds about it. As I have said, we must always bear in mind that as yet we are only at the beginning of the subject and we know very little about it. Inevitably, there will be cases—perhaps many of them—the mechanism of which we cannot explain. But in many others we shall be able to see to some extent how the cure works, and in that way we can avoid irrational credulity on the one hand and foolish and unnecessary skepticism on the other.

The Healing Service

The healing service in the Liberal Catholic Church is quite different to other services. It is arranged especially for the bringing down of the healing power of Christ to the physical plane so that it may be applied to the physical bodies of the sick who come for healing. On this occasion, we invoke an angel of the order of the archangel Raphael. The result is that the great one who is sent to help us is quite different from those who direct the work of the Holy Eucharist.

One may feel his influence as soon as one enters the church because the angel is already overshadowing, or perhaps has actually come. He does not confine his influence to those who come up for the laying on of hands and the anointing; he sheds it over the whole church and those who come to help by their prayers and good wishes. To those of us who have to do the anointing and the laying on of hands, the angel's influence is like a mighty sea of power, almost overwhelming in its strength—a force far greater than we can in any way direct or manage, so that we have to steady ourselves lest we should be overcome by it. We can only be channels for it and trust to the Christ from whom it comes and the angel through whom it comes to apply it in the best possible way to meet the different needs that come before us.

It is not we who do the healing; the power comes through us. Similarly, a priest is required to consecrate the Host, but the force that comes is not his but the power of the Christ, and it is the Christ Himself whom we receive in Holy Communion. Yet it is so ordered that human hands are needed in order that the call may be made and the necessary physical action performed.

Unquestionably the healing power could be poured out without human intervention, for angels have shown themselves physically and healed by the laying on of hands. But it pleases the Christ to work through His Church, through those whom He has ordained and set apart for that work.

The Healing Force

It is true that each priest gives his own personal touch to the healing force; one aspect or ray of force flows more easily through one person, and another through a person of different type; their personalities make them more easily able to receive a particular type of force. It may be something like a string tuned up to a certain pitch that responds to that vibration and not to any other. A string can only give one rate of vibration unless you mute it; so if we should be tuned to a certain rate of spiritual vibration, we will respond to that and be a channel for it. The quality of our nature, either of our ray or of our temperament which is a sort of sub-ray, makes us channels for one particular type of healing force. There does seem to be a good deal of difference in the power transmitted by our priests.

The force, as has been said, comes from the Christ; we ask for His power and we receive it, but it is a special section of it that we draw upon. We call upon the archangel Raphael, and I presume that the gigantic figure which appears is his representative on the same ray as himself. The healing angel uses the force which we call down and directs it in some cases to people sitting in the congregation who have not applied to be cured.

We are pioneers in the matter of sacramental healing. All through the centuries no one has ever approached healing from a scientific standpoint. They have taken it as a miraculous interposition by the Deity and therefore, since it is His action, it must be perfect. Either He cured or He did not cure, and if He cured, the cure had, of necessity, to be instantaneous. Now in many cases cures are not instantaneous; but it does not follow from that that the patients are not affected by the outpouring of the Divine Power. We know little as yet about the laws which govern such matters; I think we should try to know more.

In the case of a mentally ill person, it is not so much with the mental body as with the links between the astral and the etheric bodies that one has to deal; in most of these cases it is the links which are wrong, not the bodies themselves. There are many cases, however, in which a man has a wrong thought or a wrong emotion which has to be cleared away before healing can take place. But generally the healing force pours straight down through our hands into the etheric body of the person with whom we are dealing; we probably affect him at the same time mentally and spiritually, and that additional force flows from our own higher vehicles into his. But the main flow of the healing force upon the patient takes place at the etheric level and consequently the greater part of the power is veiled in etheric matter.

A very great deal of force is poured down and often we do not use it very economically, possibly because we do not as yet know much about it. We appear simply to flood the patients with it, making, perhaps, an effort to direct it to definite parts of the body when information is given to us of what is wrong. But as far as my own experience of our healing services has gone, the stream of power has seemed to be so strong that it has been difficult to direct it very much at all. It simply rushes through the patient like a Niagara, and anything that is in the way is combed out.

The Healing Angel

The healing angel is a very tall and dignified personage whose consciousness appears to function normally on the spiritual or nirvanic plane, although he pours his forces down to the etheric level; his aura glows chiefly with green and purple, the purple force flowing at the exorcism which precedes the anointing, while the green forces are those of healing.

During the singing of the *Veni Creator*, the traditional call to God the Holy Ghost, the church fills with a red glow like a glorious sunset shining through a faint mist, and it gives much additional power to the healing service.

The consciousness of the healing angel is most interesting to watch but very difficult to explain physically. An angel has a mind which works in many compartments, and apparently the angel is working through all his compartments simultaneously. One can see an angel's thoughts just as one can see anyone else's—only one sees a bewildering number of them because his consciousness is so complex. The angel appears to give only a part of his attention to us, for other departments of his consciousness are working with other cases.

For while he was working in the church, he as equally present in a number of other places—perhaps thirty or forty—but all connected in some way with the treatment of disease. All these scenes were reflected in little compartments in his aura like a number of vividly colored moving pictures. One that I saw was that of a surgeon performing an operation. The surgeon made some mistake; he cut something which he did not mean to cut and was unnerved and full of sick horror. But instantly the angel sent him a flash of blinding lightning that was somehow like the waving of a sword, and, in a moment, steadied his nerves and showed him what to do so that the patient's life was saved.

In another picture, some nuns were kneeling round the bed of their mother superior, who was evidently near to death. Their prayers wove a lovely colored network about the figure on the bed, and the angel took advantage of that and poured vitality into the network so gently and carefully that presently a little color came into the superior's cheeks and she raised herself in the bed and held out her hand, blessing the praying nuns. They kissed her hand and went away weeping for joy; and the mother superior drank something from a bowl into which the angel had poured his light, and then she sank into a healthy sleep. Our Lady was also helping, for She stood near the dying nun and flooded the room with Her wonderful blue peace.

These events, and many more, were happening at the same time, and the angel was taking part equally in all of them, for they were all mirrored in different parts of his consciousness.

The work of the angels touches our lives at more points than we realize. It may well be that angels watch over the sick, blessing and strengthening them. Sick people are often wonderfully cheerful under their troubles; it may be that angels are responsible for much of their optimism. There is, indeed, a great deal going on around us of which we know now very little.

29

CEREMONIAL

I n our solar system there are seven great rays or types, to one or other of which all created things belong. The power of the Logos pours into His system through these seven channels. There are seven mighty angels, sometimes called the Seven Spirits before the Throne of God, who are at the head of and represent the seven great types. Through one or other of them all evolution has come forth. We ourselves, for example, are distributed over the Seven Rays, and each of us belongs to one or other of them. Every kind of mineral, plant, and animal, every angel, every saint belongs to one or other of these Seven Rays.

Astrologers call these seven types after the seven planets, and they speak of a man as a Venus man or a Jupiter man or a Mars man. Two hundred years ago, they spoke of these types as *temperaments*; they would speak of a man as being of the lymphatic temperament, or of the sanguine temperament, and so on. But those are only attempts to classify men according to these seven great divisions or types. Now, not only do these rays affect us, but they bring their special influence to bear upon the world itself. That is to say, at one time one of these rays will be in the ascendant and will influence the world strongly with its particular force; then, although it is always present to some extent, its particular influence fades away and another ray succeeds it as the dominant factor for the time being. Do not misunderstand it. The other rays are always present also, and their influence can always be felt and drawn upon, but there is ever one which, for the time, dominates the others.

For a long time—in fact all through the Middle Ages—the ray of devotion was dominant in the world. The religion of Christianity set forth devotion and self-sacrifice as its central feature. Now, though self-sacrifice will still remain as a powerful factor, the ray of devotion is passing away, and the ray of ceremonial is coming into prominence. It is not that there will be less devotion in the world than before, but that the devotion will be less blind, more discriminating and intelligent, expressing itself through ritual. It will bring us a better understanding of what ceremonial means, and it will also bring us the power and opportunity to cooperate much more closely than formerly with the great angelic evolution which always assists in and enjoys ceremonial.

Ceremonial has been in operation all through this long reign of the devotional ray, but it has been used as an accessory of devotion. It has been thought of principally as a method of expressing devotion, as indeed it is. It has been thought of also as a means of beautifying and strengthening the various services, as indeed it does. But when the change of rays was just beginning to manifest itself, and at the same time the lower mind—the analyzing rather than the synthetic mind—was coming into prominence, people began to be impatient of ceremonial and to think of it as a useless appendage, or even as something which came between themselves and God rather than a help to worship and to understand Him. Then a great wave of Puritanism and, almost at the same time, one of atheism passed over Europe. Even then there were always those who knew better, and who understood the true function of ceremonial.

But ceremonial is more than a useful accessory of devotion, and now, perhaps for the first time in Christian history, it is beginning to be understood that it has a place of its own in the worship of God and that it is important for its own sake. It is not only that ceremonies are performed in honor of God, not merely that the Presence of Christ on the altar is rightly surrounded with glory and beauty and all that we can give of reverence; it is not merely that ceremonial is of great use to the people in lifting up their thoughts and showing them something of the beauty of higher planes. That is true, but there is very much more in it than all that; we now realize that ceremonial, since it is a channel for the outpouring of spiritual force, is in itself a definite work and that those who take part in it are doing something distinct and definite for the helping of evolution.

When we meet in church and celebrate the Mysteries of the Body and Blood of Christ, it is not only, or even chiefly, for ourselves that we come together, great as is the benefit that we derive from it, and great as is the strength that is given to us; but in performing this ancient ritual and in taking part in this holy ordinance which was ordained by Christ Himself, we help to build a mighty form which is, as it were, a storage battery of spiritual force. Into that form the Christ pours down of His fullness, and then through the Benediction at the end of the service we distribute His blessing throughout all the surrounding neighborhood. We may mention some special channel into which we ask that this mighty force be poured, and His holy angels bear it there. There are those who can see the angels gathering round at certain stages of the ceremony. We can see how, when they are dismissed at the end of the service, they each bear away a portion of the force to the object to which each has been assigned. Thus the Holy Eucharist is a mighty ceremony with a definite object, and through it spiritual power is poured out over the world with less expenditure of energy than would otherwise be the case.

It is asked why we speak of less or more expenditure of energy, since the energy of God must be infinite. The power of God is infinite, beyond all doubt, but the power apportioned to a particular piece of work is not. No doubt God's power is all-pervading and is sufficient for everything, but there is an infinity of purposes for which He intends to use it. The portion assigned to a particular church or to a particular occasion is not infinite. The more that is expended on the machinery of distribution the less there is to distribute. If we provide the machinery, we at least have done our part and the work of the angels in charge of the service, and of the patron saint of the church, is much facilitated.

St. Alban

As has been said, the seventh of the great rays is now beginning to dominate the earth. It happens that he who was once St. Alban is at the head of this Seventh Ray, and that is why we attach so much importance to him, and why we have selected him as the patron saint of our Church.[82] It is under his direction that this great work of ceremonial is being carried out. We do not pray to St. Alban, we do not ask him to intercede for us with God, because we hold that God is Love and Light and that in Him there is no darkness at all and that He always does the best that can be done for every one of us. We ask no saint to plead with Him for us, because we trust Him utterly. But we do look to the patron saint as an intermediary in the sense that we work under him.

There are many who say that they approach God directly. In one sense that is true of the God within us. But when we are dealing with the outer world it is as though a soldier declared that he would take no orders except from the commander-in-chief. But the commander-in-chief has hundreds of officers under him through whom he carries out his work. So the Logos has thousands of adepts and saints who carry out the work under His direction; and St. Alban being one of those, we enroll ourselves under him, but only that under him we may work the better and the more wisely in the service of Christ who is the Lord of All.

30

THE VISION OF ST. JOHN

Among the many visions described in the Bible, perhaps none are more remarkable than those attributed to the evangelist St. John.[83] One of the most interesting of the glimpses of a higher world that we are given is his description of the Four Beasts and the four and twenty elders who worship for ever before the throne of God [Rev. 4:10]. We have all been charmed by the flow of its poetic language; we can feel that there is somewhere about it a vast conception of something very beautiful, and yet it may well be that much of it conveys little to us.

Let us try to see a little of what that marvelous vision of St. John really means. Remember, first of all, that his testimony in this matter does not stand alone. The prophet Ezekiel, centuries before, had a very similar vision which it will be useful to compare with it [Ezek. 1:26]. St. John says: "I was in the Spirit" [Rev. 1:10]. That means that he had raised his consciousness to a higher level—that he was removed from earthly things. He saw with the eyes of the Spirit, as it were, and he heard with the ears of the Spirit; he understood spiritual things and saw the wonderful symbolism which is connected with thought at that high level.

The Throne Set in Heaven

He tells us that "a throne was set in heaven, and one sat on the throne" [Rev. 4:2]. It may be that there are some who believe that heaven is a definite place in space where God lives, and with Him live His holy angels and the spirits of just men made perfect, the dead who have passed away into His glory. It would be easy enough for them to think that there should be there a throne and a heavenly court, something like a glorified earthly court. Members of the Liberal Catholic Church know that heaven is not a place but a state of consciousness, that God pervades everything, that He is everywhere, and that all that is is part of Him. Nevertheless, there is a point of view from which the throne and the God seated upon it is literally true. That which St. John and the prophet Ezekiel saw has been seen in this our present day by others who were also "in the Spirit," who were able to raise their consciousness to a sufficiently high plane.

It is not possible to explain fully, but there is a higher consciousness to which this mighty solar system is like a great flower, to which the planets, that to us appear as separate spheres, assume the likeness of the tips of petals of incredible size—petals springing from the true Sun, the glowing heart of this Cosmic Flower, of which the sun that we see is but a reflection.

There is a point of view from which the Logos of the solar system is seen to be sitting upon the stupendous flower of His system as though it were a throne; and he who is able to see that can also see the meaning of many other mystical sayings. He will see that every planet circling round the sun is connected with that throne by the stream of devotion of its inhabitants, linked by streams of force which, from that higher side, are seen as glowing lines of living light and yet somehow like ropes of flowers too; so Tennyson was literally right when he spoke of our world as "bound by gold chains about the feet of God."[84] These chains of love and devotion are impalpable to the grosser senses, yet they bind each planet to the central sun, and to Him who sits thereon. So He may indeed be seen, as it were, seated on a throne, living His life among His peers—the Deities of the other great systems—all subordinate to the One Mighty God in whom all the universes exist.

St. John tells us that He who sat upon the throne "was to look upon like a jasper and a sardine stone" (Rev. 4:3). What are those respectively?

Jasper is an opaque stone, usually red or yellow in color. The "sardine stone" is a yellow or orange carnelian. It is not the stone itself but the color which is the important point in this description. What the evangelist means is that there is a golden-red color at the heart of all—"the colour of amber, as the appearance of fire round about with it," as the prophet Ezekiel puts it (Ezek. 1:27). We read in certain Indian books of a golden man the size of a thumb who is found in the heart of every man. That is the image of the Deity, and that is the central hue.

Then we read that "round about the throne there was a rainbow, in sight like unto an emerald." There is perhaps no more glorious or beautiful thing in nature than a rainbow, but there is none on the physical plane that looks like an emerald. Yet those who have seen at a higher level know exactly what is meant. The aura of the Solar Logos includes the whole of His system; He, in the heart of it, is golden in color, and around Him, where the next curve comes, is the glorious green of sympathy which is indeed "like unto an emerald," though Ezekiel sees it with a tinge of blue and compares it to a sapphire. We see, then, that although this is a wonderful and glorious symbol, it also represents a definite fact. It represents one of the aspects of the Deity, an aspect which can be seen only "in the Spirit," when one has raised oneself to that level.

The Four and Twenty Elders

"And round about the throne were four and twenty seats; and upon the seats I saw four and twenty elders sitting, clothed in white raiment; and they had on their heads crowns of gold." He who is privileged to see this (and remember it will come to everyone one day), sees it from his own world, from its special point of view; and so he sees twenty-four elders, who are the twenty-four great teachers who have been sent out to us in this round of our Planetary Chain. The Christian Church has translated that somewhat differently, taking the elders as its Twelve Apostles and the twelve Jewish prophets.[85] If those twenty-four were indeed the apostles and the prophets, the seer—if he was the apostle John—must have seen himself among them, which surely would have been mentioned. The elders have on their heads crowns of gold which, it is said, they cast before the throne.

In images of the Lord Buddha a little mound or a cone stands out from the crown of His head. It is as a crown, golden in color, which represents the outpouring of spiritual force from the *brahmarandha chakram* or the thousand-petaled lotus, the center at the top of the head. In the highly developed man, this center pours out splendor and glory, which makes for him a veritable crown. Thus the passage means that all that he has developed—all the splendid karma that he makes, all the glorious spiritual force that he generates—he casts perpetually at the feet of the Logos to be used in His work. Over and over again he casts down his golden crown, for it perpetually reforms as the force wells up from within him.

"And out of the throne proceeded lightnings and thunderings and voices" [Rev. 4:5]. The Logos speaks to His stellar brethren, and though, from our limited human standpoint, They are separated by vast light-years, yet is our space but an illusion and the Great Ones find no difficulty in communing as They will. The voices which penetrate those awful spaces may well seem to the seer as cosmic lightning and thunder.

The Seven Lamps

"[And] there were seven lamps of fire burning before the throne, which are the Seven Spirits of God" [Rev. 4:5]. Those are the Mystical Seven, the Planetary Logoi, who are life centers in the Logos Himself. They are the true heads of our rays—the heads, indeed, for the whole solar system, not for our planet only. Through one or other of that mighty seven, every one of us must have come—some through one, some through another.

They are the Seven Sublime Lords of *The Secret Doctrine*, the Primordial Seven, the Creative Powers, the Incorporeal Intelligences, the

Angels of the Presence. This last title is used in two quite different senses and must not here be confused with the Angel of the Presence who
appears at every celebration of the Holy Eucharist. These Seven Great
Ones are so called because they stand ever in the very presence of the
Logos Himself, representing there the rays of which they are the heads,
representing us therefore, since in every one of us is part of the Divine
Life of every one of them. For though each of us belongs fundamentally
to one ray, we have within ourselves something of all the rays; there is
in us no ounce of force, no grain of matter, which is not actually part
of one or other of these wondrous beings; we are literally compacted of
their very substance—not of one, but of all, though always one predom-
inates. Therefore no slightest movement of any of these great star angels
can occur without affecting to some extent every one of us, because
they are bone of our bone, flesh of our flesh, spirit of our spirit; this fact
is the real basis of the often misunderstood science of astrology.

We stand always in the presence of the Solar Logos, for in His system
there is no place where He is not and all that is, is part of Him. But in a
very special sense these Seven Spirits are part of Him—manifestations
of Him, almost qualities of His, centers in Him through which His power flows out. We may see a hint of this in the names assigned to them by
the Jews. The first of them is Michael, whose name means "The Strength
of God," and he is linked with Mars. Gabriel means "The Omniscience
of God," and he is connected with the planet Mercury. Raphael signifies "The Healing Power of God," and he is associated with the sun,
which is the great health giver for us on the physical plane. Uriel is "The
Light or Fire of God"; Zadkiel is "The Benevolence of God" and is connected with the planet Jupiter. The other Archangels are usually given
as Chamuel and Jophiel.

Everything is done by the Logos through the mediation of these planetary Spirits. The planets may indeed be condensations from the mass
of the nebula, but why at those particular points? Because behind each
there is a living intelligence who chooses the points so that they will
balance one another. Truly, whatsoever exists is the outcome of natural

forces working under cosmic laws; but behind every force is always its administrator, a directing intelligence.

The Four Beasts

In the midst of the throne, and round about the throne, St. John sees the strangest of all these wonderful phenomena—"four beasts full of eyes before and behind" [Rev. 4:6]. The first beast was like a lion, and the second like a calf, the third beast had a face as a man, and the fourth beast was like a flying eagle. Each of them had six wings, and they "were full of eyes within." All this has a definite symbolical meaning. In the Church, the four beasts are taken as the four evangelists. There is a verse of a hymn which runs:

> The man is Matthew's emblem,
> And Mark the lion's might;
> The ox is Luke's fit token,
> And John the eagle's flight.

But if that be so, one of them must be the very man who is giving this description!

In fact, the symbology has nothing to do with the four evangelists, for the four Gospels were chosen centuries later from a large number of other gospels. We find the same symbolism in other religions. There is the four-faced Brahman; there is the fourfold Jupiter and the gods of air, water, lightning, and land. And that leads us to the reality behind this—the four great *devarajas*, the administrators of karma, who are the gods or leaders respectively of earth, water, air, and fire. They are full of eyes within, because they are the scribes, the recorders, the *lipika*. They watch all that is, all that happens, all that is written or spoken or thought in all the worlds.

The prophet Ezekiel pictured them a little differently. Though equally impressed by their tremendous inherent vitality, he did not envisage them as animals, but as wheels, and he tries to give a description of that which is indescribable. He says that they are wheels within wheels, as though they were set at right angles to each other, making a sort of skeleton of a ball or sphere. Each one has the four symbolical faces, because each man has within him the characteristics which are symbolized by the man, the lion, the ox, and the eagle. Ezekiel was evidently greatly impressed by the readiness and smoothness of their movement, for he specially emphasizes that "they turned not as they went" [Ezek. 1:16] but in whatever direction they wished to move they followed the face that pointed that way. He, too, says that the wheels were full of eyes.

The imagery of the four-faced recurs again and again. We read in Greek philosophy of the perfect quadrilateral of the infinite circle. The *devarajas* or Lords of Karma are represented in each one of us. Each of us has in his body solid matter, liquid, gaseous, and etheric or fiery matter. They are often described in the East as the "rulers of the four points of the compass." *The Light of Asia* tells us of

> The four Regents of the Earth, come down
> From Mount Sumeru—they who write men's deeds
> On brazen plates; the Angel of the East,
> Whose hosts are clad in silver robes, and bear
> Targets of pearl; the Angel of the South,
> Whose horsemen, the Kumbhandas, ride blue steeds
> With sapphire shields; the Angel of the West,
> By Nagas followed, riding steeds blood-red,
> With coral shields; the Angel of the North,
> Environed by his Yakshas, all in gold,
> On yellow horses, bearing shields of gold.

These four most strange and wondrous beings, who manage the machinery of divine justice, are not angels in the ordinary sense of the word, though they are often called so. Neither they, nor the glorious seven, communicate directly with man.

Each has thousands of subordinate representatives, and it is with these that man sometimes has contact. Such a representative, if asked who he is, will always give the name of the head of his ray, not his own, and in doing so, he is no more guilty of falsehood or pretence than is the office-boy who, dispatched on some errand for his employer, gives the name of that employer instead of his own, realizing that what people want to know in business is not who he is, but whom he represents.

Each of these regents, we are told, has six wings. Of course, no angel has wings springing from his shoulder blades. In the poetry of ancient scriptures, wings are symbolical of power, just as are the extra arms of the Indian divinities. In this case, the wings are clearly intended to indicate the six forces or powers of nature of which we read in *The Secret Doctrine*, and perhaps there may also be a reference to the six directions of space in which these powers may be exercised.

Finally, St. John tells that these varied manifestations ever give glory to God, crying: "Holy, holy, holy, Lord God almighty, which was, and is, and is to come." Well may we follow this noble example and give glory to Him who shows Himself thus wondrously, even though it be in symbol, to the limited senses of us, His lower creatures. All attempts at description of those higher worlds are foredoomed to failure because of our limitation; but one day we shall know even as we are known; one day we shall see Him as He is, and seeing Him, we shall become one with Him. Our eyes shall see the King in His beauty; we shall behold the Land of Far Distances.

31

EXOTERIC AND ESOTERIC

The true use of speech, it is said, is to conceal our thoughts; undoubtedly in our Liberal Catholic philosophy we are constantly finding that if words do not conceal our thoughts, they certainly fail to express them. The distinction between the words "exoteric" and "esoteric" seems obvious, yet the fact that questions are constantly asked about them shows that many do not understand their meaning. People want to know what things are esoteric, and why; and many seem to be of the opinion that there should be no secrecy but that everything which can be learned or discovered should at once be put at the disposal of the whole world as is done in physical science. The wisdom of the ages, however, has not pronounced in favor of this method of instruction, and it is not difficult to see at least some of the reasons for which caution in these matters is desirable.

Those who accuse the occultist of withholding knowledge from the multitude in order that he may himself have the exclusive advantage of its possession are in error. Indeed, by advancing such a theory, they show themselves to be blankly ignorant of the very nature of the problem. Knowledge possessed by the few earnest students is sometimes not put before the general public. That much is admitted; but this is only because the man who has attained the knowledge judges that silence is wisdom, not for himself but for the world. All such knowledge as can be of practical use in daily life is freely put forward; and the ethical teaching given by the Liberal Catholic Church is invariably supported by an explanation of the exact reasons why a certain line of conduct is advisable and a certain other line is inadvisable. Whatever will do good is freely told; but the possessor of knowledge must be permitted to use his discretion as to what portion of it he will share with his fellow men.

People sometimes say that they resent being treated as though they were children; that they want to know all that there is to know, either of good or of evil, and that they feel thoroughly competent to decide as to the use which they will make of the information when they receive it. But the fact is that, with regard to this higher knowledge, the ordinary man *is* a child, and suddenly to present him with a mass of new information would not increase his years or enable him to deal with it safely. No knowledge ever is, or ever can be, withheld from the earnest student. Those who know have earned the right to know by years of study and self-development. The way by which they traveled is open to all, as it has always been open, and no man can hold another back from treading that path. The truths to be gained along this line are not of the same nature as those which are promulgated by physical science. If a man discovers a new metal, he announces the fact to the world, and the world is the better and not the worse for this additional piece of information; but it would be absurd to give equally wide circulation to the discovery of some new and deadly poison. Where secrecy is maintained, it is always in the interest of humanity. Facts which are not publicly discussed fall usually under one or other of four heads:

1. Those which are dangerous.
2. Those which might be used for evil purposes.
3. Those which are incomprehensible.
4. Those which might provoke irreverence.

1. Those which are dangerous. A large amount of knowledge falls under this head, for there are forces in nature which can only be safely handled by men who have gone through a long course of careful preparation. No one would put dynamite into the hands of child; yet that would be a light matter in comparison with the responsibility of putting the knowledge of great occult forces into untrained or unworthy hands. Examples of this danger are not wanting, even though they are fortunately superficial and insignificant. People who have learned a tiny fragment of inner knowledge in connection with the Serpent Fire, or even some elementary breathing exercises, frequently contrive to wreck their health or their sanity; and those who have been unfortunate enough to come into touch with the world below the physical have rarely lived long enough to regret the indiscretion which led them into realms that man is not meant to penetrate. Magic is a reality—sometimes a very terrible reality—and undoubtedly for the majority of mankind this is one of the cases where ignorance is bliss; for the man who keeps outside of this is reasonably safe from its dangers.

2. Those which might be misused. In occultism, as in other sciences, knowledge is power; and it is not well to give power into the hands of a man until there is some guarantee that he will use it well and unselfishly. Certain fragments of occult knowledge have escaped into the outer world, and we already see how far the world is from being worthy of even so small a gift. Of late years, people have come to accept, to some extent, the power of thought and the possibility of dominating the will of another by a determined effort. This is a small and rudimentary fact—only the merest beginning of the study of mental dynamics—yet we already see that even this first step on the road to real knowledge along that line is being misused. Already we see advertisements from those offering to teach a man how to overreach another in business by the use of thought-power—how to obtain success (and always at the cost of others) in business. The way in which this fragment of the inner knowledge has been received does not encourage its custodians to give out anything further.

Only those races which are generally considered the most backward are found at the present day to believe in the efficacy of magic; it may be noticed that those who do believe in it and employ it invariably do so for evil purposes. One reads of instances in which the practitioner of the Voodoo or Obeah rites brings disease upon his victim or causes him to waste away, but never of a case in which this gruesome power is used to make a man stronger, better or happier. It is frequently employed to blast the crops of an enemy or to make his cattle barren, but never to increase the general prosperity of the country or to diminish poverty and disease.

It is not denied that some good use is being made of this power. Cures effected by Christian or Mental Science may be cited on the credit side of the account, and the fact that in this way some people have learned to hold themselves above the possibility of depression is clearly a gain. Occult truths will, by degrees, become known in the outer world as they have been known at other periods of the world's history. It is even part of the plan that they should become so known, but not prematurely, lest the injury done should be greater, lest those should be fewer who can be saved from the evil to come.

Some of these powers were well known in the great Atlantean continent. A few employed them well and thereby made progress, but so many abused them that it was finally necessary to sink the whole continent beneath the sea. History will no doubt repeat itself. It seems certain that even now there will still be a majority who will use their knowledge selfishly; but at least it is hoped that this time the minority who use their power well will be larger—a definite sign that progress has been made.

In order that this hope may be realized, it is necessary that the knowledge should come before the world at the right moment and by slow degrees. To throw down a great mass of it before those who are wholly unprepared for it would mean danger and not progress. All new inventions which are capable of being used for purposes of destruction are so employed as soon as their secret is mastered. We see it in the case of the airplane and the submarine, just as we saw it before in the case of the balloon, the steam engine, and the telegraph. If the enormously greater power which lies dormant in every atom were put into the hands of the men of today, should we not see a further exemplification of the same evil tendency?[86] Until the nations have become sufficiently civilized to abandon the barbarities of war, it is obviously undesirable to put into their hands powers far transcending anything of which they know at present.

No doubt in due time the scientific men of the day will discover these things for themselves. All that occultists can hope to do is to strive earnestly to bring more and more people to understand the real trend of evolution, so that when the discovery comes there may be a strong public opinion in favor of its kindly and unselfish use. Surely also the world must attain a higher level of morality in regard to commercial matters before wider knowledge can be of real use to it; for at present it is, unfortunately, well known that every new discovery in organic chemistry which is capable of being used in that way always means a further adulteration of food.

People often say that there must be many secrets which can be given out without danger, that it is possible to avoid mention of these terrible physical powers and yet say a great deal which would be of general use. It is perhaps not so easy as is supposed, for one thing leads to another and the processes of nature are inextricably linked together; the responsibility for putting scientific investigators on the track of forbidden things is too tremendous to be undertaken lightly. In our Liberal Catholic Church, however, we have already lifted a little corner of the veil. Let us see whether the world will so use the fragment which has been given to it as to convince the custodians of the wider knowledge that it is ready for further revelations.

The Great Brotherhood has no other interest than the progress of mankind, and its members are therefore always watching for those to whom additional knowledge can safely be given. Many a man thinks himself fully prepared to receive and use wisely any knowledge that may come his way; but often that only means that he forms a higher estimate of his own merits than is justified by his real condition. One who, by earnestness and conscientiousness, raises himself above the mass of mankind at once attracts their attention, for he flashes out before their vision as does a brilliant light upon a background of darkness. It is quite impossible that any likely person can be overlooked, and so it follows that if any man who is earnestly trying has not yet been noticed by them, it is necessary that he should continue and even increase his efforts.

3. Those which are incomprehensible. If a man is to understand a system of thought which is new to him, it is not well in the beginning that all its details should be poured out upon him. It is better for him at first to gain a thorough grasp of its main outline; this can then be filled in by degrees, so that every new thought may be seen in its due proportion and may fall naturally into its place. Owing to the stage of evolution at which we have arrived, we are at present engaged in the development of the discriminative power of the lower or concrete mind. This naturally makes us critical, so that we instinctively pounce first upon those points in any new system which are farthest removed from our previous ideas; and precisely because they are new to us, because our mind has a tendency to resent novelty, these points are immediately exaggerated and made to loom so large in the scheme that, as a whole, it becomes distorted and we form an entirely false impression of it. This trouble is avoided if the novelties are put before us gradually; but it involves a certain withholding of detail in the beginning—a fact to which many people take exception.

There is much information in occultism which can only be appreciated at its proper value by those who have developed the faculties to which it appeals. Until this development has taken place, such truth is meaningless to them and is more likely to be harmful than useful. Yet these are precisely the people who clamor that nothing should be withheld from them. We encounter, in the course of occult study, a great deal of knowledge which cannot be communicated because it is of such a nature that only the man who has himself experienced it is able to comprehend it. All attempts to describe it to one who has not had the experience are ineffectual, and are to him but a "[darkening of] counsel by words without knowledge" [Job 38:2]. It has often been explained that the Ego in its causal body thinks in realities and not in concrete expression; naturally such thought as this transcends all words, and to try to put it into speech leads unavoidably to confusion and misapprehension.

Many other facts are incommunicable because they are intensely personal; each man experiences them for himself and in his own way, and the method by which one man has learned to appreciate them would be quite unsuitable for another. In the course of a considerable experience, it has come my way to hear from various pupils of the Great Ones something of their relations to their respective Masters, and nothing has struck me more than the remarkable diversity of the methods employed and the wonderful exactitude with which these methods are adapted to the person concerned. It is not only that no two cases are exactly alike, it is that the methods are fundamentally different, and that two pupils of the same Master may have almost nothing in common in their experience until they stand side by side at a certain level and find that, though there be many roads, there is only one goal. Obviously, any teaching that we can give on matters of this sort can be only of the most general nature, and each man is qualified to speak only of what has come within his own experience; and although what he says may be encouraging and helpful to some, it may well be quite meaningless to others whose nature requires that they be led along a different path.

4. Those which might provoke irreverence. There is a saying attributed to Our Blessed Lord: "Give not that which is holy unto the dogs, neither cast ye your pearls before swine, lest they trample them under their feet, and turn again and rend you" (Matt. 7:6). There is a vast amount of practical truth in this remark, and recent history supplies us with plenty of evidence that it is just as true now as it was two thousand years ago. Not only is priceless information cast aside as useless by those who are not yet fit for it, it is ridiculed and cast into the mud of their own impure thought and, having so disposed of it, they invariably turn upon the person who gave it to them and do their best to injure him. It is not wise to know more than the majority; at least, it is not wise to let them know that one knows more. Galileo found this out some centuries ago when the Church forced him to retract assertions which he knew perfectly well to be true. All through the darkest part of European history there were those who knew something of occult truth, but they found it undesirable to admit their knowledge. Even to speak of these things meant persecution and death at the hands of the ignorant and fanatical majority. If anyone had ventured to tell one of those picturesque crusader knights as much of science as may now be found in a schoolboy's primer, he would have been regarded as a fearsome magician and would probably have speedily found that arrangements were being made for his premature cremation at the nearest stake. Thus it is seen that what is the magical or secret knowledge of one century may become the orthodox science of the next. In these days, "swine" still turn and rend the wise man—not his physical body, perhaps, but his reputation.

This makes any attempt to teach a thankless task for the teacher; but if that were all, it would be well worth while to run the risk of the ridicule and defamation by the ignorant majority in order that the few might learn and profit. Unfortunately, that is not all, and the suffering of the teacher is a negligible quantity as compared with the harm that the swine do to themselves when they trample those pearls in the mud. It is not well to offer an opportunity for irreverence, for that irreverence brings with it the most serious results. To come into contact with one of the Great Ones offers an opportunity of rapid development such as can be gained in no other way; and to help, or to be of use to, one of these makes good karma which, on the face of it, looks altogether out of proportion to the actual service rendered. But we must remember that the converse of this is also true—that any harm done to one of them brings a corresponding weight of evil.

People often seem to think that ignorance may be pleaded as an excuse in such a case, and that a man who did not know that it was some Great One whom he was injuring ought therefore to escape the inevitable result. One can only say in reply that this is not so. First, the man ought not willfully to have injured anyone, whether he knew him to be great or not; and whatever karma comes upon him as the result of the injury is entirely his own fault; and secondly, the laws of nature work automatically and take no account of our knowledge or our ignorance. The man who takes up a red-hot iron will be burned whether he knows that it is red-hot or not. The man who steps over a precipice in the dark will fall, whether he knew that there was a precipice there or not. Therefore it is not well to cause the enemy to blaspheme, or to offer to the ignorant and self-conceited the opportunity of doing themselves harm by flouting that which they ought to respect.

For this reason, all intimate mention of the Great Ones and of the facts of their lives is avoided amongst students of the Wisdom, except in the presence of those who can be trusted to understand such reference and to adopt the right attitude towards it. It is not in the least that the Great Ones would feel themselves injured by such misconstruction or impertinent thought; it is that such thoughts and feelings do harm to those who experience them and also cause much pain to the followers of the Teacher who is thus traduced. For this reason (although when asked we always hold ourselves bound to bear testimony, even before hostile witnesses, to the fact of the existence of the Masters) we speak of them in public utterances as little as may be and give intimate details only to those of whose reverence and understanding we feel certain.

The above considerations, among others, show reason for a certain amount of reserve in speaking of occult matters. But exotericism and esotericism—the open and secret—are only two parts of one great whole which is slowly unfolding itself as mankind progresses. Consequently, the line which divides them is a shifting line and, as time goes on, many facts which at first were kept rigidly secret are spoken of openly. This advance is as beneficial as it is inevitable. It is a proof of the success of the means adopted to spread the inner teaching, that the thought of the world at large has been so far affected that the public—or a certain proportion of the public—is now prepared for much which in earlier days would have been sneered at or misunderstood. The general attitude towards occult teaching is more interested and more respectful than it was. People have not gone far, but they have made some progress; the ghost story which once would have been received with sneers and ridicule is now accepted with the remark that there seems to be something in these things. Not a great advance, certainly, but still something to be thankful for when we remember the attitude which was common in the time of our grandparents. It is still necessary for us to educate the world in these matters; but even now we must do it gradually and give it only what it is able to assimilate, for if we pour out upon it too great an installment of the vast stores of occult knowledge, we shall merely give it a kind of mental indigestion and so do more harm than good.

Let us beware lest our esoteric knowledge should lead us into pride—should bring us to look down upon those who know less than we do. It is true that our Liberal Catholic teaching gives us a vast amount of information, that it puts us into a position to deal better with the difficulties of life, to solve its problems and to explain its mysteries; yet we must remember that what has been lifted for us is only a tiny corner of the veil; and while even that little has produced for us the most marvelous results and, indeed, has entirely changed our understanding of life, it will still be wise for us to keep ourselves humble by reminding ourselves how much more there is to learn and how infinitely little is our knowledge when we compare it with all that there is to know. When we lay our ignorance beside the still greater ignorance of the ordinary man, we have, indeed, reason for thankfulness but none for conceit. When we compare our ignorance with the knowledge of an adept or a saint, we obtain for the first time some idea of the true proportion of things, and we see that deep humility is the only attitude which befits us.

The very fact that we have learned even so much makes us earnestly wish to learn more; and we know that the fullest information will be given to us only if we have made good use of the little that we already possess. Therefore, if we wish to penetrate into realms which are still esoteric to us, we must be able to show what we have done with the additional knowledge which we have already acquired. If we have been generous, yet judicious, in dispensing that, if by its means we have lightened the sorrow of the world in our neighborhood, we shall soon find it possible to acquire further information; for occultism is essentially a practical thing, and the knowledge that it gives is intended for instant application. "To him that hath, more shall be given" [Mark 4:25], but only if he has used it wisely.

However much of the truth is still esoteric to us, we have at least learned enough to feel absolute certainty that everything is managed entirely for the general good. When information is given forth, it is given with a view to that good; and we recognize with equal certainty that when information is withheld, it is always and without exception for the same reason. We seek the knowledge of God; and the more we gain of that, the more clearly we see the depth and the height of the love of God which, like the peace of God, "passeth all understanding" [Phil. 4:7]. In that peace we enfold ourselves, to that love we trust ourselves, calm in the certainty that deeper knowledge can only reveal to us still more of the glory towards which, however slowly, we are moving. From Him we came forth; to Him we shall return; and however deep may have been our sleep when we were buried in the depths of matter, we know that we are rising steadily towards a full realization of Him.

32

A New Attitude towards Sin

The attitude of Liberal Catholics towards sin is usually different from that of members of other churches.

Some of our Christian brethren, indeed, find it difficult to understand the way in which we regard it. They seem to think that we make too light of it, that we are not sufficiently impressed with its guilt and its awful consequences. Many people think that the death of Christ was to save men from sin, and they even go further than that and say that sin was actually the *cause* of the crucifixion of Our Lord.

Readers who may have belonged to the Church of England (as I did) may remember an appalling verse which occurs in one of the hymns from the "Ancient and Modern" collection.

> O Sinner, mark and ponder well
> Sin's awful condemnation;
> Think what a sacrifice it cost
> To purchase thy salvation;
> Had Jesus never bled and died,
> Then what would thee and all betide
> But uttermost damnation?

The Christ was truly crucified upon the cross of matter. We do not for one moment deny that that was a very real and inexpressible sacrifice; we do not for a moment seek to minimize the extent of the sacrifice when the Second Person of the ever-Blessed Trinity laid aside His glory and took upon Himself the limitation of matter. We cannot hope to understand how great a sacrifice that was. The true sacrifice of Christ involves not so much the painful death of a physical body as an age-long limitation of glory which is far beyond our comprehension, a shutting down of that glory into the imprisonment of earth and matter. That sacrifice was undertaken for us, not to save us from our sins, not indeed "for our salvation," but for our very existence. Had the Christ never descended into matter, there could have been no humanity as we know it now. Our very life depends upon that eternal sacrifice, not on an action once performed long ago in the past, but an eternal sacrifice being offered here and now, extending from before the foundation of the world when the Lamb was slain, until the last moment when the last human being shall have been fully absorbed into Deity. This is a sacrifice beyond all words, but it was not the consequence of our sins; however sad our sins may be, we cannot with common sense regard them as the cause of that tremendous sacrifice.

Sin is a terrible thing, but we must try to understand exactly what it is. Two great Teachers have shown two ways of looking at the problem of sin. The Lord Buddha told us that all the difficulty and trouble, the sorrow and sin of the world, come from ignorance; that if men would cast off their ignorance and learn, and become wise, there would be no more sorrow, no more suffering, no more troubles. The Lord Christ, who followed Him as World Teacher, taught us that the suffering, sorrow, and sin in the world come from lack of love.

Both these teachings are entirely true, for in their highest aspect, wisdom and love are identical. If a man could see the full result of evil, he would turn away from it, and if a man were full of love, he would at all times consider the effect upon others of his actions and words, and also of his thoughts. Thus in either way we should avoid sin; if we knew perfectly, or if we loved perfectly, there would be no more sin.

There is a fundamental difference, then, between our doctrine and others. But perhaps I should not use that expression "our doctrine," for we lay down no dogmas in the Church; we leave our followers—our friends and members—completely free to believe as they will. Our business as a Church is to administer Christ's sacraments to our people; we are not concerned with what they believe. Our altar is free to all who approach it reverently, we impose no creed, nor do we exact any expression of belief from any man. But this does not mean that we who act as ministers in the Church—its bishops and its priests—have no definite belief of our own. We have a great teaching to give to the world, and it is our right and our duty to give it, but we do not exact acceptance of it as a condition of membership in the Church, or as a preliminary to receiving the sacraments.

Original Sin

The fundamental difference between our ideas of sin and those of many of our Christian brethren of other branches of the Church is that they hold what is called the doctrine of *original sin*, and we do not. They believe that a man is essentially evil—that he is born under a curse from which he can escape only by belief in the scripture story of the Christ. That story is true in a certain sense. It is not necessary for any man to believe that Christ was born and lived and died in Palestine two thousand years ago. It is not in that sense that he must believe it; but he must believe in and recognize the Christ within himself—that "Christ in you" which, we are told, is the "hope of glory" [Col. 1:27]. This is the heart of the matter, for without that Christ within you there could be no hope of finding the Christ without. So in this sense the story is true, but it has become distorted and twisted and made to mean that which it was never intended to mean.

We do not believe that man is originally evil, or that he is full of the desire to do evil for evil's sake. We fully admit that man is ignorant, that he is selfish and short-sighted, but he is all this because he is undeveloped: he often acts without seeing the consequences of his actions; and it is even true that very often he does not care about the consequences of his deeds. A child makes mistakes, acts foolishly and sometimes passionately because he does not know. So is it with the man: he does not know enough yet; if he only understood these things he would be quite different. Sins, from our point of view, are not usually intentional outrages upon God's law, but ignorant infringements of it. Man forgets: it would not be true to say that he has never known, for God has never left Himself without a witness.

All races have had their teachers, but many men will not listen to them or follow them. In many cases they do not see why they should. Man forgets what he has been taught or is swept away by passion, or he thinks perhaps that it does not matter just for once. Men make many foolish excuses, but they make them because they do not know. If they understood the immutable law of karma, of God's justice, they would see that as a man sows, so shall he reap. The sinner is often blameworthy, but always he is more to be pitied than blamed.

Our Own Sins

Such is our attitude towards sin in others. What should be our attitude towards sin in ourselves? Undoubtedly there should be the most earnest and determined resolve to get rid of sin. But we reject servile appeals to God's mercy because they dishonor God, putting Him in a light in which not even a just and good man should be put. We believe man to be divine in origin, we believe him to be a god in the making—"I have said, ye are gods; and all of you are children of the Most High" (Psalm 82:6). The Christ made that wondrous sacrifice in order that we also might one day become like Him. "God so loved the world, that he gave his [alone-born] Son, that whosoever believeth in him should not perish, but have everlasting life" (John 3:16). Therefore our attitude towards our own sins is not one of despair or of depression, but of hope and of earnest, tireless effort. "I note that I have made such and such a mistake; with God's help I will not do that again. Other faults I may have but that particular folly I have now seen: that, at least, I will not do again." If we fight steadily, victory is certain. Of that we may be absolutely sure; it is only a matter of time and perseverance.

Therefore, be our sins what they may, we must never despair but resolve. There is no forgiveness required. It is a strange notion about God to think that He should need to be implored to forgive His children because of their mistakes and their infirmities. He knows far better than we do how those slips and weaknesses come about. He knows it all; He watches it all; in His hands lies the destiny of humanity, and He is satisfied with the progress being made. The Church gives the means of straightening out the entanglements which we make for ourselves by our own foolish and ignorant actions, and in that way she helps us to lay ourselves open once more to the play of all the good and helpful forces which are round about us.

When we do wrong we set ourselves against the current of evolution, against God's will for us. God is not shocked; He is not angry or disturbed; but by setting ourselves against those currents we disturb ourselves and our surroundings. We get ourselves into an entanglement and are so preoccupied with it that the grace of God cannot enter. He knocks at the door of the human heart, but He does not break it open; He does not force Himself upon man, but patiently stands waiting and offering. The force is flowing still, but man shuts himself off from God. What is needed, then, is not a change in *God's* attitude—a change from anger to forgiveness—but a change in *man's* attitude—a change from discord to harmony, from stubbornness and stupidity to responsiveness and comprehension, from fear and anger to love—so that he may once more be open to the sunlight of God's love which has been shining all the time.

That is what the Church does in the Absolution which she gives at every service. If you know that you have done wrong, if you are sorry for it and earnestly mean to give it up, which (as one of the Masters of the Wisdom once said) is the only sort of repentance worth anything, then the Church in the Absolution clears away the obstructions to the flow of God's light and love. It is no use sitting down and weeping over the past. Get up and go on, and do not make the same mistake again. If you do make it again, resolve more firmly than ever that this time you will succeed in your effort, and cling to that determination until you have won the victory.

Let us look at sin rationally, pityingly, understandingly, making tender allowance for others, for each heart knows its own bitterness. But let us set a rigid rule for ourselves, remembering ever that the Holy Spirit, the Great Encourager, who entered into us at the sacrament of confirmation, is all the while working within us unto righteousness and helping us to press onward to the glorious consummation of that ineffable sacrifice of Christ.

The Sin against the Holy Ghost

A curious biblical problem which has exercised the minds of many students is the nature of what is called the sin against the Holy Ghost. The question arises from a saying attributed to Christ: "All manner of sin and blasphemy shall be forgiven unto men; but the blasphemy against the Holy Ghost shall not be forgiven unto men. And whosoever speaketh a word against the Son of Man, it shall be forgiven him; but whosoever speaketh against the Holy Ghost, it shall not be forgiven him, neither in this world nor in the world to come" (Matt. 12:31–32). Commentators have usually adopted the ordinary interpretation of the words "sin" and "forgiveness"; they have supposed that anything said against God the Holy Ghost would offend Him so seriously that He would be unable to forget His resentment either in this world or in the next. Others have concluded that persistent impenitence is the unforgivable sin, and many other suggestions have also been made.

The context of the passage seems to imply that the crime against which Christ was speaking was the attribution of a good action to an evil source. He had, according to the story, been "casting out devils"— that is to say, freeing people from some form of obsession. As the crowd was greatly impressed by this, the Pharisees, who hated Him, sought to belittle His action, saying that He was able to cast out devils because He was Himself in league with the prince of devils; and it was apparently this attribution of a manifestation of divine power to a diabolical source that He condemned in such emphatic language. This is one of the commonest of crimes; we see it in evidence through the whole course of history and instances meet us, too, in everyday life. A man with the best and purest motives tries to do some action that, to him, seems good; immediately his enemies pounce upon it, distort it, and attribute to him the foulest of motives. If this be the unforgivable sin, the host of the unforgiven must be a multitude which no man can number! It is a peculiarly mean and contemptible form of wickedness; nevertheless, it cannot be that alone that is referred to in the text.

The matter is more serious than it appears to be at first sight, for this rather gruesome text seems to have an unholy attraction for many morbidly minded people. I have myself at various times received a number of letters from unfortunate people, each of whom was thoroughly persuaded that he had committed the unforgivable sin against the Holy Ghost and was consequently in the depths of despair. More than one suicide has left behind him a statement that he was driven to this rash act by the conviction that he had committed this mysterious sin. It is therefore worthwhile to say a few words about the matter, so that if any of us should meet with a deluded unfortunate we may be able to offer him some help.

In the first place it should be clearly understood that the appearance of the text in the New Testament is no guarantee whatever that the words were ever used by the Christ. The Gospels were never intended to be historical, but are rather symbolical presentations of the great Christ drama, presenting the chief stages in the spiritual history of every man as he climbs the upward path. At the same time, many of the sayings popularly attributed to the Christ were incorporated in the drama, and it is possible that this may be one of them; though even if it is, we can never be certain that it is in anything like its original form, for many such sayings have been altered almost beyond recognition.

Assuming, however, that it is a genuine saying, we must still take exception to its English form because of the mistranslation of the words which are rendered *world* and *forgiveness*. As usual, the former word is put for the Greek *aion*, which is identical with the English word *aeon*, and can mean nothing but an age or period. Then again, the sense which we now attach to the word "forgiveness" is entirely foreign to the Greek word which it represents. A man feels resentment against someone who has done him a wrong; eventually he makes up his mind to let that resentment go, and then we say that he has forgiven that person. But there would be no meaning in the word forgiveness if he did not first feel resentment.

We have no right to assume that God ever feels resentment against anyone under any circumstances whatever; we know that the divine nature is utterly incapable of any such feeling; therefore to speak of God as forgiving us is really a blasphemy against Him. Our loving Father holds no grudge against any man, nor could He possibly be angry. What we call a wicked man is one who is working selfishly against the current of evolution and therefore against his own best interests. Such a one is no doubt laying up for himself a great deal of trouble and sorrow; we may well pity him, but it is of little use being angry with him. The attitude of mind which is indicated by the word "forgiveness" is one which is impossible for God, and we must understand that the word is used here in the same sense as when it is employed in the creed—that of the readjustment of what is wrong, the combing out of the entanglements which we have made by our transgressions. Notice the meaning of the words; to *progress* is to move forward with the current of the divine Will; to *transgress* is to move *across* that current, and consequently to cause confusion. It is the straightening out of the confusion with which we have surrounded ourselves by our own actions which is inadequately described by the word forgiveness.

Having these considerations in mind, we may perhaps attempt a paraphrase of this much-disputed saying which shall contain a more intelligible meaning than that which is ordinarily ascribed to it. The Christ frequently speaks of Himself as the Son of Man, and we may perhaps assume that He is doing so in this sentence. The passage might run something like this: "However much you oppose Me or speak against Me, the resulting entanglement can be straightened out; but if you act or speak against the Holy Ghost you cannot put that straight in this age at all, and perhaps not even in the next one."

The Holy Ghost is the very symbol and agent of evolution. It was He who first set out the plan, who "brooded over" the virgin waters of space, who poured life into what otherwise would have been inert matter; so we might well think of any person who persistently sets himself to work against the current of evolution as sinning against the Holy Ghost. There can be no question that a man who deliberately sets himself to do harm, to do evil instead of good, is acting in opposition to God the Holy Ghost and laying up for himself the most unpleasant results in the future. If the Christ ever made the statement contained in the text, it is quite possible that something of this sort may be what He meant.

The attitude of mind which seems indicated here is not by any means that of the ordinary "wicked" person. We usually apply that term to one who is selfish and seeks his own interest at the cost of injury or ruin to others, or to one who plunges into all kinds of wild excesses for the gratification of his lower vehicles. People who do these things are simply ignorant; they have not yet learnt that nothing which is harmful to one person can ever benefit another; they have not yet discovered that the only things which are truly good for anyone are those which are good and helpful for all. They do not understand the course of evolution, and so they are acting without reference to it. The person who commits the sin against the Holy Ghost is one who understands the scheme of evolution and willfully sets himself to act against it. One who adopts that attitude might very well so involve himself as to need more than one age or dispensation before his entanglements could be fully straightened out.

It is unlikely that any of us are in danger of falling under such a condemnation; yet it were well that we should be on our guard against that minor form of blasphemy against the Holy Ghost which is involved in the constant attribution of wrong motives to our fellow men. Most of us have probably had the experience of being ourselves grossly misunderstood; the very actions which we meant most kindly have been regarded as evidences of depravity.

Even our Church is sometimes misunderstood in the most amazing manner. Our good is evilly spoken of and the most abominable slanders are invented and freely circulated against us; and yet we know perfectly well that all the time our intentions are of the noblest and that we are simply trying to do as well as we can the work that has been put into our hands. The attacks often seem so malicious that it is difficult to believe that they are due only to incredible ignorance; yet in truth that must be so.

We can learn from such experience to refrain from the attribution of motives, even when hatred and spitefulness seem most apparent. Let us show the advantage of the training which our Church gives by steadily returning good for evil, blessing for cursing, knowing that the future is always with those who do the work rather than with those who abuse us for doing it. And there is always the consolation that the good work is not fruitless; there are always the ignorant who mock and misunderstand, but there are also those who appreciate and those who are helped and uplifted.

33

A Rational Creed

One of the greatest needs of today is a rational creed that will commend itself to the ordinary man and woman of the twentieth century who is seeking for an explanation of the problems of life. The traditional creeds of the Catholic Church are indeed full of meaning when properly understood, but since the true interpretation of their ancient symbolism seems to have been forgotten almost entirely by the Churches, they are of but little use to the ordinary man. In our Liturgy, therefore, in addition to the older creeds, we have included a very simple statement of our belief in the act of faith which we recite in the shorter form of the Holy Eucharist and at the offices of prime and compline.[87] It is as follows:

> We believe that God is love and power and truth and light; that perfect justice rules the world; that all his sons shall one day reach his feet, however far they stray. We hold the fatherhood of God, the brotherhood of man; we know that we do serve him best when best we serve our brother man. So shall his blessing rest on us and peace for evermore.

This is not a complete or detailed statement, but it includes the principal points of our belief and is especially intended to remind our people of first principles, to comfort any who are in trouble, and to act as an antidote to the false and foolish beliefs which are so current in the present day.

From the opening assertion—that God is love and power and truth and light—it necessarily follows that, in spite of appearances, all things are definitely and intelligently working together for good; that all circumstances, however untoward they may seem, are in reality exactly what are needed; that everything around us tends not to hinder us but to help us, if only it is understood. The evolution which we are considering is a spiritual evolution—an evolution of the soul far more than of the body. The reason for the production of better and more refined bodies is that they are needed for the expression of the evolving souls; and therefore we must always remember that the true man is the soul, and this body to which we pay so much attention is, after all, only an appendage of it. We must look at everything from the standpoint of the soul; and in every case when an internal struggle takes place we must realize our identity with the higher and not with the lower.

Another important matter to realize is the method of evolution. The soul indeed is a spark of the divine fire, and so has within itself the most wonderful divine possibilities; but as yet they are but germs, and they need development. How is this development to be achieved? It will be noted that this achievement is the whole object of the descent of the Second Person of the Blessed Trinity into matter; it is very truly "for us men and for our salvation [that He] came down from heaven." The germs or latent qualities are awakened by impact or vibration from without; and since the finer movements of higher worlds cannot at first affect the undeveloped soul, it has to draw round itself vestures of grosser matter through which the heavier vibrations can play; and so it takes upon itself successively the mental body, the emotional body, and the physical body. This is birth or incarnation—the commencement of a physical life. During that life all kinds of experiences come to the soul through the physical body, and from them it should learn some lessons and develop certain qualities within itself. After a time it begins to withdraw again into itself, and puts off by degrees the vestures which it has assumed. The first of these to be dropped is the physical body, and that withdrawal is what we call death. But it is not the end of its activities, as many people suppose; it is simply withdrawing from one effort, bearing back with it the results; it returns, as is said in the Gospel, bearing its sheaves with it; and after a certain period of comparative repose it will make another effort of the same kind.

Many Lives

Thus, as has been said, what we ordinarily call this life is only one day in the real and wider life—a day at school during which we learn certain lessons. But in as much as one short life of seventy or eighty years at most is not enough to give an opportunity for learning all the lessons which this wonderful and beautiful world has to teach, and in as much as God means us to learn them all, it is necessary that we should come back many times, live through many of these school days in different classes and under different circumstances, until all the lessons are learnt. Then this lower schoolwork will be over, and we shall pass to something higher and more glorious, the true divine life work for which this earthly school life has fitted us.

We must not for a moment confound the doctrine of reincarnation with a theory sometimes held by the ignorant in classical times, that it is possible for a soul which has reached humanity to take rebirth as an animal. No such retrogression is possible; when once a man comes into existence as a human soul inhabiting a causal body, he can never again fall back into a lower kingdom of nature, whatever mistakes he may make or however he may fail to take advantage of his opportunity. If he is idle in the school of life, he may need to take the same lesson over and over again before he has really learnt it; but on the whole, progress is steady though it may often be slow.

Life presents us with many problems which, on any other hypothesis than that of reincarnation, seem utterly insoluble; this great truth explains them, and therefore must hold the field until another and more satisfactory hypothesis can be found. This, of course, is not an hypothesis to some of us, but a matter of direct knowledge, though naturally our knowledge is not proof to others.

Absolute Justice

Man's gradual growth takes place under a law of absolute justice— perhaps better stated as an unchangeable law of cause and effect—so that nothing whatever can come to a man unless he has deserved it. Everything that happens to him (whether it be sorrow or joy) is, on the one hand, the direct result of his own action in the past, and, on the other, an opportunity by means of which he can deliberately mold his future.

But this law works both ways; it does not only react upon us from our past, but it also reaches forward from our present into our future. Every thought, word, or action produces its definite result: not a reward or a punishment imposed from without, but a result inherent in the action itself and definitely connected with it in the relation of cause and effect, these being really but two inseparable parts of one whole. Just as our present is the result of what we thought and said and did in the past, so are we definitely and unfailingly building our future for ourselves by what we think and say and do now. It is in our interest to study this divine law of cause and effect very closely, so that we shall be able to adapt ourselves to it and to use it as we use the other laws of nature. It clearly follows also that it is necessary for us to attain perfect control over ourselves so that we may guide our lives intelligently in accordance with this law.

The Plan

The Plan has long been understood in older religions and was certainly part of the teaching of the Christ; but it has been forgotten, distorted and overlaid by all sorts of confused traditions. Its broad outlines have been widely known in the world for thousands of years and are so known at the present day. It is only we of the European civilization who, in our incredible self-sufficiency, have remained ignorant of the facts and scoff at any fragment of them that may come our way. As in the case of any other science, so in this science of the soul, full details are only known to those who devote their lives to its pursuit. Those who fully know have patiently developed within themselves the powers necessary for perfect observation. For in this respect there is a difference between the methods of inner investigation and those of science; the latter devotes its energy to the improvement of its instruments, while the former aims rather at the development of the observer.

This development is entirely a question of vibration. All information which reaches a man from the world without reaches him by means of vibration, whether it be through the senses of sight, hearing, or touch. Consequently, if a man is able to make himself sensitive to additional vibrations, he will acquire additional information. It is found that it is possible for a man to become more and more sensitive to various subtler vibrations until his consciousness, acting through many developed faculties, functions freely in new and higher ways. He will then find new worlds of subtler matter opening up before him, though in reality they are only new portions of the world he already knows. He learns in this way that a vast unseen universe exists around him and that it is constantly affecting him in many ways, even though he remains unconscious of it. When he has developed the faculties whereby he can sense these other worlds, he is able to observe them scientifically, to repeat these observations any time it is necessary, and to verify them with those of others.

All this has been done, not once, but thousands of times. The sight of these usually unseen portions of our worlds at once brings to our knowledge a vast body of facts entirely new to most of us, though not new to those who have carefully studied ancient religions and philosophies. But those ancient religions, like our own, have been distorted and overlaid by unnecessary accretions as the centuries have rolled on, and so are often completely unintelligible.

CHAPTER 33

A Mighty Whole

What we, who have studied these things, are really doing, is to apply modern scientific methods of investigation to these facts of the higher life that were heretofore taught as revelations from on high. We are bringing forth the secret teaching of the Mysteries for the helping of those who are able to receive and understand it. This teaching gradually solves for us many of the most difficult problems of life; it clears up for us many mysteries, so that we now see them to have been mysteries to us so long only because heretofore we saw so small a part of the facts, and because we looked at them from below as isolated unconnected fragments, instead of rising above them to a standpoint whence they are comprehensible as part of a mighty whole. It settles in a moment many questions that have been much disputed, such as, for example, that of the continued existence of man after death. It affords us the true explanation of many wildly impossible statements made about heaven, hell, and purgatory; it dispels our ignorance and removes our fear of the unknown by supplying us with a rational account of the orderly scheme of life and the world.

There may be those who will find some of the results of these investigations incredible, or at least to run entirely contrary to their preconceived ideas. If that be so, I would ask them to remember that I am not putting them forward as a theory, as a metaphysical speculation or a pious opinion of my own, but as a set of definite scientific facts that have been examined over and over again, not only by myself but by many others also. We are not offering a creed to be swallowed like a pill, but are trying to set forth a system to study and a life to live. We ask no blind faith from anyone, but we suggest that these teachings should be considered as working hypotheses, though to many of us they are not hypotheses, but living facts.

If the student of this system finds it more satisfactory than others that have been presented to him, if it seems to him to solve more of life's problems, to answer a greater number of the questions that inevitably arise for the thinking man, he will probably pursue his study further and will find in it the same ever-increasing satisfaction and joy that many others have found. If, on the other hand, he thinks some other system preferable, no harm is done; he will merely have been made acquainted with some tenets with which at present he is unable to agree. Naturally our own knowledge is not proof to others. It is simply a piece of evidence which the student is invited to take into consideration when examining and comparing systems of thought.

We must always hold clearly in our minds the difference between evidence and proof. My own evidence in the matter is this: by many years of work I have learned how to use some of the faculties of the soul as distinct from those of the body. Anyone can learn to do the same, provided he is willing to take the necessary trouble and to give the necessary time to it, but few men would care to face the utter and whole-souled devotion to this study, carried on through a very long period of time. Still, it can be done, for many have done it. How long it would take any particular person it is impossible to say, because no one knows through what thickness of crust he has to dig before he can reach the very kernel of himself, the true man.

The Advantages of This Knowledge

When this knowledge is fully assimilated, it changes one's outlook on life so completely that it would be difficult to enumerate all the advantages which flow from it. I may perhaps mention a few of the principal lines along which this change is produced, and your own thought will be able to supply some of the endless ramifications which are their necessary consequence. But it must be understood that no vague knowledge will be sufficient. Such belief as most men accord to the assertions of their religion will be quite useless, since it produces no practical effect in their lives. But if we believe in these truths as we do in the other laws of nature—as we believe that fire burns and that water drowns—then the effect that they produce in our lives will be enormous. For our belief in the laws of nature is sufficiently real to induce us to order our lives in accordance with it. Believing that fire burns, we take every precaution to avoid it; believing that water drowns, we avoid going into deep water unless we can swim.

First, then, we gain a rational understanding of life; we know how we should live, and why, and we learn that life is worth living when properly understood. To many of us it seems very little worth living for the sake of any pleasures or profits belonging exclusively to the physical plane; but it is emphatically worth living when it is regarded as a school to prepare us for the indescribable glories and the infinite possibilities which lie before us; when we regard it not from the selfish point of view of how much we can gain from it but from the higher standpoint of the opportunities that it offers us and the work that we can do for others. In learning how to govern ourselves (and therefore how to develop ourselves) we also learn how best to help those whom we love, how to make ourselves useful to all with whom we come into contact, and, ultimately, to the whole human race. We realize that it is our duty definitely to range ourselves on God's side and to stand for Him against whatever is evil and sordid in the world around us. There is not one of us who cannot do something to lighten the burden of those with whom we come into contact, even if it be only by a cheery word and a kindly thought.

A Wider View

We learn from this study to view everything from the wider philosophical standpoint rather than from the petty and purely personal. We inevitably begin to regard everything not merely as it affects our infinitesimal selves, but rather to think of its influence upon others, even upon humanity as a whole.

Because of all this, the troubles of life no longer seem so large. For many of us, our sorrows are seen out of all proportion because they are so near to us; they seem to obscure the whole horizon as a plate held near the eyes will shut out the sun. But true Christian teaching brings all these things into due perspective so that we are able to rise above the clouds of sorrow, to look down and see things as they are, and not merely as they appear when looked at from below by a very limited vision. We learn to sink altogether the lower personality with its mass of delusions and prejudices and its inability to see anything truly; we learn to rise to an impersonal, unselfish standpoint where to do right for right's sake is the only rule of life and to help our fellow men is the greatest of our joys.

God both Almighty and All-Loving

Many good men have been forced to admit that they are unable to reconcile the state of affairs which exists in the world around them with their belief that God is both almighty and all-loving. They have felt, when they looked upon all the heartbreaking sorrow and suffering, that either He is not almighty and cannot prevent it or He is not all-loving and does not care. Now we hold with the utmost strength of conviction that God is both almighty and all-loving, and we are able to reconcile the existing facts of life with that certainty by means of this teaching. Surely the hypothesis that allows us reasonably to recognize the perfection of power and love in the Deity is the only one worthy of careful examination.

We understand that our present life is not our first, but that we each have behind us a long series of lives, and by our experience in them we have evolved to our present position. Assuredly, in those past lives we must have done both good and evil, and from every one of our actions a definite proportional result must have followed under the inexorable law of justice. From good follows happiness and further opportunity; from evil proceeds sorrow and limitation. So if we find ourselves limited in any way, the limitation is of our own making or is merely due to the youth of the soul; if we have sorrow and suffering to endure, we alone are responsible. Therefore we should feel no sense of injustice with regard to our surroundings or our destiny. We know that it is use-less and foolish to grumble at what happens to us, however unpleasant it may be. It could not happen to us unless we deserved it, and so we regard it as the paying of a debt that must be cleared out of the way before further progress is made.

We have gained a totally different view of life after death and understand its place in evolution. We know that death is a matter of far less importance than is usually supposed, since it is by no means the end of existence but merely the passage from one stage of life to another. We are altogether free from the fear of death for ourselves, and our grief in connection with the death of those whom we love is very greatly mitigated.

A Splendid Evolution before Us

It also follows that we have a splendid evolution before us, the study of which will be most fascinating and attractive if we can obtain any information with regard to its nature and details. Furthermore, there is an absolute certainty of final attainment for every human soul, no matter how far he may seem to have wandered from the path of evolution, for, as is said in our Act of Faith: "All his sons shall one day reach his feet however far they stray." By our comprehension of these facts we are set free from religious fears and worries, either for ourselves or for our friends. We are no longer troubled by any uncertainty as to our future fate, but live in perfect serenity and fearlessness.

We cannot but take a serious view of life, because we know how full it is of opportunity and how much there is that we can do in it for God and for our brethren; yet our life should assuredly be calm and happy. We ought to be distinguishable from the rest of the world by our perennial cheerfulness, our undaunted courage under difficulties, and our ready sympathy and helpfulness. We should look ever for the good in everything that we may strengthen it; we should watch for the working of the great law of evolution in order that we may range ourselves on its side and contribute to its energy our tiny stream of force. In this way, by striving always to help and never to hinder, we shall become in our small sphere of influence one of the beneficent powers of nature; we shall have the happiness of knowing that we are making our small corner of the world a little better; we shall know that to the best of our ability we are working upon God's side and striving to do His will on earth as it is done in heaven.

A.M.D.G.[88]

NOTES

1. Biblical quotations, in this introduction and in Leadbeater's text, are taken from the Authorized King James Version (RS).
2. Jiddu Krishnamurti, "Truth Is a Pathless Land"; <http://www.jiddu-krishnamurti.net/en/1929-truth-is-a-pathless-land; accessed Nov. 29, 2010 (RS).
3. Stephan A. Hoeller, "Wandering Bishops: Not *All* Roads Lead to Rome," *Gnosis* 12:20 (winter 1989; RS).
4. *Koilon* in Greek literally means "hollow." The ether was posited by physics up to the early twentieth century to serve as a medium for the transmission of light, electromagnetic energy, and similar forces. As a scientific concept it is now considered obsolete (RS).
5. This is Leadbeater's own enumeration, following British usage in his day. In current American usage, a thousand million equals a billion; hence in the United States it would be written "14 billion" (RS).
6. There is no Latin word *sona* as such. There is a verb *sono*, "to make a noise," which is part of the root of *persona* (RS).
7. Literally, "Whoever wishes" in Latin. It forms the traditional opening of the Athanasian Creed: "*Quicunque vult* salvus esse, ante omnia opus est, ut teneat catholicam fidem": "Whoever wishes to be saved, before all else it is necessary that he hold the Catholic faith . . ." (RS).
8. Further details may be found in *The Hidden Side of Things*, vol. 1, chapter 4; also in *The Chakras*, chapters 2 and 3 (CWL).
9. Probably an allusion to the *Svestasvarata Upanishad* 5.8: "He [the Self] is of the measure of the thumb, of sun-like appearance": Robert Ernest Hume, trans., *The Thirteen Principal Upanishads*, 2d ed. (London: Oxford University Press, 1931), 407. "This image of the Self as thumb-sized is common in the Upanishads and other mystical texts, and perhaps has some background in the Vedic description of God the Creator standing 'ten fingers' breadth' back from the heart (Rig x.90.1). It is an attempt to draw attention inward; the size is not to be taken literally but helps one focus all concentration within": *The Upanishads*, trans. Eknath Easwaran and Michael N. Nagler (Tomales, Calif.: Nilgiri, 2007), 351n (RS).

309

10. In Buddhist cosmology, gods of the formless realms (RS).
11. This is not in the Gospels. Most likely Leadbeater is misremembering the location of Psalm 126:6: "He that goeth forth and weepeth, bearing precious seed, shall doubtless come again with rejoicing, bringing his sheaves with him" (RS).
12. The term used (principally in Eastern Orthodox theology) is *theosis* (RS).
13. Possibly a reference to the Athenian democracy, which was established in 510 B.C. and survived (with interruptions) until 87 B.C. Ancient political philosophers, including Plato and Aristotle, regarded democracy as an inferior form of government. Reasons included the ease with which laws could be made and unmade; the strong sense of individualism that it inculcated; and the general mistrust of anyone who grew too powerful: see *The Oxford Classical Dictionary*, 2d ed., N.G.L. Hammond and H. H. Scullard, eds. (Oxford: Oxford University Press, 1970) s.v. "democracy" (RS).
14. Two passages are cited most often to support this argument. The first is John 9:1–3, in which Jesus is asked by his disciples in regard to a man who is born blind: "Master, who did sin, this man, or his parents, that he was born blind?" Jesus replies: "Neither hath this man sinned, nor his parents: but that the works of God should be made manifest in him." (Jesus's answer is equivocal, however, and does not in itself validate a belief in reincarnation.) The second verse is Matt. 11:14, in which Jesus says in regard to John the Baptist: "And if ye will receive it, this is Elias, which was for to come." Jesus is sometimes interpreted as meaning that John the Baptist is a reincarnation of the Hebrew prophet Elijah or Elias. Leadbeater discusses these passages in chapter 21 (RS).
15. T.H. Huxley (1825–96) was one of the most prominent defenders of the theory of evolution in nineteenth-century England. Leadbeater is referring to an 1893 lecture of this name (RS).
16. Metempsychosis is a term sometimes used to refer to reincarnation, but as Leadbeater says here, it usually involves the idea that reincarnation into animal bodies is possible (RS).
17. A long poem about the life and teachings of the Buddha, highly esteemed by the early Theosophists (RS).
18. *Lipika* (sometimes *lipikas* in the plural) are celestial beings who serve as the recorders of karma: H.P. Blavatsky, *The Secret Doctrine* (Wheaton, Ill.: Quest, 1993 [1888]), 1:104 (RS).

19. The primordial energy of the cosmos: Philip S. Harris, et al., eds., *Theosophical Encyclopedia* (Quezon City, Philippines: Theosophical Publishing House, 2006), s.v. "Fohat" (RS).
20. Probably Isaak Vossius, Dutch humanist (1618–89): Wikipedia <http://en.wikipedia.org/wiki/Isaac_Vossius>; accessed Nov. 4, 2010 (RS).
21. From Henry Wadsworth Longfellow's poem "Retribution" (RS).
22. "Aeonian" is Leadbeater's translation of the adjective αιωνιος (*aiōnios*) in the original Greek of the New Testament (cf. Matt. 25:41, 46). It is derived from the word αιων (*aiōn*), which means "age" or "epoch" (as in Matt. 13:22): Henry George Liddell and Robert Scott, *A Greek-English Lexicon*, ed. Henry Stuart Jones (Oxford: Oxford at the Clarendon Press, 1968), s.v. αιων. Leadbeater is saying that the punishment Christ foresees for the wicked is not eternal but is limited to the particular world dispensation that we are living in. For another esoteric perspective on this concept, see Maurice Nicoll, *Living Time and the Integration of the Life* (London: Vincent Stuart, 1952), chapter 6 (RS).
23. The *Pistis Sophia*, as Leadbeater says, is a long and discursive dialogue of Christ with his disciples after the Resurrection; Mary Magdalene plays an important role. The work consists of four discrete sections, which are of different ages but which are generally dated to the third century AD: Wilhelm Schneemelcher, *New Testament Apocrypha*, rev. ed., trans. R. McL. Wilson (Cambridge: James Clarke, 1991), 1:361–69. Like many Gnostic texts, the *Pistis Sophia* is supposed to have originally been written in Greek but survives only in a Coptic translation. G.R.S. Mead produced an edition of this work; he made his own translation from a Latin version produced in the nineteenth century: Mead, *Pistis Sophia* (London: Watkins, 1921). Hence Leadbeater says the text has passed through three translations: from the (now-lost) Greek to the Coptic; from the Coptic to Latin; from Latin to English. Another version can be found in Violet MacDermot, *The Fall of Sophia: A Gnostic Text on the Redemption of Universal Consciousness* (Great Barrington, Mass.: Lindisfarne, 2001; RS).
24. "Wisdom" is an unusual translation of γνωσις (*gnosis*), since σοφια (*sophia*) is the word usually so translated; it is the word Paul uses in the passage cited here. (RS).
25. Quoted in Charles Biggs, *The Christian Platonists of Alexandria* (N.p.: 1886), 62 (CWL).

26. The subject of this and following chapters has also been dealt with in some detail in the author's earlier work *The Christian Creed* (St. Alban Press; CWL).

27. Tyrannius Rufinus (c. 340–410), a Roman monk, scholar, and historian. He is chiefly remembered for his translation of the works of the Church Father Origen into Latin; <http://en.wikipedia.org/wiki/Tyrannius_Rufinus>; accessed Nov. 5, 2010 (RS).

28. Meaning "God from very God, Light born from light, true God coming forth from the true God" (CWL).

29. This statement is extremely important in evaluating much of the material in this chapter, which is at variance with the prevailing scholarly opinion of both Leadbeater's time and ours. "Clairvoyant investigation" probably refers to a method that attempts to read the Akashic Records, which, according to some occult theories, contain imprints of all that has ever taken place (RS).

30. The Essenes were a monastic Jewish sect that flourished in the first century AD. The classic primary source that discusses them is Flavius Josephus, *The Jewish War*, 2.8. Josephus praises them highly for their piety and fastidiousness. In Leadbeater's time it was common to assume that Jesus had studied or lived with the Essenes, but this view has fallen out of favor in recent decades because of the evidence of the Dead Sea Scrolls, which most scholars believe contain fragments of the Essenes' library. (See, for example, James M. VanderKam, "The People of the Dead Sea Scrolls: Essenes or Sadducees?" in Hershel Shanks, ed., *Understanding the Dead Sea Scrolls* [New York: Random House, 1992], chapter 4.) If in fact the Dead Sea Scrolls reveal the Essenes' beliefs, it is hard to connect them with Jesus, since their attitude toward the Jewish Law was, unlike his, hyperobservant. Moreover, there are no first-century sources that connect Jesus with the Essenes (RS).

31. Leadbeater speaks of different levels of initiation throughout this work. Essentially, the first initiation constitutes admission to the Great White Brotherhood. "The Initiation which admits [the individual] to the ranks of the Brotherhood also insures him against the possibility of failure to fulfill the divine purpose in the time appointed for it. Hence those who have reached this point are called in the Christian system the 'elect,' the 'saved' or the 'safe,' and in the Buddhist scheme 'those who have entered the stream.' . . . That first Initiation corresponds to the matriculation which admits a man to a University, and the attainment of Adeptship to the taking of a degree at the

end of a course. Continuing the simile, there are three intermediate examinations, which are usually spoken of as the second, third, and fourth Initiations, Adeptship being the fifth": C.W. Leadbeater, *A Textbook of Theosophy* (Adyar, India: Theosophical Publishing House, n.d.), 147–49 (RS).

32. A reference to the widely accepted theory that the book of Genesis is a composite of several earlier sources. The first creation account that Leadbeater mentions is attributed to the Elohist, so called from his use of the name *Elohim* for God; the second is attributed to the Yahwist, so called because he refers to God as Yahweh: see, for example, E.A. Speiser, *The Anchor Bible: Genesis* (Garden City, N.Y.: Doubleday, 1964), xxii–xxxvii (RS).

33. While it is true that it was the Romans and not the Jews that practiced crucifixion, most scholars would vehemently disagree that the Gospels are not set in the time of Roman occupation. (The Romans controlled Palestine through client kings from 63 BC on; they occupied Judea and ruled it directly after AD 6.) Leadbeater is probably alluding to a theory, promulgated by Mead and widely accepted among Theosophists of the era, that Jesus actually lived around 100 B.C.: see G.R.S. Mead, *Did Jesus Live 100 B.C.?* (London: Theosophical Publishing Society, 1903; RS).

34. This idea is known as the adoptionist theory of the Incarnation. As Leadbeater indicates, the idea is that the man Jesus was overshadowed by the being known as Christ at the time of his baptism. This doctrine is not accepted by the majority of Christian churches (RS).

35. Leadbeater is referring to *The Gospel of Thomas*. In his time this work was known only in fragments discovered at Oxyrhynchus, in Middle Egypt, in 1905. These fragments are in Greek, the language in which this Gospel was written, but they are so incomplete that the identity of the text was not known until the discovery of the Nag Hammadi texts in 1945, which included a full translation of *Thomas* into Coptic—the only complete text of this work that we have. See Schneemelcher, 1:111, 117–29 (RS).

36. This is dated to 586 B.C. (RS).

37. The use of the word "symbol" here reflects the usage of the Orthodox Church, which refers to the creed as the *symbolon* (RS).

38. This rebellion took place in 1884, when a Sudanese boatman, Mohamed Ahmed, claimed to be the Mahdi, the long-awaited Messiah of Muslim tradition, and started a rebellion against the Sudan's Egyptian rulers. Since Egypt itself was under British occupation, the British sent an expeditionary force under General George "Chinese" Gordon to suppress the rebellion, but the force was overwhelmed and Gordon killed. It was not until

1898 that the British smashed dervish power at the Battle of Omdurman: "The Sudan: The Mahdi's Return," <http://www.time.com/time/magazine/article/0,9171,854292,00.html.; accessed Nov. 8, 2010 (RS).

39. Probably a reference to Luke 2:39–40. Leadbeater is conflating the concept of a Nazarene, a native of Nazareth, with that of a Nazirite, an individual consecrated as one apart in the Israel of biblical times. The role is probably best understood as a kind of temporary monasticism. Numbers 6:1–21 gives the stipulations for Nazirites: they may not cut their hair, they may not eat or drink of the fruit of the vine in any form, and they may not touch any dead body. After a stipulated period, the Nazirite is to offer a sacrifice, shave his head, and resume his former life. The two principal examples in the Bible are Samson (Judges 13:5) and Samuel (1 Samuel 1:11). But they are unusual in that their mothers dedicated them as Nazirites before their births, and they were to remain such for their entire lives.

40. Liddell and Scott's Greek lexicon does not support Leadbeater's interpretation, defining μονογενης (*monogenēs*) as "the only member of a kin or kind: hence, generally, only, single" (RS).

41. The Greek is προ παντων των αιωνων (*pro pantōn tōn aiōnōn*), literally, "before the aeons" (RS).

42. This passage is slightly confusing because Leadbeater implies that the error appears in the subhead as he has just given it. But actually he is saying that the error lies in translating this phrase as "Incarnate of the Holy Ghost *by* the Virgin Mary," as some English versions do, rather than as "Incarnate of the Holy Gnost *and* the Virgin Mary" (RS).

43. The Latin equivalent is *incarnatus est de Spiritu sancto, in Maria virgine homo factus,* which has two prepositions, like the English but unlike the Greek (RS).

44. Πιλητος (*pilētos*) literally means "made of felt"; its secondary meaning is "compressible": Liddell and Scott, s.v. πιλητος. Pontius Pilate was prefect of Judea from AD 26 to 36. Leadbeater, as before, is arguing that Jesus lived before the Roman annexation of Judea, which took place in AD 6 (RS).

45. See W. R. Inge, *Christian Mysticism Considered in Eight Lectures* (London: Methuen, 1899), 89 (CWL).

46. In Scottish Rite Freemasonry, the eighteenth degree is called "Knight Rose Croix," i.e., "Knight of the Rose Cross": Albert Pike, *Morals and Dogma of the Ancient and Accepted Rite of Scottish Freemasonry* (Charleston, S.C.: Supreme Council of the Thirty-Third Degree for the Southern Jurisdiction, 1871), 276–311 (RS).

47. "An indulgence is the extrasacramental remission of the temporal punishment due, in God's justice, to sin that has been forgiven, which remission is granted by the Church in the exercise of the power of the keys [cf. Matt. 16:19], through the application of the superabundant merits of Christ and of the saints, and for some just and reasonable motive": *Catholic Encyclopedia*, 1911, s.v. "indulgences"; <http://www.newadvent.org/cathen/07783a. htm>; accessed Nov. 15, 2010. Indulgences are granted by the Catholic Church usually for special forms of devotion, such as pilgrimages, prayers, and similar observances. The Church also teaches that communicants can obtain indulgences for themselves or apply them on behalf of the souls in purgatory: *Catechism of the Catholic Church* §1498; <http://www.scbor-romeo.org/ccc/para/1498.htm>; accessed Nov. 15, 2010. While there has been commercial traffic in indulgences—which were sometimes sold for cash—the present-day Church regards this practice as an abuse and condemns it (RS).

48. The *Garuda Purana* is a Hindu scripture that includes a list of punishments in the afterlife for various types of sins: *The Garuda Purana*, trans. Ernest Wood and S.V. Subrahmanyam, 1911; <http://www.sacred-texts.com/hin/gpu/index.htm>; accessed Nov. 15, 2010. Yama is the Hindu god of death (RS).

49. An apocryphal work also referred to as the *Acts of Pilate*. See Schneemelcher 1:522–526 (SVK, RS).

50. According to Buddhist teaching, an *arhat* is an individual who has reached a high level of attainment. In Theravada Buddhism, the term is generally applied to one who has reached full enlightenment; in Mahayana Buddhism, it is a term indicating a somewhat more limited form of liberation: "Arhat," *Wikipedia* <http://en.wikipedia.org/wiki/Arhat_%28Buddhism%29>; accessed Nov. 15, 2010 (RS).

51. Probably Mark 16:19. This section is today generally acknowledged to be a later addition to the original text of the Gospel (RS).

52. Marcion was a Gnostic teacher of the second century AD; Apelles was one of his chief disciples. Apelles' *Regula fidei* ("Rule of Faith") was a kind of creed for the Marcionite Church: Adolf Harnack, *History of Dogma*, trans. Neil Buchanan (London: Williams & Norgate, 1894), 1:255 (RS).

53. Literally, "Come, Creator" (RS).

54. The Greek verb παρακαλεω (*parakaleō*), the root of the word *Paraclete*, has a much wider range of meanings than Leadbeater suggests here. Its principal meaning in the Greek of most periods is "to call for," "to summon."

While it does mean "exhort" or "encourage" in some classical passages, it only means "comfort" in the Septuagint and the New Testament: Liddell & Scott, s.v. παρακαλεω (RS).

55. The Greek is το κυριον και ζωοποιον (*to kurion kai zōopoion*); *zōopoion* literally means "maker of life" (RS).

56. Sir William Crookes (1832–1919) was a British scientist. Among his discoveries were the metal thallium, the radiometer, and the high-vacuum tube used in X-Ray techniques. He was also active in the Society for Psychical Research. A. P. Sinnett (1840–1921) was a journalist and author. His works include *The Occult World* and *Esoteric Buddhism*. He was the recipient of many of the letters that were believed to be sent by the adepts who were behind the founding of the Theosophical Society. See A. T. Barker and Vicente Hao Chin, Jr., eds., *The Mahatma Letters to A. P. Sinnett in Chronological Sequence* (Quezon City, Philippines: Theosophical Publishing House, 1997; SVK, RS).

57. Drawings of these atoms and further details may be found in *Occult Chemistry* by A. Besant and C. W. Leadbeater (London: Theosophical Publishing House, 1919; CWL).

58. C.W. Leadbeater, *The Chakras* (Wheaton, Ill.: Quest, 1974), 25–30 (SVK).

59. St. John Damascene, *De Hymno Trisagio*, §28. St. John Damascene was a Church Father who died in AD 749 (CWL, RS).

60. Charles W. Leadbeater, *The Christian Creed: Its Origin and Signification*, 2d ed. (London: Theosophical Publishing Society, 1904), 69–70 (SVK, RS).

61. The word εκκλησια (*ekklēsia*) is derived from εκκαλεω (*ekkaleō*), "to call out" or "call forth" (RS).

62. There were apostles certainly, and from them came our faith and apostolic succession, but when we made clairvoyant investigation into the times, we did not find those particular twelve men called the apostles in the Gospels (CWL).

63. The Greek word is αφησις (*aphēsis*), from αφιημι (*aphiēmi*). The verb has a wide range of meanings, from "send away" to "get rid of" to "release." This is the same verb used in the verse of the Lord's Prayer in the Greek New Testament "Forgive us our debts, as we have forgiven our debtors" (Matt. 6:12; RS).

64. This is incorrect. While it is true that Origen (c. 185–c. 253 AD) taught "the passing of the soul from one body to another," he explicitly repudiates the doctrine of reincarnation, or transmigration, on more than one occasion: "The dogma of transmigration . . . is foreign to the church of

God, and not handed down by the apostles, nor anywhere set forth in the Scriptures": Origen, *Commentary on Matthew* 13.1; in Allan Menzies, ed., *The Ante-Nicene Fathers: Translations of the Writings of the Fathers down to AD 325* (Edinburgh: T & T Clark, 1990), 5:474. In *Contra Celsum* ("Against Celsus"), Origen refers to "the foolish doctrine of re-incarnation": Origen, *Contra Celsum* 3.75, trans. Henry Chadwick (Cambridge: Cambridge University Press, 1953), 179. In *Contra Celsum* 7.32, Origen refutes the claim by the pagan polemicist Celsus that the Christian doctrine of the resurrection was a misunderstanding of reincarnation. Origen held that the soul was immortal and preexisted the physical body and in the afterlife would constellate a body around it that was in accordance with the soul's own level of development; see, for example, his *On First Principles*, 4.4.8. In the passage of the *Commentary on Matthew* quoted above, he denies that this includes the possibility of reincarnation. Origen makes these comments in regard to Matthew 11:14, discussed immediately below by Leadbeater. (RS).

65. A slightly misleading statement in that by conventional etymology the name "Mary" is derived from the Hebrew "Mariam"; in Greek it is Μαρια (*Maria*). But Leadbeater is correct in saying that the word is the plural of "sea" in Latin (RS).

66. A traditional altar has two lecterns: from the one on the left (from the congregants' point of view), the text from the Gospel is read; from the one on the right, the text from the Epistles is read. "Generally speaking, the positive or masculine Rays are represented on the south or Epistle side and the negative or feminine Rays on the north or Gospel side": C.W. Leadbeater, *The Science of the Sacraments*, 2d. ed. (Adyar, India: Theosophical Publishing House, 1929), 221. The north and south orientations are based on the fact that churches are generally built with the altar facing east (RS).

67. Leadbeater's etymologies for the names of angels here do not always agree with conventional scholarship. The usual etymology of the name Michael is that it means "Who is like God?" Gabriel is usually thought to mean "the strength of God." Raphael is, as Leadbeater suggests, usually connected with the Hebrew verb *raphah*, "to heal," and Uriel is "light of God." Zadkiel, however, is more likely derived from *tzedeq*, "righteousness," rather than benevolence as usually understood: Francis Brown, S. R. Driver, and Charles A. Briggs, *A Hebrew and English Lexicon of the Old Testament*, 2d. ed. (Oxford: Clarendon Press, 1953), s.vv. *Gavriel, Mikhael, raphah, aur, tzedeq*.

68. St. Dionysius, or Dionysius the Areopagite, is traditionally associated with a certain Dionysius who was converted by Paul (Acts 17:34). The works attributed to him include a highly influential work on angelology entitled *The Celestial Hierarchies*. Today it is usually assumed that the author of this text lived in the fifth century AD; his identity is otherwise unknown. Hence he is frequently referred to as Pseudo-Dionysius: "Dionysius the Pseudo-Areopagite," *Catholic Encylopedia*; <http://www.newadvent.org/cathen/05013a.htm>; accessed Nov. 18, 2010 (RS).

69. A reference to the diagram known as the Kabbalistic Tree of Life. This consists (in its most familiar form) of a series of ten principles known as the *sephiroth* (the singular is *sephirah*). The three supernal sephiroth are Kether, "Crown"; Chokmah, "Wisdom"; and Binah, "Understanding" (RS).

70. The Greek philosopher Pythagoras of Samos (c. 570–c. 495 B.C.) probably did not teach a heliocentric theory of the universe. He appears, however, to have taught that there was a "central fire" around which the earth and the planets, as well as the sun, moved: Paul Edwards, ed., *Encyclopedia of Philosophy* (New York: Macmillan, 1967), 7:39 (RS).

71. The passage in question is Deut. 32:8. Leadbeater is correct in saying that the Septuagint reading differs from the standard Masoretic Hebrew text, reading "sons of God" (meaning "angels of God") instead of "sons of Israel." Remarkably, the version of Deuteronomy found among the Dead Sea Scrolls and dating from the first century AD (which was only discovered after Leadbeater's death) also has "sons of God," indicating that this may have been the original reading: Margaret Barker, *The Great Angel: A Study of Israel's Second God* (Louisville, Ky.: Westminster/John Knox, 1992), 5–6 (RS).

72. More commonly, "dominions": Col. 1:16 (RS).

73. John Bunyan, *Pilgrim's Progress*, 2.3 (RS).

74. "Alcyone," *At the Feet of the Master*, 3d. ed. (Adyar, India: Theosophical Publishing House, 1999), 87. Alcyone was the pseudonym of the spiritual teacher Jiddu Krishnamurti; the work was written in 1910, when Krishnamurti was fourteen: *Theosophical Encyclopedia*, ed. Philip S. Harris et al. (Quezon City: Philippines, 2006), s.v. "*At the Feet of the Master*" (RS).

75. Henry Suso (c. 1300–66) was a German mystic whose writings dwelt powerfully on spiritual mortification. In his autobiography, he says that he was told by the Lord, "If thou wouldst truly arrive at my naked divinity thou must tread the thorny path of my suffering humanity": Henry Suso, *The*

Exemplar, trans. Sister M. Ann Edward (Dubuque, Iowa: Priory Press, 1962), 1:32. John Ruysbroeck or Ruusbroec (1293–1381) was a Flemish monk who spoke of the highest mystical state as "a darkness which [the spirit] cannot enter by the power of reason": John Ruusbroec, *The Spiritual Espousals and Other Works*, trans. James A. Wiseman (New York: Paulist, 1985), 183. But the actual work entitled *The Dark Night of the Soul* was written by the Spanish mystic John of the Cross (1542–91) and is probably what Leadbeater is referring to in the following paragraph. *Asekha* literally means "nonlearner" and refers to a stage of spiritual perfection in which no more learning is necessary or possible: *Theosophical Encyclopedia*, s.v. *asekha* (RS).

76. Angelus Silesius (CWL).

77. "The Liturgy begins with the asperges, or purification ceremony. *Asperges* is simply the Latin for the opening words of the antiphon 'Thou shalt sprinkle,' for it is constantly the custom in the Church to use the first word or words of a psalm or canticle as its name": Leadbeater, *Science of the Sacraments*, 28 (RS).

78. For a detailed description of this process, with illustrations, see Leadbeater, *Science of the Sacraments*, chapter 2 (RS).

79. An allusion to the Latin roots of the word "substance": *sub*, "below," "under"; *stare*, "to stand" (RS).

80. C.W. Leadbeater, *The Hidden Life in Freemasonry* (Adyar, India: Theosophical Publishing House, 1926), 259–61 (RS).

81. Mark 6:5. But the passage makes no specific reference to Capernaum, merely saying that Jesus was "in his own country" (RS).

82. The Seventh General Episcopal Synod (1976) confirmed St. Alban as the patron saint of the Liberal Catholic Church (SVK).

83. Scholars today generally agree that Revelation was written "by a Jewish Christian prophet named John who was neither John the son of Zebedee nor the writer of the Johannine Gospel or of the Epistles": Raymond E. Brown, *An Introduction to the New Testament* (New York: Doubleday, 1997), 774 (RS).

84. Alfred, Lord Tennyson, *The Idylls of the King*, "The Passing of Arthur" (CWL).

85. Traditionally the minor prophets in the Hebrew Bible: Hosea, Joel, Amos, Obadiah, Jonah, Micah, Nahum, Habakkuk, Zephaniah, Haggai, Zechariah, and Malachi (RS).

86. This was written in 1924 (SVK).
87. Prime and compline are traditional parts of the canonical Hours of the Church. Prime takes place at 6 a.m.; compline takes place after sunset: E.J. Quigley, *The Divine Office: A Study of the Roman Breviary* (N.p.: Bibliobazaar, 2007), 17 (RS).
88. An abbreviation for *Ad maiorem Dei gloriam*: "For the greater glory of God" (RS).

INDEX

Bold indicates diagrams

Quest Books

encourages open-minded inquiry into
world religions, philosophy, science, and the arts
in order to understand the wisdom of the ages,
respect the unity of all life, and help people explore
individual spiritual self-transformation.

Its publications are generously supported by
The Kern Foundation,
a trust committed to Theosophical education.

Quest Books is the imprint of
the Theosophical Publishing House,
a division of the Theosophical Society in America.
For information about programs, literature,
on-line study, membership benefits, and international centers,
see www.theosophical.org
or call 800-669-1571 or (outside the U.S.) 630-668-1571.

Related Quest Titles

The Cross and the Grail, by Robert Ellwood

A Dictionary of Gnosticism, by Andrew Phillip Smith

The Divine Seed: The Esoteric Teachings of Jesus, by Pekka Ervast

Echoes from the Gnosis, by G. R. S. Mead

Esoteric Christianity, by Annie Besant

Gnosticism, by Stephan A. Hoeller

Hidden Wisdom in the Holy Bible, by Geoffrey Hodson

A Rebirth for Christianity, by Alvin Boyd Kuhn

To order books or a complete Quest catalog,
call 800-669-9425 or (outside the U.S.) 630-665-0130.